Christian Ritual and the
Creation of British Slave Societies
1650–1780

RACE IN THE ATLANTIC WORLD, 1700–1900

SERIES EDITORS

Richard S. Newman, Rochester Institute of Technology
Patrick Rael, Bowdoin College
Manisha Sinha, University of Massachusetts, Amherst

ADVISORY BOARD

Edward Baptist, Cornell University
Christopher Brown, Columbia University
Vincent Carretta, University of Maryland
Laurent Dubois, Duke University
Douglas Egerton, LeMoyne College
Leslie Harris, Emory University
Joanne Pope Melish, University of Kentucky
Sue Peabody, Washington State University, Vancouver
Erik Seeman, State University of New York, Buffalo
John Stauffer, Harvard University

Christian Ritual and the Creation of British Slave Societies
1650–1780

NICHOLAS M. BEASLEY

The University of Georgia Press
Athens & London

Paperback edition, 2010
© 2009 by the University of Georgia Press
Athens, Georgia 30602
www.ugapress.org
All rights reserved
Designed by Walton Harris
Set in 10.5/14 Garamond Premier Pro

Printed digitally in the United States of America

The Library of Congress has cataloged the hardcover edition of this book as follows:

Beasley, Nicholas M.
Christian ritual and the creation of British slave societies,
1650–1780 / Nicholas M. Beasley.
xii, 223 p. : ill., maps ; 24 cm. — (Race in the Atlantic world, 1700–1900)
Includes bibliographical references (p. 189–211) and index.
ISBN-13: 978-0-8203-3339-7
ISBN-10: 0-8203-3339-5
1. Church of England—History. 2. British—America—Religion.
3. Plantation life—South Carolina—History. 4. Plantation life—Jamaica—History. 5. Plantation life—Barbados—History. 6. Great Britain—Colonies—America—Religious life and customs. 7. Great Britain—Church history. 8. South Carolina—Church history.
9. Jamaica—Church history. 10. Barbados—Church history. I. Title.
BR757.B43 2009
283.086'25—dc22   2009008550

Paperback ISBN-13: 978-0-8203-3645-9
          ISBN-10: 0-8203-3645-9

British Library Cataloging-in-Publication Data available

CONTENTS

List of Illustrations *ix*

Acknowledgments *xi*

CHAPTER ONE.
Christian Ritual in British Slave Societies *1*

CHAPTER TWO.
Ritual Time and Space in the British Plantation Colonies *21*

CHAPTER THREE.
Marriage and Baptism in the British Plantation Colonies *54*

CHAPTER FOUR.
The Meanings of the Eucharist in the Plantation World *84*

CHAPTER FIVE.
Mortuary Ritual in the British Plantation Colonies *109*

CHAPTER SIX.
Revolution, Evangelicalisms, and the Fragmentation of Anglo-America *136*

Notes *145*

Bibliography *189*

Index *213*

ILLUSTRATIONS

MAPS

Barbados Parishes, ca. 1700   *4*

Jamaica Parishes, 1723–69   *7*

South Carolina Parishes   *9*

PHOTOS

Interior of St. Andrew's Church, South Carolina   *23*

Exterior of St. Andrew's Church, South Carolina   *24*

Interior of St. Michael's Church, Charleston, South Carolina   *28*

Exterior of St. James's Church, Goose Creek, South Carolina   *97*

Reredos of St. James's Church, Goose Creek, South Carolina   *98*

The Church of St. Jago de la Vega, Spanish Town, Jamaica   *124*

Exterior of St. Michael's Church, Charleston, South Carolina   *138*

ACKNOWLEDGMENTS

The research and writing that resulted in this book would not have been possible without the generosity of numerous institutions and friends. Teaching and research fellowships from the Department of History at Vanderbilt University were essential. I am also thankful for grants and intellectual stimulation from the Interdisciplinary Seminar in Social and Political Thought and the Center for the Study of Religion and Culture at Vanderbilt. My final year of writing was supported by a generous dissertation fellowship from the university's Center for the Americas. That support enabled me to use a variety of research resources. Among several archives, I was helped by particularly fine people at the South Carolina Historical Society, the South Carolina Department of Archives and History, the South Caroliniana Library, the Jamaica Archives, and the Barbados Archives.

I enjoyed much hospitality during my research. In Kingston, the Franciscan Sisters of the Immaculate Conception Convent in Constant Spring were gracious hosts, as was the United Theological Seminary of the West Indies. James Robertson kindly entertained me at the University of the West Indies at Mona and was an invaluable guide to the Jamaica Archives. In Barbados, Pedro Welch and Amparo and Mark McWatt welcomed me to the Cave Hill campus of UWI and furthered my exploration of the island. In Charleston, David T. Gleeson and W. Scott Poole of the College of Charleston brightened the end of the research day. Horry Parker kindly opened the door to St. James's Church in Goose Creek for me.

Beyond Vanderbilt, a postdoctoral fellowship at the Candler School of Theology at Emory University provided an opportunity to begin teaching students of Christian liturgy. There portions of this book benefited from the reading of E. Brooks Holifield, Jonathon Strom, and Elizabeth Bounds. Just prior to that, my two weeks at the International Seminar on the History of the Atlantic World at Harvard University were an intellectual turning point. In Cambridge, Massachusetts, I first received the helpful critique of Eric Seeman, later a reader of this manuscript. At a later stage, Suzanne Linder Hurley graciously shared her photographs of low country churches with me. I am thankful to the editors of *Church History* and *Anglican and Episcopal History* for their permission to reprint portions of my essays that appeared in those journals.

I served in three Episcopal parishes during the time this book was written. St. George's Church in Nashville offered me an office, many friendships, and an atmosphere entirely different from campus. Holy Trinity Parish in Decatur, Georgia, welcomed me with open arms during a brief sojourn in Atlanta. I completed this project at the Church of the Resurrection in Greenwood, South Carolina, a parish that has shown remarkable patience with my academic interests. Remembering other ecclesial debts, I give thanks for a timely grant from the Historical Society of the Episcopal Church and a generous fellowship from the Episcopal Church Foundation. I will always be thankful for the people of Christ Church in Greenville, South Carolina, where I first led the rites described in this book.

Daniel Usner has been a generous and gentle advisor through many transitions. He and Jane G. Landers eased me into early America and the Atlantic world at a critical moment, a great kindness that I will always appreciate. Joel Harrington allowed me to keep one foot in early modern Europe and in the social history of Christianity. Kathleen Flake and James Byrd were rigorous readers and guides in the historiography of American religion. I owe my professional interest in history to members of the History Department at the University of the South, particularly W. Brown Patterson, Charles R. Perry, and Susan J. Ridyard. I am deeply thankful for all of their guidance.

My parents and my wife's parents always encouraged me. To be sure, Elizabeth Irwin Beasley has forgiven me many things during the writing of this book. She made a home for us in Nashville, Atlanta, and then Greenwood, endured my archival wandering, and gave us a son. My greatest debts will always be to her.

Nativity of John the Baptist, 2008
Greenwood, South Carolina

Christian Ritual and the
Creation of British Slave Societies
1650–1780

CHAPTER 1

Christian Ritual in British Slave Societies

IN 1627, THE ENGLISH BEGAN their colonization of Barbados and the creation of a British plantation world that would span the circum-Caribbean. They adapted to their new setting ably, creating a creolized English culture that celebrated metropolitan mores even as it made concessions to life in a tropical environment. That culture proved both durable and replicable. In 1655, Barbadians joined the English forces that sailed across a thousand miles of sparkling Caribbean sea to join in the conquest of Jamaica, an island twenty-six times the size of Barbados and of enormous economic potential. Founded another fifteen years later, South Carolina had roots in Barbados's fertile soils as well, with more than half of the earliest migrants to that continental colony, both black and white, coming from Barbados. In both of the younger colonies, lessons learned on the older island served settlers well as they created highly successful plantation entrepôts. Growing from a common cultural hearth in Barbados, the British plantation colonies thus shared a colonial experience as slave societies in the strongest sense of the term.[1]

In Barbados, Jamaica, and South Carolina, Africans and their descendents composed the majority of the population for almost all of the colonial period. Most of them were enslaved and engaged in plantation agriculture. After short periods as societies with slaves, all three became paradigmatic slave societies, places in which "slavery stood at the center of economic production, and the master-slave relationship provided the model for all social relations."[2] In all three colonies, the growth of the enslaved population aroused fear among a white elite that thought African slavery both indispensable and dangerous. Those minorities composed of planters, merchants, and their employees profited from the labor of the enslaved and used those profits to maintain connections to London, from whence came the consumer goods, information, and colonial officials that

1

reinforced the imperial connection. In addition to common origins, similar economic models based on racial slavery, and abiding cultural and commercial connections, these plantation colonies shared a largely common religious history that furthers their usefulness as a unit of analysis.

The Church of England was by law established in all three colonies, and social and political privilege was associated with membership in that church. Establishment meant that the church enjoyed some measure of financial support from the colonial governments, for ministers' salaries and the maintenance of church buildings in particular. Each parish was a geographic district that elected a vestry, the lay board that handled the temporal matters of the parish, including poor relief, elections, the employment of the minister, roads and bridges, and other duties assigned by the provincial government. Though frequently pretending to it, the Church of England in these colonies enjoyed no monopoly on matters of the divine, surrounded as it was by practitioners of various African religious systems and numbers of Protestant dissenters, especially in Carolina. The subject of this book is the cultural meaning of the worship offered in the established church in these vibrantly diverse and rapidly developing slave societies.[3]

The three plantation societies of this study were founded in an era in which religious difference between Catholics and Protestants and between Protestants themselves was a central issue in British, European, and imperial affairs. The early settlers of Barbados and Jamaica indeed found their colonial experience directly shaped by the English Civil War and its aftermath. In the 1640s, some Barbadians rioted in support of the Book of Common Prayer and later resisted Parliamentary rule; many of the first English Jamaicans were Parliamentary soldiers, officers, and chaplains, intent on both riches and beating back the pope and the Spanish. The foundation of Carolina in 1670 reflected the legacy of the Civil War's religious dimension through John Locke and Lord Shaftsbury's plans for a colony of wide religious tolerance, excepting only Roman Catholics. Though certainly a struggle over the relationship of the monarchy and Parliament, the violence of the 1640s was also inspired by differences regarding the office and power of bishops, the balance of power between clergy and laity, church property, and the furnishing and decoration of churches.[4] While the clergy of the Church of England in England would reemerge at the Restoration in 1660–62 with many of their prerogatives restored, in these Anglican colonies the balance of power shifted decisively toward the laity for several reasons.

The Church of England did not appoint bishops for the colonies, an issue that was revisited over and over during the colonial period in North America. This omission, a striking one when compared to the practice of the Catholic empires, was due to a variety of metropolitan and colonial factors. The Whig ministries of the eighteenth century hesitated to create more bishops, an act, Horace Walpole wrote, that could well inflame passions around the "distinction of High Church & Low Church which has occasioned great Mischiefs in this divided country in former Reigns." Colonial resistance to the appointment of bishops was also stout. Anti-episcopal dissenters were predominant in New England and other colonies and were heirs to a long tradition of Whiggish thought that connected episcopacy, the divine right of kings, crypto-Catholicism, and political tyranny.[5] Without supervising bishops nearby, Anglican ministers and vestries functioned under the distant and vague authority of the bishop of London and the more immediate authority of the colony's governor. English clergy were accustomed to lay patronage and a degree of lay control, but colonial clergy found themselves without the countervailing episcopal hierarchy of their metropolitan experience.

Unlike the Spanish they sought to replace as a colonial power, the English pursued their colonization of Barbados and Carolina by essentially private means and without supervising bands of clerics to regulate their worship, morals, and relationships with indigenous and African persons. Unlike the English who settled New England, the first colonists of the plantation world were predominantly male. Many were soldiers and adventurers, men unlikely quickly to re-create the Church of England in their locales.[6] When Anglican parishes were created and clergy arrived in the English colonies some years after the foundation, both institution and personnel were cultural additions to already evolving plantation societies. To be sure, they were familiar additions from deep in the English experience, but these latecomers were easily subjected to the demands of these new societies. While Cromwellian army chaplains were present from the first at the conquest of Jamaica in 1655, their influence on the later civilian society was negligible; indeed, their political and theological convictions were accounted treasonous by 1660. The church and clergy would flourish in all the plantation colonies in their most prosperous days, becoming vital locations for the negotiation of power as colonists sought to refine their rude corners of the world. Yet church and clergy flourished within the decidedly limited parameters offered them by the white elite on the one hand and the African majority

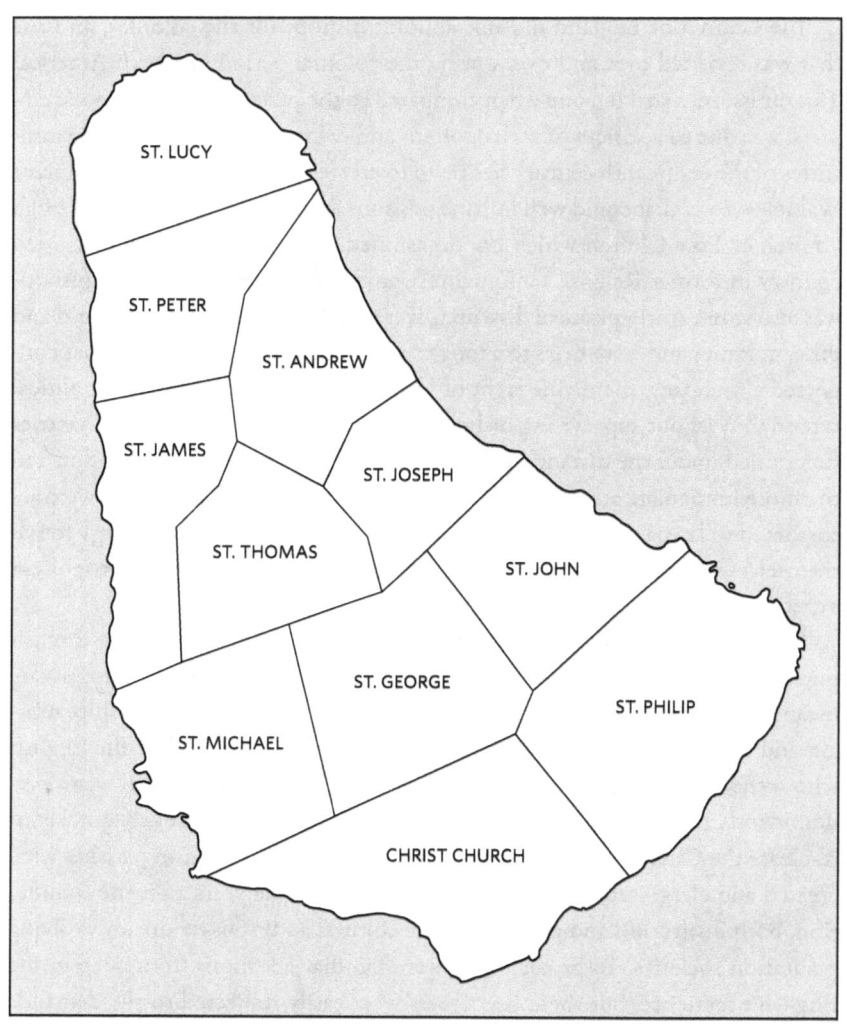

Barbados Parishes, ca. 1700.

on the other. The cultural power of the church and its liturgy grew from the mid-seventeenth century to the late eighteenth but as a later refinement to societies whose fundamental cultural scripts were rooted in race and slavery.

Thus English religious culture was selectively translated to the colonies in ways that augmented the power of white laypersons in parish affairs and pastoral relationships. Clergy who served in the plantation colonies found themselves removed from the structures of English church life that gave them power over laypersons. Financial considerations deepened their dependence. The revenues of the clergy in colonial America were also less secure than in most English parishes, with their income-producing glebe land and other endowments. Clergy in the colonies depended on the beneficence of the London-based Society for the Propagation of the Gospel (SPG), the provincial legislatures, fees for services, and free-will offerings. Prudent clergy in the colonies learned quickly the importance to their own well-being of understanding local culture and personalities. As examples in the following pages will show, the most dangerous area in which clergy might depart from colonial norms was in ministry across the developing color line.

Of the three colonies at the center of this study, a typically English parish system and social and political role for clergy emerged earliest and most fully in rapidly settled and geographically manageable Barbados, functioning by the mid-seventeenth century. The development of the institutional life of the church in Jamaica was hampered by that colony's general precariousness until the second half of the eighteenth century. Challenged by Maroons, the Spanish, frequent slave rebellions, and earthquakes and hurricanes, Jamaican planters could plead that they could ill afford to share much of their power or money with church or clergy. Until after 1750, churches were built slowly, if at all, in the island's rural areas, and clerical positions were often unfilled. Yet Jamaica and Barbados were characterized by a high degree of religious uniformity among whites. Though religious minorities existed, the establishment of the Church of England was unquestioned in both colonies. That was decidedly not the case in Carolina, where Anglicans were no more than a substantial plurality among whites and where the establishment of the Church of England was only achieved after considerable struggle and intrigue in 1706. Establishment in Carolina meant no more for the social and political power of the clergy than it did in the West Indies. Still, a church and clergy with reduced coercive power proved to be a more interesting venue for the expression of the cultural hopes of laity in the plantation world. Thus this book does not tell a story of dramatic change over time, but of the gradual elaboration of a set of ritual habits in societies whose most powerful members were committed to a fundamental racial and cultural stasis.

The main changes pursued by whites from the foundation of these colonies to the Revolution were the augmentation of their fortunes and the related refinement of their personal and social lives. Both goals fostered the further growth of slavery and thus white anxiety, deepening the need for cultural means of wrestling with that anxiety. The white minorities that controlled the export economies of these colonies focused production on sugar in the two West Indian islands and on rice in Carolina. Those economies produced great wealth at higher rates than anywhere else in British America. A sugar revolution in the 1640s and 1650s brought Barbados its wealth early, making the island "the richest colony in English America" by the end of the seventeenth century.[7] Barbados's daughter colony Jamaica would easily surpass it in the eighteenth. The per capita net worth of free white Jamaicans in 1775 was an enormous £12,000. While that dwarfed the 1774 wealth for whites in the area around Charles Town in Carolina, Carolinians' £2337 per head easily quadrupled the average net worth of haughty Virginians, who had a plantation world of their own. In short, the richest men in the first British Empire were the West Indians and Carolinians of the plantation colonies.[8]

That great wealth was accompanied by an enormous cultural challenge. It was difficult for Europeans and Creoles to maintain their claims to Englishness in the face of clear evidence that their colonies were not settler societies that faithfully reproduced English culture. Hot climates, fierce hurricanes, and dismal swamps all reminded white colonists that they were far from home.[9] With black majorities in all the plantation colonies, indeed reaching 90 percent in Jamaica, claims to be English- rather than African-dominated societies strained credulity. Though caricatured and criticized by metropolitans for their addiction to slavery, low social origins, and *nouveau riche* materialism, residents of the plantation colonies boisterously claimed the liberties of Englishmen even as they constructed societies rooted in the perpetual and brutal subjugation of a large body of non-English laborers. In the face of black majorities that threatened to absorb or even annihilate them, re-creating as much as possible of English political, consumer, and religious culture was vital to white residents' pretensions to dominance.[10]

White anxiety increased as the slave population reached the tipping point of majority population and increased well beyond it in some regions. Jamaica

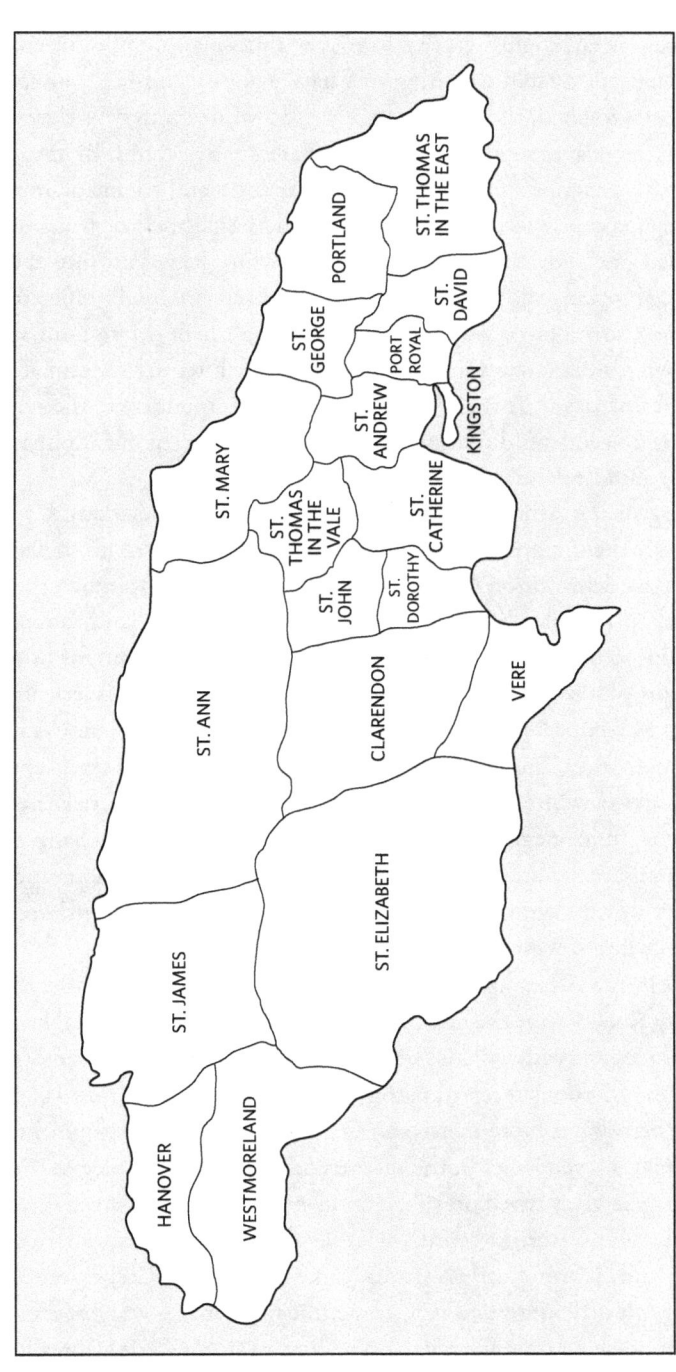

Jamaica Parishes, 1723–69.

began its existence as an English colony in 1655 with a small number of enslaved persons but made a rapid transition to a slave majority. In 1673, population parity had been reached; there were roughly 7700 whites and 7700 slaves. By 1693, over 40,000 slaves significantly outnumbered 7300 whites. By 1774, whites were 6 to 8 percent of a total population of 210,000 and commentators like Edward Long nervously insisted on the increasing Englishness of Jamaica, even as he warned of the descent of some common white Jamaicans into the ways of Africans, absorbing the "tricks, superstitions, diversions, and profligate discourses, of black servants, equally illiterate and unpolished." More modest growth in the slave population in Carolina still led many whites to overestimate vastly the number of slaves in their hand-wringing correspondence, though Africans and their descendents did compose more than 60 percent of Carolina's population in the middle decades of the eighteenth century.[11]

Awareness of growing African majorities prompted colonial legislatures to restrict periodically the importation of Africans, yet their resolve to do so was limited by relentless demand for African labor. The provincial government in Carolina worked to recruit white Protestant colonists, offering land, bounties, and townships to immigrants, some of these incentives being paid for by a duty on the import of slaves. The fair response they received from the German, French, and Irish who relocated to the backcountry only altered the colony's racial demographics slightly. The Jamaican Assembly fined landowners who kept insufficient numbers of white supervisors on their plantations, a practice that did more to fill government coffers than change population.[12] Nothing changed the fact that colonists felt sure that their economies required slave labor and that the brutality of the regime required continued importation of enslaved Africans, especially in the West Indies.

The moments in the Africanization of the plantation colonies that aroused the greatest white anxiety were the great slave rebellions. Jamaica's colonial history is particularly replete with violence between Europeans and Africans, more frequent before the Maroons received autonomy and began to function as an arm of the plantocracy but more massive in the years after that development. Slaves rose in Jamaica seven times in the seventeenth century and twice in the eighteenth before the great rebellion (Tacky's) in 1760; further massive rebellions occurred in the nineteenth century. Carolina's great rebellion, one of a handful in mainland British North America, came in the Stono Rebellion of 1739. Barbados, with little unsettled land to permit maroonage, was not conducive to rebellion, facing only unrealized plots until 1816.[13] While whites in

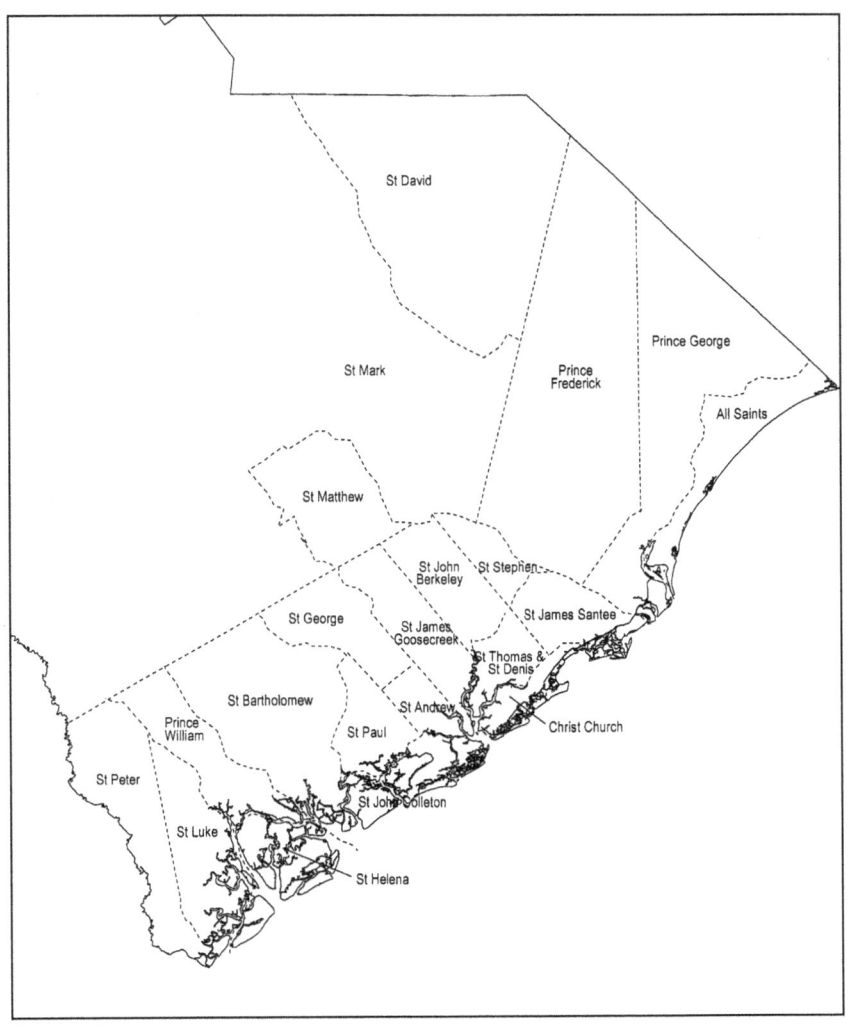

South Carolina Parishes. The geographically smaller Charleston parishes of St. Philip's and St. Michael's are not pictured. Map by Marta Thacker, reprinted with permission of the Episcopal Diocese of South Carolina, from Suzanne Cameron Linder, *Anglican Churches in Colonial South Carolina* (Charleston: Wyrick Press, 2000).

Barbados and Carolina faced fewer rebellions than in Jamaica, their papers and correspondence with the rest of the Atlantic world provided lurid accounts of every plot and rebellion, from St. John's in the Caribbean, to New York City, to the great conflagration of St. Domingue.[14] The whites of the plantation world were well informed about the collective danger of the world they had made.

For every realized rebellion, whites lived through numerous plots, rumors of plots, and imagined plots. Every threat of foreign invasion, every rumor of European war, left whites wondering about the intentions of those they enslaved. Even when rebellion and large-scale violence seemed unlikely, quotidian interaction between Africans and Europeans was hardly reassuring to white elites. Their violence was frequently reciprocated, and the deference the master class expected was frequently in short supply at home, in the field, and on the streets. Long- and short-term running away was common; verbal resistance was a daily reality; slaves assaulted and killed their owners. Slaves colluded with indentured servants, formed relationships with men and women beyond their masters' control, tippled in punch houses, and worshipped in the night. They assembled in large groups to mourn, to celebrate, and to trade. Yet whites dealt with the pressing anxiety of their slave societies not by altering demographics but by cultural construction and obfuscation.

The translation of English religious culture to the plantation colonies held together European cultural identity and articulated a profound set of desires for the ordering of colonial experience. In the familiar structures, repetitions, and drama of Christian worship, white residents of the plantation colonies reproduced sacred moments from their collective English and European past, erasing the difference and distance that separated them from the mother country. While I stress whites' studied continuity with early modern English religious culture, it is also clear that much about English religious culture was transformed in the colonial experience, especially in the presence of majority populations of Africans and their descendents. Though inheriting an inclusive parish community tradition, colonists violated that tradition as they excluded most persons of color from Christian worship throughout the colonial period. By rendering their Christian ritual life largely free of the presence of Africans and their descendents, white worshippers were able to deny the social reality of life in the plantation colonies, thus eliding the difference and distance that separated them from the metropole.

That denial was often pursued in the setting of parish churches constructed at public expense. Chapter 1 takes up the meaning of sacred space in the British plantation colonies, arguing that the ordering of liturgical space and especially seating in it were essential to colonists' efforts to remind themselves of their Englishness. Working within their understanding of the parish community, colonists fashioned liturgical spaces that created community for whites and offered only a low place in their hierarchy to free persons of color and a few slaves. Demonstrating that demand for seats in church was great, the chapter also disputes hoary arguments about the meaninglessness of religion in the plantation colonies. Adding temporality to that spatial argument, the first chapter also shows that the cycles of Christian time, from the weekly worship of Sunday to the festival cycles of the liturgical year, had profound social meaning in the plantation world. Control of ritual space and time, the most public aspects of religious devotion, was essential to obscuring the ritual lives of the plantation regions' black majorities.

Even as whites sought to dominate public life by controlling ritual space and time, they also largely withdrew to private places for the initiatory rites of marriage and baptism, treated in the second chapter. Europeans readily embraced higher expenses for these rites in order to have them celebrated at home. When celebrated mostly in domestic spaces, marriage and baptism served to legitimate the sexuality and reproduction of Europeans. Removed from the public discourse of the parish church, baptism and marriage were largely unavailable to the enslaved. While free persons of color were often baptized and married in Christian rites, most were obliged to celebrate these rites in the more public venues that whites had largely abandoned for those purposes. By removing baptism to the domestic sphere, whites effectively evacuated it of the spiritual egalitarianism inherent in the rite and reserved its celebration of legitimate reproduction to themselves. Similarly, the celebration of marriage at home symbolized the manner in which that rite was privatized, giving Europeans ideological room to develop a long-running discourse on the supposed illegitimacy of the marital and reproductive habits of enslaved Africans and their descendents.

Except when provided for the sick, Anglican discipline forbad private celebrations of the Eucharist, that sacrament being the topic of the third chapter. Christians in the plantation colonies inherited a long tradition of experiencing the Lord's Supper as a rite that had the power to bind diverse parishioners together as a living manifestation of the Body of Christ. They also knew the long tradition of translating that corporate, pastoral practice into the political realm through legislation such as the English Test Act. Given the diversity among Europeans in the plantation colonies, it is not surprising that whites in the plantation colonies continued to see Protestant Eucharistic theology as a useful marker of national loyalty and political reliability, in relation both to white foreigners and to persons of color. The exclusion of most persons of color was vital in a rite that required whites to carry themselves with a humility they preferred to see only in their slaves. While some persons of color responded by seeking inclusion in the whites' Eucharistic community, many others waited for opportunities to take places at tables of their own authority. An examination of the rich material culture of the Eucharist further shows that sacramental practice in the plantation colonies was far more vigorous and socially meaningful than many historians have admitted.

Anglican communicants received the bread and wine with a reminder from the priest that the sacrament was intended to "preserve thy body and soul unto everlasting life." Hope for eternal life, be it variously understood, was articulated in the mortuary rituals of the plantation colonies. The final chapter turns toward the grave to examine the ritual practices that residents of the plantation colonies used in the face of the death that so often surrounded them. There were highly visible differences in the elaborate cultures of death that surrounded the distinct rites of Europeans and Africans, differences that both groups and some of their descendents sought to preserve as they constructed New World identities. Sharing many practices from the beginning, others blurred lines between the practices of distinct groups among Europeans as well as across emerging racial lines. Even under the reign of death that characterized life in these deadly places, residents of the plantation world found ritual a lively forum for creating and contesting the racialized power structures of the Americas.

This book is thus mostly concerned with the white minorities of the plantation world. Yet it is concerned with them as they and their ritual ways were transformed in slave societies, surrounded by the cultural power and numerical superiority of Africans and their descendents. Francis Le Jau, Anglican priest at Goose Creek, South Carolina, wrote home that slaves came "constantly all of them near and about the Windows of Our Church, which cannot contain them when the Parishioners are met."[15] The white parishioners who filled that small, elegant church shared a liturgy that connected them to England, a place they plaintively continued to call "home." Gathered on Sunday, they might imagine themselves for a moment in their ancestral parish churches in London, Bristol, or Plymouth. Yet even a glance out the window would remind them of Carolina's black majority and the different world they now inhabited. As Goose Creek Africans looked in those same windows, gauging the spiritual power of their oppressors, whites tightened their grip on the comfort and power of their worship. For diverse groups of Africans, Europeans, and their descendents, Christian liturgy was a central venue for finding a place in an inchoate, violent, and rapidly developing colonial world.

In all the plantation colonies, persons who had heritages both African and European featured prominently in the ritual life of the church. Free persons of color, many of them mulatto, found power and meaning in Christian worship. In baptism, they earned a distinction from most slaves and created a legal identity for themselves in parish records. In matrimony, they found theological support for their unions and legitimacy for their children, who when baptized themselves became second- (or more) generation Christians. Elite Creole slaves, some of them mulatto, were similarly the most likely of the enslaved to find meaning for their lives and power in the ritual life of the church. While slave religion and the black church have been important areas of historical inquiry, the ritual lives of free persons of color and elite slaves have often suffered a historiographical neglect rooted in the image of the tragic mulatto and in historians' distaste for persons who explored the religion of their oppressors. They feature prominently here.

This book seeks to explore Christian ritual in places that historians have long found devoid of any meaningful Christian practice. Historians have paid little attention to religion, especially in its ritual dimension, in the British plantation colonies. Given the vitality of the historical literature on religion in early modern Europe and other parts of early America, such as New England and the Middle Colonies, this omission is striking. It is as though the Englishmen and Englishwomen who colonized the plantation regions shed their religiosity in the middle of the north Atlantic, becoming secular protocapitalists who worshipped only the main chance. Emerging from an English religious landscape that provided them with a rich cultural repertoire of socially useful rituals and a nationally cohesive Protestantism, it seems highly unlikely that settlers would abandon those resources just as they faced the challenges of a colonizing project fraught with cultural anxieties.[16] Failing to understand liturgical Christianity, ignoring the social meanings of ritual, and subjecting the religiosity of the plantation colonies to an evangelical hermeneutic has obscured an essential process by which social power was created and contested in the British colonial world.

Built into the documents historians have cited for many years on religion in the plantation colonies is a bias that has led to significant confusion. In the absence of diaries and other personal papers, historians have long relied on travelers' accounts, documents produced by sometimes hostile outsiders whose experience in the colonies may have been quite short. Indeed, many of those visitors were Roman Catholics, Quakers, or evangelicals, persons whose negative interactions with Anglican hegemony hardly inclined them to view the Church of England sympathetically. One French Catholic priest who visited Barbados in the 1650s saw nothing there to remind him of Catholic religious culture, which he recorded in his account as "no sign of religion in this island." Even as he reported rigorous enforcement of the Sabbath, the priest insisted that the colonists "have almost no religion." Written in the same decade that Barbadians rioted to preserve the use of the Book of Common Prayer, the suggestion that colonists had no religion seems unfair.[17] While we might forgive the priest this misrepresentation, especially given English treatment of Roman Catholics, it is hard to look so charitably on historians citing this account as evidence of the irreligion of the British Caribbean.[18]

The British plantation colonies have also been regarded as irreligious simply because their establishments were not evangelical in nature, paling in comparison to a sometimes unstated Puritan ideal.[19] Even historians without any evangelical commitments of their own have struggled to understand a legally established and liturgical version of Christian belief and practice. They have reproduced, often uncritically, the complaints of evangelicals about Anglicanism. When New Englander Josiah Quincy visited Charles Town in 1773, he found the worship of St. Philip's Church no more than a "*solemn mockery*," largely because the minister lacked the evangelical *gravitas* Quincy expected and because the people were too sociable. While Quincy was entitled to criticize Carolina worship based on his allegiance to New England's religion, it is unfortunate how often his critique has been assumed by later historians. Puritanism and then revivalism are often seen as the dynamic and democratic American religious traditions as the standards of period evangelicals became the standards of most historians. As John K. Nelson explained this evangelical synthesis, "worship is equated with preaching; spirituality with individual conversion; and institutional authenticity with voluntary association and congregational autonomy."[20] This strand of the historiography of religion in the United States has been profoundly unhelpful for understanding a period in which early modern European precedents are far more important than nineteenth-century developments.

That failure to attend to the established church on its own terms is situated in a larger failure to evaluate the plantation regions outside of comparisons implicit and explicit with other regions of early America, New England in particular. The values that most historians bring to their inquiry have long led to a valorization of the New England way. For many years, free labor, small-scale agriculture, widespread literacy, and the early establishment of permanent cultural institutions like churches and schools drew historians' attention and marked New England as the seedbed of the later nation. The plantation regions failed to achieve in ways that marked them as divergent from the hopeful national narrative. Even historians who resist the teleology of looking through the wrong end of the telescope at the colonial experience have found the British plantation regions to be pathological places. Peter Wood's seminal *Black Majority*, Richard Dunn's *Sugar and Slaves,* and Carl and Roberta Bridenbaugh's *No Peace Beyond the Line* found dismal colonies populated by paranoid white minorities with little interest in founding real societies. Two of the Bridenbaughs' chapter titles illustrate the point: "Incomplete Societies" and "Material Success and Social Failure."[21]

These important books share a common foundation in the powerful social history model dominant in the second half of the last century, one that exposed plantation societies from the ground up. Wood's careful demographic analysis and nuanced recovery of varieties of work, for instance, recovered black life in Carolina in ways many had imagined impossible. Yet its drawback was an inability to approach the difficult-to-quantify religious lives of its black and white subjects. The social history of religion can be inclined to a skeptical instrumentalism that sees all religious practice as a proxy for more fundamental social processes, indeed, as ideological cover for efforts at social and political domination. That reading is deeply attractive for understanding the meaning of ritual in the plantation colonies, yet it has the capacity to flatten religious culture in ways that lead us away from, not deeper into, the archives. While resisting that interpretation in its crudest form, I recognize that religion must have social meaning for most persons to bother with it at all. But I draw back from instrumentalist readings that perpetuate some historical subjects' manipulation of the Christian tradition by insisting that those manipulations are the total meaning of religion. Pushing back against social history methodology and a New England bias can thus correct persistent misunderstandings of the plantation colonies.

The decentering of New England in the historiography of early America that has occurred since at least the 1970s has offered useful correctives that are enabling researchers to provide a clearer picture of the plantation colonies. Jack P. Greene's essays and the work of his students are at the center of this shift. Greene has argued that rather than being typical and thus normative, "New

England was in many respects exceptional," its culture "scarcely penetrat[ing] into the area west and south of the Hudson River."²² While later developments would render the South and British Caribbean strange and slavery peculiar, it is now clear that they were far more typical of the early American experience than was that of the Bible Commonwealth. Their exploitative structures were sadly conventional, not uniquely pathological. Thus one recent scholar of Jamaica points to planters who were "more unified, less debauched, less selfish, and less self-serving than some think," persons who "did manage to create a viable society in the Caribbean that was characterized by more than just untrammeled individualism, self-centeredness, and lack of concern for the commonweal."²³ Indeed, West Indians and Carolinians celebrated their successful creation of "identifiably *English* political institutions and a corporate identity that centered upon allegiance to the metropole and replication of that metropole's most cherished norms of behavior and identity."²⁴ Spending less time castigating the plantation colonies has predictably opened the way to understanding them better, even without granting them absolution. Yet the work of Greene and scholars associated with him has often had a tin ear for religious themes in the southern colonies.²⁵

From a different scholarly direction, the past thirty years of scholarship on religion in the Chesapeake have offered a substantial revision of long-received wisdom about the cultural meaning of religion in that region, a place that offers New England some competition as seedbed of the later nation. Shibboleths about the economic basis of colonization in Virginia and the purer mission of New Englanders have given way to careful studies of the Anglican religious culture in Virginia that point to a church that was, at the least, not exceptionally deficient in its ministrations.²⁶ The richness of that scholarship shapes the present inquiry in many ways, though important differences between the social history of Virginia and the British plantation colonies included in this study should be noted. Sharing much, the Chesapeake and the plantation colonies of this study diverged in terms of race and population, in ways that affected their respective religious histories. If Virginia (founded 1607) was the first British plantation colony in North America, the colonies in this study saw the development of that system beyond any early Virginian's expectation. Yet the plantation colonies of the lower South and Caribbean are not offered here as paradigmatic for understanding the religious or racial history of the United States or of early America generally. Such an intellectual project would either ignore or essentialize the disparate regions and peoples of early America in ways that are by no means helpful at this moment in the development of the historiography.

The demographics of race place Barbados, Jamaica, and Carolina in a category apart from Maryland and Virginia. The Chesapeake was a society with slaves that became a slave society, but its European population never faced the majority and supermajority African populations typical of Carolina and the West Indies.[27] While Barbados shared with Virginia an economy initially established with indentured European labor and featuring relatively small units of production, its transition to African slavery and large-scale plantation agriculture in the 1640s was early and rapid.[28] Virginia's more famous, similar, but not so thorough transition came in the wake of Bacon's Rebellion in 1676.[29] Jamaica and Carolina had still less in common with early Virginia; they were practically established as slave societies, rooted in the later Barbadian colonial experience. Though much contemporary scholarship warns us away from underestimating the cultural and political coherence of the European regimes in the southerly plantation colonies, it remains the case that there were many more whites in Virginia than in the colonies in this study. In 1730, for instance, there were over 100,000 whites in Virginia and fewer than 10,000 in South Carolina.[30] Thus Europeans in Virginia were able to achieve the critical mass of population necessary for the creation of a more complex set of cultural institutions than was to be found in the plantation colonies: a better developed parish and local government system, a provincial college, and a larger political class buttressed by more white freeholders. Those differences with the islands were furthered, to a degree that should not be overstated, by West Indian absenteeism. While Carolina planters did not repatriate nearly as frequently as West Indians, the colony's fractious political culture and the dominance of Charles Town prevented the development of a wider set of cultural and political institutions.[31] Whites in the plantation colonies thus faced a level of cultural anxiety persistently higher than residents of the Chesapeake.

The African experience differed between the Tidewater and the other plantation colonies as well. The first generation of Africans in the Chesapeake predated the full-scale plantation regime, allowing for a charter generation experience that included access for some to the church, the courts, and, sometimes, to freedom. While the earliest generation of Africans in most American colonies experienced some period of the saw-buck equality that often accompanied frontier conditions, those periods were much shorter in the plantation colonies.

After the end of the charter generation experience, Afro-Virginians lived in smaller groups than did Africans in the plantation colonies, under closer white supervision and greater European cultural regulation of African ways. Unlike economies relentlessly focused on sugar and rice, Virginia's tobacco monoculture gave way to an agricultural economy that included substantial cereal production across the eighteenth century.[32] The larger-scale monoculture production of the plantation colonies did offer enslaved Africans moments of greater personal and cultural autonomy, even as it lowered their life expectancy and reproductive capacity to dismal levels.

Across the decades, whites in the plantation colonies were thus persistently surrounded by African languages, religions, and cultures in a way that Virginians were not. While travelers might say that Carolina was "more like a negro country," Virginia visitors could be sure that whites there preserved a much greater degree of cultural suzerainty and faced a generally lower risk of violent reprisal from slaves. Those cultural differences also rested on the basic fact that both Europeans and Africans in the Chesapeake lived longer and better than their counterparts farther south; that demographic difference produced more creolized populations in both racial groups. Slave populations in the plantation colonies contained many more Africans than increasingly creolized Virginia.[33] Vastly outnumbered by a decidedly foreign people they oppressed, it was inevitable that those engaged in Christian worship in the plantation colonies would experience it differently than Virginians.

Yet a relative dearth of books on religion in the plantation colonies suggests that Virginia and its literature on religion and society have, in the historiography of early America, often stood in for the rest of the colonial South, an approach with obvious shortcomings, including serious inattention to the British Caribbean.[34] Historians of Christianity have produced a few monographs on the established church in the plantation colonies, often from an institutional perspective. Those books have not been noteworthy for their impact on the wider social and cultural history of these locales, particularly the important history of slavery and race.[35] Indeed, both Anglicanism and religion generally in the British Caribbean and, to a lesser degree, in the early South are underdeveloped fields in the historiography of religion in early America.[36] Some new studies are exploring vitality in Christianity in Carolina before the advent of evangelicalism. Thomas J. Little points to a highly churched people and a resurgent Anglicanism as keys to understanding the emergence of evangelicalism.[37] An attractive interpretive field thus remains largely open for historians willing to explore the place of Christian ritual in the slave societies of the plantation colonies, aided in part by recent accomplishments in the Virginia historiography.

Freed from unflattering comparisons with both evangelicalism and New England and from the national narrative of the United States, the ritual lives of the plantation colonies can be seen in an Atlantic frame, as part of a "pervasive Anglican culture" that linked them "not only with contemporaries across the Atlantic but also back across the centuries that had witnessed the fashioning of the institutions, beliefs, and traditions of Western Christendom."[38] That Atlantic frame makes available the analytical tools of scholars of early modern European religion, drawing the analysis of these colonies toward deep European precedents. While American historiographical traditions offer few useful tools for understanding liturgical phenomena in this early period, studies of European Christianity abound in potentially useful cultural perspectives on ritual life, many building on anthropologists' attention to the ways in which ritual behavior serves to mediate both continuity and change in societies.[39] While some social historians can be criticized for always seeing religion as a conservative instrument, anthropologists like Victor Turner have shown that ritual "is not necessarily a bastion of social conservatism; its symbols do not merely condense cherished sociocultural values. Rather, through its liminal processes, it holds the generating force of culture and structure." A ritual approach to religion offers a better sense of the dynamics of power in these British plantation colonies, where "the capacity for ritual action to embrace and even celebrate ambiguity" in power relations was also made manifest. Following the invitation of David D. Hall, the study of ritual is particularly useful for understanding religion in regions where sources would reveal little about the ordained ministry or the history of theological ideas, topics that have unhelpfully dominated religious history.[40]

The Atlantic frame also allows my analysis to transgress later political boundaries that have often distracted historians and that are entirely irrelevant to understanding religion early in the period covered here. The prenational approach that long dominated colonial American history marginalized the study of places like Barbados and Jamaica on account of their failure to rebel in 1776.[41] Yet "the thirteen colonies in North America represented only half the colonies of British America in 1776," as a recent study of the Revolutionary-era Caribbean insists. In their religious experience, the plantation colonies were linked by the "movement of Africans and Europeans in both directions" between the mainland and the islands, by "metropolitan-based institutional links" to the Church

Christian Ritual in Slave Societies **19**

of England, and by the movement of the African American missionaries who created black evangelical churches late in the eighteenth century.[42] This book shows how state-sanctioned liturgical religion, black majorities, and plantation economies created a common set of experiences that render the British plantation colonies a unit of analysis as useful as nearly any grouping of the thirteen North American colonies.

Sharing demographic profiles, economic structures, and deep-seated drives to Anglicize the colonial experience, the colonies of the British plantation world were rooted in a common religious culture. The churches of the plantation colonies did not produce theological luminaries like Jonathan Edwards, powerful preachers like Cotton Mather, or intensely introspective spiritual diarists like Samuel Seawell, the usual heroes (sometimes villains) of religion in early America. Christians in the plantation colonies instead experienced their faith on levels considerably more mundane and hardly knew how to respond to the occasional spiritual prodigy who rose up among them. The religious culture and ritual life that whites and some persons of color shared in these slave societies was rooted in an early modern English religious experience, one that readily translated from a gentry- and merchant-dominated metropole to colonies in which power was heavily concentrated at the upper ends of the social and economic spectrum. While emerging American systems of race changed everything about ritual life in these British slave societies, those changes were within a socially situated Christian ritual tradition that had endured and sometimes transcended its manipulators for 1700 years. Uncovering the translation of that tradition and its social meanings in practices of ritual time and space is the subject of the following chapter.

CHAPTER 2

Ritual Time and Space in the British Plantation Colonies

IN THE BRITISH PLANTATION COLONIES, the legal establishment of the Church of England meant that locally elected vestries supervised the building of parish churches and chapels-of-ease, providing for everything from their exterior structures to the furnishings of their interiors. They purchased reading desks and pulpits for the reading of scripture and preaching, and communion tables and chancel appointments for the celebration of the Lord's Supper. Vestries also guided the construction of pews for congregational seating. This provision of liturgical space and the securing of a minister made available the resources for following the liturgical year established in the calendar of the Book of Common Prayer and required by the Act of Uniformity. In those spaces and in that particular sort of time, colonial Christians offered their worship in ways that allowed them to strive for the comforts of both hierarchy and community and to order their experience in ways that maintained metropolitan connections and dealt with colonial realities, particularly the reality of societies in thrall to racial slavery.[1] Faced with physical separation from the metropole and disquieting social realities, colonists translated venerable practices of ritual time and space to their new homes, hoping to elide the difference between those places and the world they had left behind. European colonists' persistent fidelity to ancient ritual practices even became a resource to enslaved Africans and their descendents, who explored their own power in the cultural interstices that this hoped-for "supercession of place" provided.[2]

Church Seating

The parish churches constructed in Barbados, Jamaica, and South Carolina shared in the idiom of English churches built in the seventeenth and eighteenth centuries. Their usually anonymous designers often shared Christopher Wren's desire to provide churches that permitted worshippers to hear and see the actions of the liturgy without impediment. These preaching boxes were usually rectangular in shape, though cruciform churches with transepts were popular in Jamaica.[3] Their shallow chancels, simple communion tables, and towering pulpits topped with elaborate sounding boards articulated an Anglican vision in which word and sacrament were balanced in the worship of the church. Yet the social intruded on any theologian's ideal. The floors of these churches were often composed of gravestones, inscribed with pious phrases and evidence of gentility. Their walls were covered in memorial tablets, some ordered from London to commemorate the wealthy dead. And pews and seats filled nearly every available space, some so large and ornate as to be nearly monumental, others so simple and light as to be readily moveable. Sold, rented, granted, inherited, pews ordered the communities of the plantation world as they gathered for divine worship.[4]

Demand for seats in church was considerable in the plantation colonies, where congregations were not always as slim as some reports had them, especially in the urban parishes. The first SPG missionary to South Carolina, Samuel Thomas, reported at Goose Creek a "Congregation [that] was so numerous yt the church could not contain them, many stood with out doors the poor people were very attentive." St. Philip's in Charles Town reported 260 regular worshippers in the 1720s. When that parish needed a new minister in 1745, the bishop of London was assured that "the usual auditory" was "Six or Seven Hundred People," likely a very full house.[5] The same was reported in nonliturgical churches. Charles Town Independents found by 1729 that their meeting house was "too small and inconvenient to receive and contain the whole number of People which repair thither for Worship," since "by means of the vast growth of our Trade, a great Number of Sea-faring and transient persons come to, and frequent this Port," and apparently wanted to worship as well. Eliza Pinckney noted that "St. Phillips Church in Charles Town is a very Eligant one, and much frequented. There are several more places of publick worship in this town and the generality of people [are] of a religious turn of mind." St. Andrew's parish, up the Ashley River from Charles Town, had sixty or seventy families (thus many more individuals) most Sundays. None of the country parishes in Carolina reported fewer than fifty worshippers on Sunday in the 1720s. St. Thomas's and Christ Church had as many as seventy, while the Goose Creek and Santee parishes regularly accommodated one hundred worshippers. While

Interior of St. Andrew's Church, South Carolina. Courtesy of Suzanne Linder Hurley.

these numbers are not overwhelming, they likely came close to filling the small churches of the rural low country.[6] The spiritual and social comforts of divine worship were recognized in early Carolina.

Barbados in the 1720s also reported a respectable level of church attendance. The rector of St. Michael's in the Barbadian metropolis of Bridgetown reported that "in dry weather every pew in it is pretty full, so that I can . . . affirm yt are no congregations in England more regular, very few larger, and not many so large as mine." Even in the plantation districts of the island, Joseph Holt of St. Joseph's could report that when "ye Weather is favourable we have a full & (blessed be God) conformable Congregation." The rectors of St. Philip's and St. Peter's assured the bishop that their services were well attended. St. Thomas's had as many as 120 worshippers, while St. Andrew's had 70 or 80. John Oldmixon's English readers were assured that St. Michael's Church in Bridgetown was "as large as many of our Cathedrals," clearly meant to seat large numbers of persons. Indeed, seventy years later, the clerk of St. Michael's recorded the destruction of the church by a hurricane, lamenting the loss of a fine building that "had often

Ritual Time and Space **23**

Exterior of St. Andrew's Church, South Carolina. Courtesy of Suzanne Linder Hurley.

held more than 3000 souls at one time."[7] The neglect of public worship in the plantation colonies reported by some visitors (and reiterated by many historians) is often not borne out in the archival record.

Even the Jamaican parishes in Kingston, Port Royal, and Spanish Town reported tolerable congregations in the 1720s. William May of Kingston found that on Sunday morning, "the Church is generally pretty full, but very thin at other times." Enlargements of the Kingston parish church over the eighteenth century eventually produced a building that could seat 1300 worshippers. John Scott of St. Catherine's parish in Spanish Town wrote that he could "assure your Lordship a considerable Number of the Parishioners constantly and religiously attend." But the country parishes in Jamaica were sparsely attended. Only John Kelly of St. Elizabeth's parish reported "a large & Devout Congregation" for his ministrations. Nicholas McCalman at St. Thomas's in the East explained his congregation of no more than twelve by noting that his parish was "three times larger than Barbados: but has only 62 families." Richard Marsden of St. John's also pointed out that the few European families in his parish largely consisted of overseers and a few white servants, amounting to a congregation of no more than eighteen, including "six Negros." Edward Reading of St. Thomas's in the Vale had between ten and thirty at his services.[8] Outside of its largest towns, Jamaica in the 1720s was a place with little observance of Sunday liturgy, largely because there were relatively few Europeans in those parishes to serve as the nucleus of parish communities.

The popularity of divine worship in most parts of the plantation colonies meant that sometimes pews could only be had at premium prices or were simply unavailable. The experience of the Independent Church in Charles Town was typical of Christian congregations in the larger towns. They initially desired in 1732 "to divide, ascertain, allot, and settle the Use of the Pews in the said House, in the most equal manner." They set aside pews for the minister's family and for strangers, reserving the gallery seats for persons without pews.[9] If that "equal manner" indicated a lack of pecuniary interest, that policy was abandoned in 1734 when the Corporation agreed "to Allot the Vacant Pews to such Person or Persons as are or shall become Supporters of the Church and Ministry . . . and That in making the Allotment the highest Subscrib^s and Payers to the Building of the said Meeting-House be allowed the preference of Exchanging their Pews or parts of Pews." The church in use in 1759 was again found too small since "many Persons had made Applications to the Managers for Pews in this Meeting-House, which they could not accommodate said Persons with, as there was not one Pew in the Meeting-House Vacant."[10] Clearly the Independent Church was not often found empty, filled as it was pew by pew, according to the pew holders' means.

As it had for the Independents, the growth of Charles Town meant that the Anglicans of St. Philip's Church would eventually outgrow their building as well. When the new Charles Town parish of St. Michael's was organized as a result in the 1750s, many people jumped at the opportunity to get a pew, often noting their inability to get a pew at St. Philip's.[11] An older man complained that "I have been Twety Odd years an Inhabiter and never yet been master of One."[12] Younger members of prominent families also took advantage of the opportunity. Daniel Ravenel Jr. wrote to express his desire for "a Pew in the New Church of St. Michael" to be shared with Alexander Mazyck, since "we both Hold Land and Houses In the Parish of St. Philip, and have not Pews in the Church"[13] Yet even with the addition of St. Michael's, one evangelical minister noted "the enormous price of Pews, some of which have sold for £1,900 in the Church of England," a price that "puts it out of the power of People in poor or middling circumstances to be the owners of them, and by this means a great number of the good people of this place are deprived of the Benefit of attending Worship, unless they will impose themselves upon the real Estate of others, which few chuse to do, and which indeed few owners of Pews would long

Submit to."[14] In Bridgetown the vestry received sundry "complaints of several of the inhabitants for want of seats for their families in the Church" in 1726. They agreed to move the pulpit to make more room for new pews, having earlier allowed persons to make an addition to the gallery and to build new pews in it.[15] Demand exceeded the limited supply of church seating available in the plantation colonies, a situation that dominant themes in the historiography of the early South and British Caribbean would not lead us to expect.

Persons had definite values in mind when they sought a seat in church. One applicant for a seat in St. Michael's in Charles Town complained of being "left in the dark in the Choice of our pews in St Michaels Church," which was an issue because he and his wife were "both in years & Consequently cannot hear at a distance So well as youth." Thus "without hearing a preacher distinctly our coming to Church is in vain, And our money laid out Unprofitably." He went on to offer a sliding scale subscription to get the best pew possible for his money.[16] John Giles wrote to pledge £211, crossed out and raised to £235, for "a large family" but only "on condition the said sum shall entitle me to one of the following Numbers, vizt, 78, 88, or 91"; otherwise he would offer only £111. John McQueen requested "a good pew in St. Michael's Church" and insisted that it be "not in the Gallerys."[17] The building of a new church was an opportunity for members of the community to secure a seat in church that would cement their place in the community and allow them the spiritual and social benefits of participation in the worship of the church, about which many seemed to care deeply.[18]

At a similar moment in the mid-eighteenth century, the vestry of St. Michael's in Barbados reviewed its nearly 120-year history of granting pews in that Bridgetown church as part of a substantial rebuilding, a process that reveals how important church seating was in the principal town of that island colony. In 1754, they posted notices on "the Church Door & the Doors of all the Public Offices & Taverns of Town," informing inhabitants that they would be available in the vestry room from 9:00 to 12:00 in the morning and from 2:00 to 6:00 in the afternoon the next Wednesday through Saturday to "ascertain the property of the Old Pews & Settle with the Proprietors the cost of Rebuilding them, & also to Dispose of the New Pews to such Persons as are Dispos'd to purchase the same." Putting aside twenty-eight hours for these meetings reveals what an important undertaking adjusting the pews of the church was for the Bridgetown community, a place where even tavern-goers would be interested in church pews. After the meetings, the vestry published the results of their deliberations in the local newspaper, assigning pews and their respective costs. These assignments were not always well received; twenty-eight persons refused to pay for the pews assigned to them and numerous others requested and received pews other than those initially assigned by the vestry.[19] These were clearly not indifferent matters.

Applicants for seats in newly pewed spaces desired to be able to see and hear the officiating minister above all but also desired seats that reflected their understanding of their proper place in the parish hierarchy, especially as revealed by one's ability to pay. While English parishes often used older, naturalized concepts of gentility and quality, colonial vestries could not rely on the customs of time out of mind. Fortunately, the market offered attractive solutions to their problem. New pews built in St. Michael's in Charles Town in 1766 were to be rented "to the highest biders by the year."[20] The building of the church in Prince Frederick parish in South Carolina was partially funded by a subscription with a £15 minimum; "the highest Subscriber shall have the first choice of a place in the Church to build their Pew on, and so in proportion."[21] Even with competitive subscribing, pew purchasers in Prince Frederick still had to pay more for better locations. The largest pews nearest the pulpit and altar were valued at £22 by the vestry, while number 13 at the very back could be had for only £12.[22] St. John's parish in Colleton County did set a standard £17 for all its pews in 1742 but then distributed them based on the amounts paid in the initial subscription. St. Michael's in Bridgetown seems to have assigned seats based on the amount parishioners were paying in the parish levy. These systems based on economic reality were far simpler than the customary one that sought to gauge the quality, degree, or state of each member of a more static parish community, as many parishes did in England.[23] Colonists thus adapted an older English practice to the social reality of their protocapitalist plantation colonies.

Pews were not always, however, distributed all at once in systems based on economic criteria. When pews were sold or rented on demand over many years, applicants had more discretion to request particular areas of the church for their pews, usually built at their own charge and sometimes by carpenters of their own hire. James Cowse had built his eight-foot-square pew on the south side of the communion rails of St. Michael's in Bridgetown in 1707. Five years later, he requested to move the pew to the vacant north side of the rails "and to place one side of the pew close to the Inner Communion rails, he consenting to move the sd. pew back again if any inconvenience shall happen." Others slowly established some customary right to certain pews. Edward Croft of Bridgetown

Interior of St. Michael's Church, Charleston, South Carolina. Courtesy of Suzanne Linder Hurley.

found his imagined right to such a pew violated when William Bipsham and family were given permission to take part of "the pew where Mr. Edwd. Crofts usually sits, the pew being a publick pew in which the sd. Edwd. Crofts has no property." Any complaint he offered would have fallen on deaf ears, the vestry being more interested in legal right than any argument from long usage. Some Barbadians sought to construct family pews in close proximity to the intramural graves of their families. In 1697, three residents of Bridgetown were granted permission "to erect a pew at the West End of the Church for themselves and family near the place where some of their relations are interred."[24] Finding a proper place in church could mean joining generations both living and dead when gathered for divine worship.

Controversies over pews were not infrequent in the plantation colonies; indeed, readers could follow metropolitan disputes in their newspapers. The publisher of the *South Carolina Gazette* capitalized on the perennial interest of male readers in public disputes between women with an account in 1734 of an argument over a pew in Durham Cathedral. That "warm and loud Dispute" was serious enough "that the Service of the Church was interrupted by it for some time."[25] When trespassers invaded, vestries ordered locks put on pews. St. Michael's in Bridgetown did so when some unapproved women presumed to sit in the women's pew in a prominent position "under the Governor's pew."[26] In the same parish, the vestry adjudicated a dispute between Dorothy Maxwell and unknown persons who had attempted "to prevent her and her family from sitting in a pew which was granted to Alexander Skeen Esq." Her right to sit there was preserved.[27] There must have been a serious discussion around the vestry table before Alexander Garden, the rector of St. Philip's in Charles Town, agreed to allow four pews to be built in the chancel in 1738, "provided, and on the express Condition, that the Said Pews Shall not be Sold," but leased on an annual basis to produce income "towards the Repairing of the Chancell," an area of the church that the rector traditionally controlled. In the 1760s, when St. Stephen's parish was divided from St. James's Santee in Carolina, two of the commissioners for building the new church resigned in protest over the "late proceedings in regard to the pewing of St. Stephen's Church," which were "of a very Singular Nature" and highly "disagreeable."[28] Like their English forbears, residents of the plantation colonies were willing to fight over seats in church.

Beyond any infringement or dispute were the elaborate pews provided for colonial governors, pews that manifested the governor's power as representative of a distant English monarch and as the local defender of the faith. Sir Jonathan Atkins, the governor of Barbados, arrived at church one Sunday in the fall of 1676 to find his pew newly recovered, the vestry having paid 400 pounds of sugar for a craftsman's services.[29] In Jamaica, the governor had his own pew in both Kingston and St. Catherine's parish churches. In Spanish Town, the communion rails ran "about the Altar and the Governors Counsellors and other Contiguous pews," putting these seats of power nearest the visual center of Eucharistic celebrations. The governor's pew was outfitted with a canopy to increase the dignity associated with it.[30] The governor took a real interest in the pew in 1765, indicating that "it would be more agreeable to his Excelly to have the same rail'd" in place of the existing "Freeze Pannells." In Kingston, the vestry took pains to order "that Mr. James Baines Supply Green Cloth & Cushions & other Necessarys for Lineing his Excellency's Pew against Easter Sunday" and later "ordered that Mr. Sparkes alter the Governours pew answerable to his directions," another case of a governor taking an interest in his pew. The South Carolina legislation for "Erecting of a new Brick Church at Charles Town" in 1711 included provision for a "Great Pew; designed to be built in the said Church, for the Use of the Governour and Council, which shall be built in such Place in the Church, and of such Dimensions and Form as the Governor and Council shall direct." No private pews were to rival these official ones; in 1715, the Bridgetown vestry ordered "all the tops of the pews . . . be cut (as the Governors and Councillors pews formerly were)."[31] So identified were colonial governors with their pews that the Antiguans who murdered Governor Daniel Parke in 1710 ripped his pew out of the church as the culmination of their violence.[32] From these prominent and highly decorated seats, luckier governors took a central place in the liturgy that their royal instructions charged them to support.[33]

Besides political elites, parishes reserved pews for other particular groups of people, gathering the parish community in its ranks. By 1663, St. Michael's in Barbados had reserved "ye great pew over against ye pulpit . . . for such Women as ye Churchwardens shall think fitt" and another for the justices of the peace. In order "to make a place for [the rector's] scholars to set in," the vestry reserved a portion of the gallery in 1682, and schoolchildren seem to have often been seated together.[34] For some years there was a "Churchwarden and Vestrymen's pew" in St. Michael's and one for lawyers as well.[35] St. Andrew's in Jamaica had two "Green Pews," with cushions that made some select persons, like the vestry and justices of the peace, more comfortable.[36] St. Catherine's in Spanish Town had "several Seats . . . in the Church for the Soldiers adjoining the Organ Loft." The minister was granted a pew for his family in St. Helena's parish in Beaufort, South Carolina, "to be payd for by the parish."[37] The leaders of the Independent Church in Charles Town awarded the "vacant half-part of Pew No. 30 (by the Consent of many of the Congregation) . . . for the Use of Mr. Chas. Warham, so long as he shall continue to Set the Psalms." By the 1760s, St. Philip's vestry in Carolina had appropriated the chancel "for the poor of the Work house" and forcefully reminded the sexton that "you are not to suffer any other persons to sit there."[38] Reserving such prominent seats for the parish poor reminds us that seating practices were not rigidly hierarchical and were prone to frequent anomalies. Community sometimes carried the day.

Parish leaders found room for outside elements in the arrangement of their churches, and it seems that visitors regularly worshiped in the port cities of the plantation world. In 1700, a pew "for the use of Captains of Ships or Strangers" was established near the Great Door of St. Michael's in Bridgetown. By 1727, strangers in that church were lucky to find a seat on the simple benches provided for them "in the vacant places in the church." Later in the year, a more hospitable solution was found when Captain Richard Barret donated four pews in the old gallery for the use of "non residents and strangers," as an inscription on the front of the pews reminded worshippers. St. Philip's in Charles Town created a pew in 1734 for "Comanders of Vessells," directing the sexton to keep all others out of the pew "unless there be a vacancy after the first lesson is read."[39] St. Helena's in Carolina added common benches to its church more than once in the eighteenth century, at one point using funds arising from the sale of prominent pews in the east end of the church to make six new benches "to be placed on the vacant Ground at the west End of the Church between the Pews."[40] Thus could the vestry simultaneously legitimate the social standing of elites and provide seating for regular folk, bundling community and hierarchy in a deft move. While pew ownership was clearly desirable, there were usually common spaces in the church where others could find a seat.

Sextons and other church personnel made seating systems work as they seated persons arriving at church on Sunday, especially strangers and visitors. Charged with keeping order in a variety of ways, they used visual clues to determine the quality of persons who did not have regular seats. The sexton of St. Philip's in Charles Town was reminded by his employers that only "strangers who are in decent apparel" could be seated in the captain's pew. Peter Manigault wrote from London at midcentury to acquit himself of his mother's suspicion that he was spending too much on fancy clothes. He insisted that his one lace coat was a necessity, for "they won't even give one a Seat in Church, without a good Suit of Clothes on." He explained that "on Sunday Evening, I went with Billy Drayton to hear the celebrated Mr. Foster, I was drest quite plain, my friend had a Laced Waistcoat and hat, he, or rather his Laced Waistcoat, was introduced in a pew, while I, that is, my plain Clothes, were forced to stand up, during the whole time of divine service, in the Isle."[41] While Manigault's letter suggests that a lace coat was not a necessity in Carolina, he clearly expected his mother to recognize the context and nature of the affront he received from parish officials who did not recognize his status.

Such affronts were regular in the lives of the persons of color who worshipped in the white-controlled churches of the plantation colonies. Many readers will be familiar with church galleries or balconies reserved for people of color in the American South in the nineteenth century. The situation in the colonial period was not nearly so clear, with some slaves and free people of color taking seats in different locations throughout the church. The records reveal little on this point; the seats taken by people of color were rarely matters of controversy, which is often the necessary criterion for these matters to turn up in correspondence or church records. The bishop of London's queries to all colonial clergy in 1724 asked if there were "any Infidels, bond or free, within your Parish, and what means are us'd for their Conversion?" but did not ask how many people of color might already be Christians and where they might be sitting in church. As a result, few ministers mentioned the people of color worshipping in their churches. South Carolina's Church Act of 1706 charged the keeper of the parish register to "make true entry of all Vestry proceedings, and of all births, christenings, marriages and burials (Negroes, Mullatoes and Indian Slaves excepted)."[42] If records such as these, for which a fee was usually charged, were not kept of important moments such as these, it seems clear that the simple act of showing up for worship would not often be recorded. While we will never know how often people of color worshipped in the Christian churches of the plantation world, scattered evidence does make it clear that appreciable numbers of them, many of them free and many of them mulatto, did participate in Sunday worship, taking their places in the parish community.

It should be admitted that while some churches counted good numbers of people of color among their worshippers, those worshippers were a tiny percentage of Africans and their descendents in the colonies. We might take St. George's parish in South Carolina in the late 1730s as an example. In a parish containing over 3000 slaves, 100 of them were Christians, a small percentage indeed. Yet a small white population meant that those 100 persons represented one-fifth of the baptized persons in the parish. In the 1720s, the parish had reported up to 50 "parishioners [read whites] attending it, besides 25 or 30 of Mr. Skeene & Mrs. Hagues Negro's," meaning that some Sundays St. George's might actually have reflected Carolina's black majority.[43] Indeed, slaves made up one-third of Easter communicants. Francis La Jau reported that "several" slaves came "constantly to Church" in the early eighteenth century in Goose Creek and that his Sunday afternoon catechism services for slaves attracted about 50 persons. By the middle of the century, one of his successors reported that "such numbers crowded the church before, that they were very off[ensive] to the whites." Twenty to thirty people of color attended services in St. Thomas's parish in Carolina in 1712. These figures led Robert Olwell to argue quite correctly that "while the church may have been of small importance in the lives of most slaves, slaves played a significant part in the life of the church."[44]

The following chapter shows that most free people of color were baptized in the plantation colonies, especially in Barbados and Jamaica.[45] While not all baptized persons necessarily attended church, we would expect clergy and others to complain if baptized persons, especially people of color, failed to attend. This complaint is not to be found in the records. Instead, there are modest indications that their attendance was regular and unremarkable, even as early as the 1720s. In St. Elizabeth's parish in Jamaica, there were "a few" free persons of color who "attend Divine Service frequently & orderly." Added to Richard Marsden's small Jamaican congregation of no more than twelve whites were about "six Negros yt very often come to Church and behave with reverence and great Signs of devotion." More dramatically, the rectors of the parishes in Spanish Town and Kingston reported that their parishes contained respectively "a good many free slaves . . . the most of them are Christians" and "106 Free Negroes & Mulattoes most of which (I Believe) are Baptiz'd." In the middle of the eighteenth century, free people in Jamaica were uniformly Christian and some of them were regular churchgoers. By the end of the century, a Jamaican clergyman could report that "on Sundays the people of Colour make three fourths of my Congregation, nay, many times I would not have A Congregation without Them."[46] While we lack good information for Barbados in the eighteenth century on this point, it seems likely that the pattern held there as well; a few slaves and many free people of color attended Sunday worship in numbers that increased across the eighteenth century.[47]

Having established that people of color were present on Sunday, it remains to be seen where they sat, another tangled question for which little evidence has survived. It is likely that most free people of color took common seats in churches, those set aside at the rear of churches, between the sections of pews, and in galleries, sometimes in "the most distant part[s] of the Meeting-Place," as Morgan Godwyn put it.[48] While individual seats in those areas were not likely shared with whites, these unpewed areas were the common domain of all persons lacking better seats. When large numbers of whites without seats turned up for worship, it is likely that free persons were squeezed out of the church. Certainly there are no records in the period before 1800 of any person of color owning a pew.[49] People of color were thus permanent guests in churches with pew ownership systems, liable to losing their seats when conditions in the common areas became too crowded. Still, one looks in vain for any *consistent* pattern of segregation in seating in the colonial era.[50]

Though the thinking of whites would become increasingly racialized across the eighteenth century, older concepts of family, household, and the parish community held sway at times, concepts that could be extended to bring some enslaved and free persons into that community and its seating. Thus while some slaves occupied free seats, it seems likely that other slaves were seated with their owners, especially the liveried slaves of the plantation elite. In 1676, the vestry in Bridgetown had put a pew aside for "ye use of Lady Byron and her subalterns," a group that might have included slaves engaged in domestic service.[51] Fifty years later, it may have been that slaves took some of the seats reserved "for the use of his Excellency's servants" at St. Michael's in Bridgetown in 1734.[52] Slave owners like Alexander Skeene of St. George's in South Carolina, who may have insisted on slaves' church attendance, may have been seated with their slaves in family pews.[53] Such a practice was in keeping with the early modern understanding that servants and slaves were a certain sort of members of the family or household and that a parish community properly included all members of all the households in a parish.

Many slaves waited just outside the church during divine worship, outside the parish community but close to it. Leaders at St. Philip's in Charles Town complained about noise made by slaves during Sunday liturgy and in 1756 required its sexton "to employ at his own Charge, a white person to take care of the Church in time of Divine Service, & prevent the disturbance and Noise of Negroes & of Children that too frequently happen at those times." Earlier, the bearers who carried the dead poor people of Bridgetown to their graves were also charged with monitoring "the negroes who attend the parishioners to Church," who often made "a great noise in the Church yard in the time of divine service." Some white worshippers made a habit of "delivering their arms to negroes or other slaves to keep while they are at divine worship," presumably outside the church. While some of the slaves outside the church had no interest in going inside, some may have passed in and out, as many whites did during the long service, punctuated as it was by discrete sections of morning prayer, antecommunion, and sermon. Francis Le Jau noted that slaves came "constantly all of them near and about the Windows of Our Church, which cannot contain them when the Parishioners are met."[54] With large open windows and multiple open doors, these tropical and subtropical churches allowed even those outside to witness worship as auxiliaries to the community gathered inside.

The persons of color worshipping at St. Michael's in Charles Town late in the period seem to have furnished benches in the church for their own use. These "Benches the property of Negroes" were placed in two areas: the aisle between the north and south doors of the church, running across the breadth of the church about halfway to the rear and somewhere "near the Pulpitt," areas interspersed among the pews of wealthy whites. We only know this because the vestry received a request from some "Poor White People" to bring their own chairs to church in 1773. To accommodate these white worshippers more hospitably, the vestry ordered the sexton "accordingly to remove the Benches the property of Negroes, now place'd in those places, either into the Gallerys, or under the Bellfry." The latter is actually a space almost outside the church, its view of pulpit and table impeded by a doorway. The vestry ordered new benches made for the poor whites, to be placed in the areas recently vacated. In case their intentions to remove these black worshippers to the liturgical hinterlands was not clear, the vestry included an order "that no Negroes shall be permitted to sitt on the Benches so ordered to be made."[55] This late eighteenth-century development signaled the increasingly racialized direction of seating practices in the nineteenth century.

In Barbados in 1817, various parishes reserved galleries, particular pews, and benches in the aisles for persons of color, preserving something of the flux of seating that may have characterized an earlier period, even as racial regulation was becoming more intentional. But seating was more carefully regulated in St. Michael's in Bridgetown, the parish with the largest number of free black worshippers in Barbados. When slaves occupied the gallery seats usually used by free persons there in 1831, some in the latter group rebelled against white control that had developed of the main floor of the church, occasioning a serious and physical confrontation with the churchwarden.[56] Kingston parish in Jamaica resolved in 1813 to reserve the pews in the east and north aisles for whites, permitting persons of color some seating on the main floor and in the organ loft. Though free people of color still took seats on the main floor of some Charleston churches in the nineteenth century, many would eventually either join the slaves confined to gallery seats or leave white-controlled churches entirely.[57]

The increasing racial anxiety that whites experienced as the eighteenth century passed thus resulted in increasingly segregated worship spaces. Moving persons of color farther and more consistently into galleries and toward the rear removed them from whites' lines of sight, giving them views of pulpit and altar unimpeded by the presence of black worshippers, who were persistent reminders of how far the plantation colonies had diverged from colonists' lily white metropolitan ideal. Across the eighteenth century, colonists thus employed and altered traditional English modes of church seating to obscure the social realities of life in black majority colonies, translating a cultural practice initially about status into one that reified race. Yet as whites' control of seating and church space became increasing racialized, an older sense of the meaning of the gathered parish community was vitiated, and many persons of color in Carolina and the Caribbean responded by leaving for sacred spaces they could control.

The Ritual Year

Within the spaces of the plantation world's parish churches, inhabitants also lived with the cycle of Christian time, one that ran concurrently with the cycles of sugar and rice culture more familiar to historians of these locales.[58] To be sure, secular seasons and cycles structured time's passage in the plantation colonies. The tropical and subtropical climates of the Caribbean and Carolina differed greatly from English meteorological experience. Early Carolinians advised English readers that "the *Heats* of Carolina are indeed troublesome to Strangers in *June, July,* and *August*" and compared Carolina's February and March to April and May in England and Carolina's April and May to England's June and July. Yet the English in Carolina complained about extreme weather generally, including winter's chill. Thus the best time for a new colonist to arrive "is *September*; for then they have eight Months moderate Weather, before the Heat comes, in which Time the Climate will become agreeable." A low country woman found the summer of 1711 comparable to being "baked in an Oven." The hearty Eliza Lucas Pinckney permitted herself to complain that "4 months in the years is extreamly disagreeable, excessive hott." Relief came in the winter when the colony was "invigorated with purifying cold winds from the Cherokee Mountains, which recovers us from the languid habit acquired in the warm months." Thus Carolina's climate offered greater seasonality than Pinckney's native Antigua, which shared in the seemingly unvarying tropical climate that many colonists understood to be enervating.[59] Careful observers did note the relative cool and lesser humidity of a Caribbean winter, as well as the rise in temperature and precipitation that characterized much of the second half of the year, the season in which hurricanes might make their fearful appearance, in both the Caribbean and Carolina.

By the end of the seventeenth century, some years of experience in the hurricane zone taught the English to expect and prepare for the great storms within a fairly well-defined season, including the months of September, October, and November. By the 1670s, the people of Nevis took care to pack up their goods in the stormy season to minimize potential losses. Sugar planters too removed parts of their mills in advance of the season, hoping to reduce wind damage to their capital improvements. Ships' captains hoped to clear Caribbean ports no later than August, in advance of what one early slave trader called "the Michaelmas storms," locating the storms in the season around Micheahmas on September 29. Indeed, wise seafaring men realized that leaving southern ports in advance of the hurricanes also allowed them to arrive in England before the North Atlantic gales threatened shipping in winter. Some ships that missed the window of safety took their chances, but many that found themselves in the sugar ports in late fall would spend a pleasant Caribbean winter there, waiting to load the new sugar crop sometime in the first quarter of the year.[60]

That sugar and the rice that made Carolinians rich were produced in carefully considered agricultural cycles, summarized in manuals for new residents. Those headed to Carolina were advised that "our Season of Sowing is from the First of *March* to the tenth of *June*. The principal Seed-time of Rice, from the first of *April* to the twentieth of *May*; of *Indian* Corn, Pease and Beans, the last Week of *March*, all *April, May,* and the *first* ten Days of *June*. In *March* and *April,* we set Potatoes, Pompions, Cucumbers, Melons, Kidney-beans, &c." Rice was to be harvested in September, Indian corn and peas in October. Planters were advised that Indigo would not thrive in autumn and that they were "never to cut the Herb in a Wet Season." In early Carolina, spring planting was also combined with the gathering of recently born calves. "In the Spring of the year, when the Cows have Calved, we ride out in search for them in the Woods, and bring them home, then separating the Cows from the Calves, keeping the Calves Inclos'd."[61]

African knowledge of the seasons of rice agriculture was as important to the success of the Carolina economy as was African labor. Carolina planters intervened, however, by eliminating traditional labor cycles' moments of harvest rest. The international market for the grain permitted no such respite. In Carolina, rice work was year round. Labor-intensive water management systems and soil preparation occupied slaves from December to March. Rice in tidal zones had two plantings, in early and later spring. The growing season was punctuated by four floodings, each followed by hoeing and weeding. Harvest from late August into October was followed by the exhausting work of processing the rice in time for export to Europe, where peak prices would only be earned if the rice arrived in time for the increased demand of Catholic Europe's Lent. Planters thus aimed for a February delivery to southern European ports; here the liturgical year and economic cycles dovetailed.[62]

Sugar had its seasons as well, a definite calendar even in a region of fairly constant temperatures. Samuel Martin of Antigua was sure that "there is not therefore a greater error in the whole practice of plantership than to make sugar, or to plant canes at improper seasons of the year." Those who failed to plant between June and October and to harvest between the first of January and last of June would find themselves grinding cane later in the year, missing the relative dryness of the first quarter of the year, always better for cutting cane and boiling than for planting.[63] They thus risked both "the destruction of our wind-mills by hurricanes" and the making of "bad sugar, at infinite expence of time and labor, both of negroes and cattle." One poorly timed crop could affect an estate for years, since "by mismanagement of this kind every succeeding crop is put out of regular order."[64] Crop time meant seven days of work per week for slaves, for the mill and boiling house could not be kept waiting. Other times of year provided little respite, though tasks might be different. Just as on the rice plantations of the mainland, enslavement on a sugar plantation meant year-round work, punctuated by some seasonal variation.[65]

Disease cycles also shaped the calendars of low country whites. In the first half of the eighteenth century, those who remained in rural areas in late summer and fall took a considerable risk. Parish registers reveal that more than 40 percent of a parish's deaths could occur between August and November. The fall was particularly dangerous to the young: nearly 80 percent of residents of Christ Church parish in Carolina who died before the age of twenty did so in the sickly season. Planters gradually learned that spending summer in Charles Town had the advantage of sea breezes and distance from the malarial swamps in which their rice thrived, nonetheless complaining "that the vile fall-fevers should keep one pent up in Charleston the most agreeable season of the year." By the late eighteenth century, even German readers might have learned the Carolina calendar: "Carolina is in the spring a paradise, in the summer a hell, and in the autumn a hospital."[66]

Seasons of intensified social activity were typical of the plantation colonies, especially in Carolina and Jamaica. Shaped by the weather, politics, and agricultural and shipping cycles, the seasons drew some of the rural population into Charles Town and Spanish Town, filling boarding houses, rental property, and second homes. The social season in Spanish Town in Jamaica was tied to the meetings of law courts and the Assembly, a display of balls, horse races, and lavish meals more opulent than anywhere else in British North America.[67] Jamaica's governors, resident in King's House on the Parade, hosted the balls that were "the social peak of an Assembly season." Lordly Jamaicans like the Prices of Worthy Park enjoyed a Spanish Town house that occupied a city block, which might serve as both a welcome escape from the "sickly stink of the boiling sugar" on the estate and as a convenient perch from which to ensure planter domination of the colonial government. Carolina's main legislative session also coincided with a social season. Thus wealthy Carolinians, many maintaining a home in the city, flocked to Charles Town for a winter season that culminated in a February race week by the later eighteenth century. In the concerts of the St. Cecilia Society, dramatic productions, and dinner parties, Carolinians did their best to sustain the fiction that their metropolis was a little London.[68] As in London, a sacred calendar ran alongside dates of commercial and meteorological importance.

During its fitful Reformation, the Church of England had reformed rather than eliminated the cycles of the Christian liturgical year, intending "to be more studious of unity and concord, than of innovations and new-fangleness, which . . . is always to be eschewed."[69] While some Puritans would have preferred otherwise, the church retained three great festivals in Christmas, Easter, and Whitsunday (Pentecost). Each Sunday of the year had proper readings and prayers that anchored it in its particular season, be it a preparatory one like Advent or the ordinary time of the season after Trinity Sunday. Holy days included those based on events in the life of Christ (Circumcision, Epiphany, Ascension) and two based on events in the life of the Virgin Mary (Purification of the Blessed Virgin and Annunciation). Thirteen other days were based on key personalities of the New Testament, chiefly apostles and evangelists.[70] All Saints' Day on November 1 and St. Michael and All Angels Day on September 29 were also retained. Every Friday in the year, the Rogation and Ember days, and the forty days of Lent were appointed fast days. To these colonists added a variety of new fast days based on colonial events. Also added to the older holy days were various state holidays, including Gunpowder Treason Day (November 5), a day to observe the martyrdom of Charles I (January 30), Restoration Day (May 29), and the Accession Day of the reigning monarch.[71] The first three in particular were important to Protestant national memory and provided opportunities for Anglicans to differentiate themselves from their dissenting neighbors.[72] The feast days of St. George (April 23), St. Patrick (March 17), and St. Andrew (November 30), patrons of England, Ireland, and Scotland respectively, also developed as opportunities to gather those particular nationalities together

Ritual Time and Space 39

in the British colonies. While colonial practice would never rise to the level of the prayer book's ideal, some of these days provided a basic framework for corporate life and the passage of time, especially in cities and towns.[73]

The most basic time cycle in the plantation colonies was that from Sunday to Sunday. Evidence presented above shows that Sunday worship in many places was well attended, with worshippers filling many churches to capacity. Though usually lacking the sabbatarian rigor of their New England cousins, residents of Barbados, Jamaica, and South Carolina put the Lord's Day aside as a special one in the week. The "time of divine service" was meant to be a quiet time apart in the community's life, one that was sometimes observed both morning and afternoon.[74] In addition to opportunities for divine worship, Sunday offered time for recreation that other days did not permit and a chance to wear Sunday-best clothing. For slaves, the arrival of Sunday usually meant the week's one day of respite. The suspension of regular work meant a chance to gather the dispersed slave community for social, religious, and commercial purposes. Sunday was thus a day apart, one that offered the entire community relief from the ordinary strictures of the six days that followed. Because of the black majorities of the plantation colonies, this was a freedom that whites both welcomed and feared.

Sabbatarian laws established the basic outline of Sunday in the plantation colonies. In the seventeenth century, a Barbados act required those within two miles of a church to come to church morning and evening on Sunday. Those more than two miles away were to come at least once per month. Constables, churchwardens, and sidemen were to patrol during divine service, especially "where they do suspect leud and debauched Company to Frequent." Persons found "misdemeaning themselves" were to be put in the stocks for four hours unless they paid a 5 shilling fine, to be used for poor relief.[75] South Carolina law similarly authorized a 5 shilling fine for those who failed to go to church and "there abide orderly and soberly, during the Time of Prayer and Preaching." It forbade "publick Sports or Pastimes, as Bear-baiting, Bull-baiting, Football playing, Horse-racing, Interludes, or common Plays," and required church wardens and constables in Charles Town "in the Time of Divine Service, [to] walk through the said Town, to observe, suppress, and apprehend all Offenders whatsoever" and put them in the stocks. The same act provided that slaves were not to be obliged to work on Sunday.[76] Grand juries empanelled in Carolina consistently complained about persons who did not honor the Christian Sabbath, especially "the Prophanation of the Sabbath Day by Barbers and others, who keep open Shops for the Convenience of their Customers, to the great Scandal of Christianity and Offense to all Sober and well disposed Persons." In early 1747, Governor James Glen of South Carolina had "Sentinels . . . placed at the Town Gates every Sunday, to prevent as much as possible the Prophanation of the Lord's Day, to restrain all loose and idle Persons from going a pleasuring on that Day during the Time of Divine Service, and to stop all Drovers, Butchers, and their Servants with their Carts and Horses from coming to Market on that Day," in keeping with the 1712 law for observance of the Sabbath.[77] Jamaican legislation also established fines for those who permitted any "to tipple or drink in time of divine Service."[78] While there was distance between elite prescription and popular practice, Sunday was not the same as every other day in the plantation colonies.

Worshippers invested the basic Christian duty of Sunday worship with a variety of additional social and cultural meanings. Church attendance, for instance, consistently required a special level of dress. In early eighteenth-century Jamaica, it was one of the few places where men did *not* wear a ruffled or "furbelowed Cambric cap," attire judged too hot by succeeding generations. Men did wear wigs, silk coats, and vests trimmed with silver to church in Jamaica, court time being the only other occasion that called for such formality.[79] A letter from a devout old maid named "Mary Meanwell" published in the South Carolina newspaper in 1732 complained that her "constant and devout Attendance on publick Worship" was undermined by her "misfortune to sit in the next Pew to a parcel of Girls and young Fellows, who are, three Parts of the Service, *Giggling* and *Prating*."[80] Even if the letter is a total fiction, it captured the reality of the church as one of the few public places for young people to gather. Late in the period, "several young Men made a practice of assembling under the Piazza at the West Door" of St. Michael's in Charles Town, "walking backwards & forwards, trailing sticks on the Flaggs & talking loud during Divine Service on Sunday forenoons."[81] Thoroughly impious, the young men nonetheless recognized that church was still the place to see and be seen. Bridgetown resident Thomas Harrison knew as much and earned "the Esteem of his Acquaintants," who noted his "Constant attendance at Divine Service," as his memorial tablet in St. Michael's Church still records.[82] Sunday worship was also a time to take in the civic spectacles of political elites. In seventeenth-century Barbados, the governor went to church with "his marshall going before him" bareheaded, a posture some found too grandiose.[83] In Spanish Town early in the period "every Sunday there is 250 foot and 60 horse in army, to Guard his Grace [the governor] to, and from the Church."[84] Gathering for worship on a Sunday was thus both a sacred duty and a social opportunity.

This mixture of the transcendent and the mundane meant that the sacred time and space of Sunday worship was an atmosphere charged with the authority of a community gathered together, a place for important things to be done and said. Banns of marriage were published for three Sundays in all the plantation colonies, offering the wider community time to consider the upcoming nuptials of those who did not purchase marriage licenses. In Barbados, from the seventeenth century on, parish churches were the location for publishing new legislation.[85] In 1666, the legislators of the island issued a grand compilation of all acts still in force, to be put into "one fair copy of all said acts" and "sent to the Minister of the Parish of St. Michael, to be by him published in the said Parish-Church the next Sunday, and so from thence to some other Parish, to be published the next Sunday after that; and so successively from Parish to Parish."[86] Individual acts often included a provision for their publication by the minister in church and sometimes for their annual repetition.[87] Worshippers thus heard the "Act for the governing of Negroes" read twice annually, with its provision that a master's murder of a slave incurred only a £15 fine. Twice a year, this requirement could put on the lips of the minister, vested and perhaps speaking from the pulpit, the assertion that Africans were "of a barbarous, wild, and savage nature."[88] Those abandoning the Roman Catholic faith did as Christopher Gilmor "did in the Parish Church of St. Michael in the Island of Barbados, on the 14 of July 1734 before the Congregation there assembled," when he "openly, publickly, and Solemnly read all what is Contain'd in the Above declaration and renunciation."[89] Writs for elections were published in church, which themselves were often held in parish churches in the plantation world.[90] In Carolina, probate matters such as the appointment of administrators were announced in church.[91] Landowners in Barbados did well to be present in church when their portion of the parish tax was announced on three successive Sundays as required by legislation. Jamaican horse-catchers had to give notice in the parish church the Sunday before they intended to mark any animals.[92] Surrounded by the trappings of divine authority, these announcements were imbued with a power beyond their mundane subject matter.

Some avoided that authority, preferring the opportunities for sociability and travel that Sunday afforded. Lawmakers in Barbados passed a law "for preventing the selling of Brandy and Rum in Tipling Houses" and bemoaned that on Sundays "many lewd, loose, and idle persons, do usually resort to such Tipling-houses, who, by their drunkenness, swearing, and other miscarriages, do in a very high nature blaspheme the name of God, profane the Sabbath, and bring a great scandal upon true Christian religion." Some in Jamaica made "the Sabbath day . . . the chief day for their drinking and pastime." Later, in Charles Town, "disorders in Punch-houses" were not uncommon on Sunday. It is possible that these recreations took place after church, like the traditional church ales and pastimes of many an English parish. The Barbadian Sunday witnessed by Père Labat in 1700 was a long morning's work for his ministerial host but was followed by dinner and "the pleasure of watching a revue of the cavalry and infantry of the country."[93] No matter their timing and moral status, these activities reveal all the same how the rhythm of the Christian week structured life even for the irreligious in the plantation colonies.

Africans and their descendents made the most of the relative freedom of Sunday. When slave owners extracted regular work from slaves on Sunday, other whites took notice. In Carolina, "in several Parts of the Country" masters erred "by laying Negroes under a Necessity of labouring on that Day, contrary to the Laws of God and Man," complained the grand jury in 1737. Clergy complained about slaves working on Sunday in their own provision plots, an activity that was sometimes a necessity and sometimes part of slaves' limited arena of personal control. Le Jau thought it a great sin that slaves "are suffered, some forced — to work upon Sundays, having no other means to subsist." Similarly in Jamaica, a minister found that working six days for their masters did not obviate slaves' need to work for themselves on Sunday, the alternative being starvation. One Jamaican clergyman regretted that the three towns on the island "hold their great weekly market on Sunday Morning from day light till an hour before Church time."[94] These "Negro Markets" were supervised by parish authorities. In 1736, the vestry of Port Royal parish in Jamaica "ordered That Joseph Barton, Jacob Cordoso and Isaac Pinto, Constables, doe Attend with their Staff's on Sunday Morning next at the Negroe Markett, in Order to See there be no Injustice done to the Negroes," a mysterious and rare intervention in favor of Afro-Jamaicans. Kingston paid an attorney for "drawg the Articles of Agreement between John Hacker & the Vestry to make a Negro Markett place" in 1730. Whites complained that Afro-Barbadians used Sunday for "drumming, dancing, and riot, practicing frenzied incantations over the graves of their deceased relatives and friends." In the hands of slaves, the Christian Sabbath thus offered an interstice of economic and personal freedom amid six days of domination.[95]

Their Sunday initiatives were not welcomed by white authorities. Persistent complaints and regulation mark white response to slaves' use of Sunday. Barbados legislation of 1688 required that no master "give their Negroes or other Slaves leave on Sabbath-days, Holidays, or any other time, to go out of their Plantations, except such Negro or other Slave, as usually wait upon them at home or abroad, wearing a Livery."[96] In Jamaica's Port Royal, the constables were ordered by the vestry one Sunday to go to the Negro Market "in the Afternoon in Order to destroy the Drums and other Noisy Instruments to Prevent the Disorders that arise from their Caballing and Dancing." Time and again, the Carolina grand jury took note "that it is a Grievance that the Negroes are suffered publickly to cabal in the Streets of this Town on the said Day, while the Inhabitants are at divine Service, which if not timely prevented may be of fatal Consequences to the Province." Thirty years later the grand jury was still complaining that the law "restraining negroes from riots, &c on the Lord's day is not executed." Sunday's ritual time changed slowly, if at all. A law in Carolina and prudence elsewhere required white worshippers to attend church well armed. Johann Martin Bolzius told his German audience that in Carolina "one goes to church with swords, guns, and pistols."[97] The announcement of that law in 1739 may have contributed to the timing of the Stono Rebellion, which began on a Sunday morning just weeks before the legislation took effect. Sunday was a persistently dangerous day for planters in the plantation colonies.[98] The Antiguan conspiracy of 1736 was furthered during Sunday dancing in a pasture outside the town of St. John's.[99] The order that Christians imposed on the passage of time thus gave one day of the week a greater potential for disorder.

Within the basic weekly cycle of Sundays, the great festivals of Christmas, Easter, and Whitsunday punctuated the year in ways that affected almost all the inhabitants of the plantation regions.[100] No Anglican church could fail to be open these days, on which the Lord's Supper was nearly always celebrated and when the doctrines of the Incarnation, Resurrection, and gift of the Holy Spirit were proclaimed. Churchwardens were responsible for decorating the church for these high holy days and for purchasing the bread and wine that would be consumed in the ritual meal. Kingston parish paid 10 shillings to Edith Welsh for "dressing the Church At Easter," while Edith Newson earned £1 for the same service at Christmas in 1724.[101] The parish also laid out £2..2..6 for "Bread & Wine @ the Eucharist 88 Oz. Christmas" in December 1722. Port Royal paid Nathaniel Swivany for "Providing Boughs for the Church" in 1736, that greenery likely being gathered by some of the five slaves he owned. The same expenses can be found in all the principal parishes of the plantation regions.[102] Preparation for Easter was made in the season of Lent, which brought special opportunities for worship and instruction in the plantation colonies. In Bridgetown, ministers from all over the island preached in rotation on Lenten Wednesdays and Fridays and were entertained at the vestry's expense.[103] In many places, Lent offered opportunities for catechetical instruction. William May of Kingston reported that he devoted part of his Wednesday and Friday to catechizing during that penitential season. In South Carolina, William Guy of St. Andrew's and Francis Varnod of St. George's both took up this traditional practice of Lenten teaching as well.[104] Five Barbadian parishes provided catechism classes during Lent, some on the traditional Wednesdays and Fridays.[105]

The great feasts were also days when slaves demanded freedom from work. Hans Sloane reported that Jamaican slaves were free from coerced labor "*Saturdays* in the Afternoon, and *Sundays*, with *Christmas* Holidays, *Easter*, call'd little or *Pigganinny*, *Christmas*, and some other great Feasts allow'd them."[106] More specifically, slaves could count as "their own time" some "three days at Christmas, two at Easter, and two at Whitsuntide," thus adding the prayer book's Monday and Tuesday holy days to the Easter and Whitsun Sabbath days. These days were times for gatherings of Africans, "those of one and the Same Country . . . [to] feast, sing, and dance." As a result, the great feasts required extra vigilance on the part of nervous whites. A rector of Vere on Jamaica's south coast noted that "ordinarily at the great feasts in the Church particularly at Easter wch falls on a Sunday there is a Patroul or a part of the troop of horse rides about the Parishes to see that no Negroes should assemble." The men on patrol managed to celebrate the holiday even in the midst of their vigilance, drinking healths as they moved through the parish. Failure to exercise such vigilance could be deadly; Tacky's Revolt in St. Mary's parish in Jamaica began in the evening on Easter day in 1760, with a further outbreak in Westmoreland on Whitsunday.[107] Slave owners who attempted to ignore customary holidays could face rebellion, as when fifteen Coromantee men in Antigua rose up on December 27, 1701, and decapitated their owner Samuel Martin.[108] White servants also had liberty on the great feasts and the days following. One Barbadian servant enjoyed too much his leave "on Easter Monday, last past . . . to visit friends of his." When he was "overtaken in Drink," he stayed away on Tuesday as well. Though a trial judge sentenced him to an extra year of service as a result, the Council, perhaps recognizing that the Tuesday after Easter was a holy day as well, threw out that sentence.[109]

Slaves and servants sometimes received gifts from their owners and employers on these holidays. Eliza Pinckney insisted to her sons' guardian in England that the boys "should make your Servants some acknowledgement for their trouble at holi-day times — what you think proper. It is what they always did to our own." That included "Whitsuntide [when] they used to make Mrs. Greene a present of a guinea for a pound of tea." These holy days' related commercial importance for city merchants is revealed by the *South Carolina Gazette* heading for May 27, 1751: "ADVERTISEMENTS. WHITSUN-MONDAY, 1751." Carolinians and others dated events in their lives around the great days of the Christian year, as when a Carolina medical student dated his departure "Good Friday April 1st. 1768," while his arrival in Portsmouth was "on the following Whit-Sunday." An aged father told his son that it was on "the Eve of Whitsunday 1759" that "I married your mother" in Jamaica.[110] The Christian year was thus built into the minds of many in the plantation colonies.

Sunday and the great feasts were hardly the only days for worship in the colonial world. Unnoticed by the many historians who have described the irreligion of the plantation colonies was a tradition of weekday corporate prayer. In 1717, public prayers were read in St. Michael's Church in Bridgetown "every Day, twice every Holiday and Saturday." In the 1720s, services there were "perform'd every morn, at which we have a numerous Congregation." This duty likely fell to the curate, a junior clergyman employed by the rector. In 1732, during a dispute with his vestry, the rector of the same parish was "unwilling the Parish shd be depriv'd of daily Prayers" and paid the curate himself. In Speightstown's St. Peter's Church farther up the leeward coast, there was "divine Service every morning between the hours of eight & nine [with] a considerable number of constant attendants." The minister provided catechetical instruction "on Tuesdays after the Second Lesson at Morning Prayer." St. Philip's in Carolina held prayers every Wednesday and Friday, with up to fifty persons in attendance. Forty years later that pattern held true at St. Philip's and the newer Charles Town parish of St. Michael, both of which offered services "with Great Decency and Order: both on Holidays and Week Days." Port Royal in Jamaica also held services every Wednesday and Friday, but the minister admitted that the congregation was thin compared to Sunday worship. The same schedule and result were to be found in Kingston parish. When the duke of Portland was governor of Jamaica, his domestic chaplain "read prayers every Morning in his Grace's family and in a Chapel in Spanish Town (built by Sir Wm Beiston some time Gover. of this Island) every afternoon and Preach[ed] a Sermon Every Thursday in the sd Chapel." The rector of St. Catherine's seems to have led daily morning prayer in the same chapel. While churches in the rural plantation parishes were unlikely to be open during the week, a tradition of weekday prayer was to be found in the great port cities. These weekday corporate prayers supplemented the private devotions of families, so difficult to recover from the few surviving diaries and personal papers of the plantation colonies.[111]

Minor holy days and state holidays also punctuated the passage of time. In Barbados, only the parishes of St. Lucy, St. Peter, and St. John (three out of eleven) failed to report that they held divine service on the feasts and fasts of the church year in the 1720s. St. Michael's in Bridgetown offered a sermon, not just prayers, on all "State Holy Days." On those days the political elite of the colony usually attended church *en masse*. An early example was the attendance of the Assembly, Council, and governor at church together on November 5, 1684, which the lower house reminded the upper was the reason "that they could not finish any Business to waite upon them this morning Before Church time . . . it being Gunpowder Treason day." In Jamaica, the perennial liturgical laggard, only St. Catherine's parish in Spanish Town and the Kingston parish reported keeping "all holy days," while Vere, Westmoreland, St. Thomas's in the Vale, and St. Thomas's in the East reported divine service on at least some holy days. In the 1720s, South Carolinians could worship on the holy days in St. Philip's, St. Andrew's, St. Thomas's, St. Denis's, and St. James's Santee, in five out of eleven total parishes.[112] In the decade before, Le Jau of Goose Creek had lost his battle to observe holy days, since "the Negroes took that opportunity and wou'd not work, which made the Masters angry and none Came to Church."[113] Though short lived, Le Jau's holy day celebrations were quickly appropriated by slaves in the struggle against their owners. A governor of Barbados similarly felt that keeping the modest number of holy days in the Anglican calendar was "the greatest obstacle" to slave baptism, "most of the planters thinking Sunday too much for being spared from work."[114] More dramatic was the possible retention of Kongo-Angolan military and liturgical practices related to the Catholic feast of the Nativity of the Virgin Mary on September 8, which may have contributed to the timing of the Stono Rebellion in Carolina in 1739.[115] Antigua's slave plot of 1736 was planned around the coronation day festivities, some of them ecclesiastical, which marked the anniversary of the accession of George II.[116] The ritual calendar lent itself to efforts at both domination and resistance.

The Goose Creek Anglicans and other sorts of Christians in the plantation colonies felt differently about the wisdom of following a liturgical calendar, exposing a cleavage in the European community. Quakers and Christians in the Reformed tradition disapproved of many Anglican holy days. When Charles Woodmason held services on All Saints' Day in the Carolina backcountry, he heard that "the Presbyterians disliked the Service and Sermon of the Day saying it was Popish." They felt similarly about Good Friday, which also "savour'd of Popery." But Woodmason's service for Gunpowder Treason Day attracted even Quakers. A rousing sermon against Catholicism "gave Satisfaction" to the diverse group of Protestant worshippers.[117] Indeed, many non-Anglican Protestants in the plantation regions likely joined Charles Town Lutherans in observing the English state holidays. The Lutheran leadership resolved that "every new minister should be admonished to follow George III's order of the year 1761, namely to conduct special services of thanksgiving on November 5, January 30, May 29, and October 25, as was announced in the book of Common Prayers."[118] While theological convictions kept many dissenters from joining in the celebration of saints' days, the state holidays offered opportunities to join members of the national church in a general Protestant consensus that connected them to British national life.

These weekday festival services were attended by congregations smaller than those that attended Sunday services. Yet these observances were still enriched with various social and cultural elaborations. In the port cities, the congregations were large enough that organists were usually required to play. Kingston parish ordered its organist John Daniel D'luski "be obliged to attend Divine Service on all Festivalls" for his £130 annual salary, as did St. Michael's in Bridgetown and St. Philip's in Charles Town.[119] In the 1730s, the January 30 anniversary of the execution of Charles I was marked in Charles Town "as usual," prayers being supplemented with the flying of flags at half staff and the firing of guns. As late as 1753, the people of Charles Town still gathered for "the Anniversary of our happy Deliverance from a most horrid *Popish* Plot, and of the glorious Revolution by the landing of King WILLIAM in *England*," though the newspaper only noted that the "Day was observed here as usual."[120] The feast of St. John the Evangelist on December 27 was also widely celebrated, often as it was in St. Kitt's with freemasons processing to church.[121] In Carolina, that feast featured the illumination of ships in Charles Town harbor, "which made a very grand and agreeable Appearance," theologically appropriate for a day whose collect asked God "to cast thy bright beams of light upon thy church" for its enlightenment.[122] Bridgetown residents were treated to the sound of St. Michael's ring of eight bells every holy day.[123] Civic rituals thus extended the observances of the

Christian year into the arena of everyday life in ways that few historians have noticed.

Something much like the political-liturgical spectacle of a state holiday occurred when new governors arrived in the plantation colonies. When the duke of Albemarle arrived in Port Royal, Jamaica, in 1687, he was processed around town with other officials carrying a sword, mace, and staff before him. They went "from the King's house to the Church, all the way being covered with green Cloth." Arriving at the church, he found "at the East end a Chair of State, covered with Azur velvet." After prayers in the church, "there in publicke Audience the Secretary of the Island read his Grace's Commition from his Majesty." Similar ceremonies were still in use in Barbados late in the period. In July 1780, "his Excellency, Majr. General James Cunningham Esq. landed. . . . Previous to his going to the Government House, he was attended, by a numerous Congregation, to St. Michael's Church, where there was an Excellent Sermon preached by the Revd. Mr. William Duke, taken from the following words, vizt. 'When the righteous are in authority, the people rejoice.'"[124] These colonial political holy days marked the beginning of a new phase in the political life of the plantation colonies.

Colonial governors added to the ritual calendar when they responded to political events and natural disasters by proclaiming days of fasting and humiliation, some of them becoming annual observations. The rector of Kingston convened the clergy at the governor's behest after the devastating hurricane of August 28, 1722, "to consider what Form of Prayer wou'd be proper to be used on the 3d of October, which day was appointed to be kept as a day of Fasting & Humiliation." The form they created was sent to the governor, who then ordered it to be printed.[125] The governor's proclamation, suffused with the language of Providence, affirmed that "the Divine Majesty's afflicting Dispensations to his People is to reclaime them from Sin, and that repentance of Sin, prevents the Continuance of God's Sever Judgements." On the day of the fast, "no Person or Persons whatsoever neither by them Selves, Servants, or Slaves, [could] presume to do any Manner of Work, in their Respective Trades, or Calling, on the Said Day, nor any Shop, Tavern, or Punch House be Kept open on the Same, on Pain of our Highest Displeasure, & that the Clergy of our Said Island, do in their Respective Stations, take Such Rule & Order therein as Shall be Suitable to So Solemn an Occasion."[126] Later, June 7 and August 28 were "two days of Fasting and humiliation Set a part by publick authority" in Jamaica, "upon the Account of the great Earthquake, and the late terrible Storme." There were services in St.

Ritual Time and Space **49**

Catherine's and St. Thomas's in the East's churches on those days and must have been at Kingston and Port Royal as well.[127] An early historian of Jamaica found that the two days were "most devoutly kept," when Jamaicans at least kept "the exterior Shew of Religion."[128] With much to repent of, annual fast days gave Jamaicans an opportunity to atone for their apparent neglect of divine worship in comparison to Barbadians and South Carolinians.

Days of fasting and humiliation were especially common in South Carolina and were clearly meaningful occasions to political elites. After James Moore ousted Robert Johnson from the governor's chair during the revolt against the proprietary government, he ordered a day of "fasting & humiliation on Wednesday ye Twentyth of July," while the displaced Johnson appointed the 22nd for the same purposes. The Anglican clergy followed Johnson's directive, leading Moore's supporter John Fenwick to raise "a very great Disturbance in the Church Yard both before & after Divine Service ye Lord's Day before ye Fast was to be observed." He commanded the minister "to observe ye Day appointed by Col. Moor & strictly forbad ye People to repair to Church on ye Fast Day."[129] Disease could occasion such observances, as when an outbreak of smallpox led Governor William Bull to appoint July 5 "a Day of publick Fasting and Humiliation throughout this Province, requiring all Ministers of the Gospel and their Congregations to pay a due Regard thereunto." War in 1740 prompted another day of fasting "to pray for Success to his Majesty's Arms in General, and, in particular to the Troops from this Province and Georgia."[130] A "dreadful and consuming Fire" in Charles Town later the same year led the governor to require both Anglican and dissenting ministers to preach and lead prayers, and "all Persons to abstain from all servile Labour, and to repair to the respective Places of Divine Worship, and to dedicate the said Day wholly to religious exercises" on November 28. Bad news from Europe and the rebellion in Scotland in 1745 led Governor James Glen to declare a fast day, reminding the province that since "afflictions rise not out of the Dust, it is the Duty of all Ranks to humble themselves before God, and to offer up their fervent Prayers to the Divine Majesty." Glen called for another in 1756 on receiving news of the great earthquake in Lisbon and Indian attacks on other colonies.[131] Though the clergy of the established church were quick to lead fast day liturgies, dissenting ministers like William Hutson also embraced days of "pub[lic] Humiliation & Supplication . . . That our Hrts might all be bound together before the Lord."[132] While we cannot be sure how many residents repaired to church on these days, their continuing proclamation suggests no small level of attendance and importance.

The ethnic-patronal holidays of St. George, St. Andrew, and St. Patrick were popular celebrations as well. In the month of April, the "ENGLISH SOCIETY" of Barbados invited "All Englishmen and their descendants . . . to join their countrymen on Wednesday the 23rd instant by ten o'clock in the morning, at the house of Mr. Richard Hovell., vintner, to breakfast, and to walk from thence in procession to church; after which to dine at Free Mason Hall, and as friends and countrymen to celebrate the day with harmony."[133] Scots and their descendents in Charles Town formed a St. Andrew's club for similar observances on November 30.[134] Joseph Dumbleton submitted an "Ode for St. Patric's Day" to the South Carolina newssheet in 1749, "inscrib'd to the President and Members of the Irish Society," which likely also gathered for worship and conviviality. In a Postscript dated March 20, 1749, he submitted "A RHAPSODY ON RUM," which he called "Confusion's angry Sire," an indication that excess might have accompanied the celebration of their patronal feast. We know that St. Patrick's Day was observed in Bridgetown in the 1720s, only because a recalcitrant organist had to be ordered to play for the service. Both Scots and Irish Masons gathered for procession, sermon, and "mirth and chearfulness" on their respective days in Kingston. These feasts allowed the scattered residents of the discrete British nations to gather in time, even though great amounts of space divided them from their native lands.[135]

This hoped-for "supercession of place" through the manipulation of time's passage leads us back to this chapter's beginnings.[136] Though four thousand miles of ocean divided the plantation colonies from the English metropole, the re-creation of English ritual ways was central to the ordering of the colonial experiences. When colonists imposed parish boundaries and institutions on the landscapes of the plantation colonies, they rendered those foreign shores instantly and appreciably more English. Within parish boundaries, colonists built churches in which the parish community could gather for the worship of the English national church. They took their seats for that worship in a manner much in keeping with metropolitan practice, offering "higher" and "lower" places to persons of different means and degrees and special seats for persons in certain social categories. Seated in this manner, the parish community presented both its hoped-for unity and the status diversity of its members. Re-creating an English liturgical forum made those churches spaces of great authority, performative settings for speech and actions that sought to naturalize the power structures of the plantation world, especially as white colonists explored the meaning of race through their traditions of church seating.[137]

Essential to the creation of these English ritual spaces were the limitations placed on the attendance of Africans and their descendents. The free people of color, mulattoes, elite slaves, and former Catholic slaves who were carefully seated in these parish churches did not represent the great majority of plantation slaves, who instead preserved African religious and cultural life in the relative autonomy of their own communities. The seating of some people of color in worship, especially those with closer cultural connections to whites, likely allowed some white residents of the plantation colonies to cling to a sense that their churches were meaningful manifestations of the parish community ideal they brought from England. At the same time, the absence of the great majority of slaves allowed whites to imagine that their yearning for an African-less metropolitan ideal was possible. In the ritual life acted out in the parish's liturgical space, whites thus grappled with their manifest failure to evangelize Africans and their abandonment of the ideal of creating English settler societies bound by English norms. The ritualized seating of the plantation parishes was thus "a means of performing the way things ought to be in conscious tension with the way things are," as Jonathan Z. Smith explains.[138]

So too the preservation of the English liturgical year and its ritual dimensions offered opportunities to connect colonial experience to metropolitan ideal. Confronted with seasons and crops that did not square meteorologically with English experience, especially in Barbados and Jamaica, colonists sought the comfort of maintaining English calendrical norms as much as possible. The English Sabbath was central to the passage of time in weekly units, a day set apart for the church's liturgy, rest from labor, and social gatherings. The great and minor festivals of the Christian year offered similar opportunities for Christian teaching and social fellowship. The celebration of state holidays connected these distant outposts of the empire to the Protestant national narrative that held an increasingly British people together. These ways of ordering time lent meaning to days that otherwise slipped by amid the routines of agricultural, commercial, and domestic life.

The keeping of important English days and seasons also marked a difference between those who claimed the rights of British subjects and their slaves. The free white men who processed to church on St. George's Day claimed that worship in the most public manner, so that even the ephemeral nature of the event could be overcome in the records of their newspapers. Slaves and even free people of color had little access to any public event related to the passage of time. Their ritual lives were rendered private or domestic by the elites who sought to restrict the public gatherings of slaves that they strangely called "caballing," something usually done in private. At the same time, the ritual calendar of English Christians created moments of increased personal freedom for slaves on Sunday and at feasts during the year. The master class quickly sensed the danger of these days and responded with an increased vigilance meant to reduce slaves' appropriation of these days for their own purposes. Any doubts about the cultural importance of these habits of ritual time are relieved when we consider that the master class clung to their holy days and holidays even after they had proved to be the most dangerous days of the year.

Those who occupied the pews of the plantation colonies, walked in holy day processions, and listened to the bells of Easter participated in the construction of a comprehensive ritual environment, one in which they could continually experience the seeming naturalness of the hierarchies they were creating and, at times, contesting. Yet this ritualization of time and space was not merely some devious strategy for dominance, created by plantation colony elites for the purposes of controlling the slave societies of the New World. Indeed, the roots of these often unconscious practices ran deep into the faith and practice of early modern European Christianity and beyond it, even into the early churches of the Mediterranean world. These ways of experiencing ritual space and time ultimately grow out of the stress Christianity lays on the body and on time in its doctrine of the Incarnation and its eschatology. Seeking to experience the comforts of both community and hierarchy in time and space thus came quite naturally to colonists of the British plantation world. The comforts of the domestic rituals of marriage and baptism, rites that covered the distance between the social and familial, are the subject of the following chapter.

CHAPTER 3

Marriage and Baptism in the British Plantation Colonies

THE BRITISH PLANTATION COLONIES were fertile in only one sense: as places where warm climates and rich soils produced exportable commodities that made some planters very rich. For Africans and Europeans and their descendents, Barbados, Jamaica, and South Carolina were often places of demographic decrease, where typical human reproductive activity usually failed to sustain population levels.[1] This basic demographic problem and the culture it engendered have led many historians to speak of the failure of the colonial project in the plantation regions, creating a historical literature of the Caribbean and the early South that reveals stunted societies, composed of violently materialistic planters and slaves ever on the cusp of rebellion.[2] Mostly ignored by historians have been the ways in which residents of the plantation world forged new kinds of human communities, tragic as they might have been, in their ritual lives. In addition to their theological import, the Christian rites of passage of baptism and marriage were vital to the life of the European community in the plantation regions as rites that displayed the legitimacy of the sexuality and reproduction of Europeans. The emerging community of free persons of color and small numbers of slaves also found meaning in rites that had the power to constitute family life against the constant threats of a hostile planter and merchant elite committed to racial slavery and white supremacy. Privatizing marriage and baptism by celebrating them at home rather than in church, Europeans reserved these rites and their legitimating power to themselves. Potentially meddling clergy and free persons of color thus found these domestic rituals largely beyond their control, while the enslaved majority was nearly completely cut off from them. Both situations were essential features of whites' desired control of the Christian ritual repertoire and its power in the plantation colonies.[3]

The Culture of Marrying

Though most whites in these regions were baptized as infants, at the beginning of the life cycle, it will be helpful here to begin with marriage, since it was the moment that created a new family that in turn produced young candidates for baptism, "for Matrimony Supposes Children," as one Barbadian noted.[4] Though travelers were more likely to comment on the frequency of interracial sexual relationships outside marriage in the plantation colonies, Europeans there largely preserved the ritual ways of marriage from their cultures of origin.[5] A wedding was a private or nearly private celebration of a new domestic and sexual relationship and of the partnership between the two natal families. It was an opportunity to celebrate well-ordered sexuality and the preservation of European ways and to deny the extramarital interracial sexual relationships so obvious to outsiders. Whatever their particular ideological subtext, weddings in the period admitted considerable variation; they could be celebrated with more or less conviviality, on a variety of days, and in a variety of settings. Recovering something of the texture of the ritual culture of marrying in the British plantation colonies is this chapter's first task.[6]

Marriage was much desired by colonists, who were quick to seek the legitimacy it conferred on their domestic arrangements. When a Jamaican parish in the countryside lacked a minister, as they often did, the minister from the next parish over could be prevailed upon to take "a Journey to them to Christen and Marry such as shall desire it." At other times, Anglicans bereft of a minister would allow a dissenting minister to conduct their marriages, as did some people in Beaufort in South Carolina when their frontier parish was vacant. At the same time, cohabitation was an option for those without access to a minister. Complaints came in from the Carolina backcountry about the difficulty of living without "any to marry People so yt they marry each other when & how they please & separate . . . as they please," a situation "which has caused the vilest Abominations & that Whoredom & adultery overspread our Land." When the opportunity presented itself, however, many persons cohabiting were quick to embrace marriage by a minister. When backcountry missionary Charles Woodmason offered free weddings to those already living together, "numbers accepted of my Offer," including "some Whores and Rogues," whom he also married without fee.[7]

The Book of Common Prayer was quite specific in its direction that marriages were properly solemnized in the parish church.[8] There the minister was supposed to be in control, able to exercise the church's authority over the marriage of its people. At home in England, the Church of England's authority over the sexual and domestic lives of its people was wide.[9] The celebration of marriage was reserved to Anglican clergy, forcing even dissenters into the national church at a key moment in their lives and reserving the attendant fee for Anglican ministers. Church courts were charged with the punishment of sexual activity outside marriage in fornication and adultery. Vestries sought out the fathers of children born outside marriage and took responsibility for their support when none could be found. At the death of a spouse, church courts and the lawyers who practiced in them regulated the disposal of assets and minors in the probate process. The couple who entered their parish church for a wedding in England thus submitted to the church's comprehensive supervision of marriage and unapproved deviations from it.

In the colonies, however, the great majority of marriages took place in homes rather than in parish churches. That location was symbolic of a general disruption of the Anglican Church's discipline of domestic and sexual life in the plantation colonies. There were no Anglican bishops in early America and thus no episcopal courts for the punishment of vice. Colonial legislatures in Jamaica and Barbados banned the creation of any church courts that might perpetuate parts of an English system of discipline that many settlers were glad to have left behind.[10] Clergy in the colonies often complained to the bishop of London and the SPG about their lack of coercive authority.[11] Their occasional efforts to create church courts, even those restricted to the discipline of wayward clergymen, were viewed with deep suspicion by the colonial political classes who felt themselves quite competent to regulate their family lives without the prying and expensive regulation of the church. Many of the powers of an English bishop were vested in royal governors, including issuing marriage licenses and regulating probate matters. Marriage in houses was thus a fitting symbol of this quiet lay revolution against church discipline in the midst of colonization. At the same time, vestries wanted their clergy compliant, nearby, and ready to be summoned to perform pastoral rites, to minimize "ye Inconveniences to the Parishioners."[12] The minister who presided at a wedding in a Charles Town drawing room or in a Barbadian great house was a guest in another's space, the inconvenience of his going there reminding all just "who was working for whom."[13]

This preference for marriages at home seems constant across the decades in the plantation colonies, even though it usually cost the marrying parties more than a church wedding. An early eighteenth-century resident of Barbados told his reader that "as most Countrys have some particular Customs to themselves so hath this," including the practice of "their marriages, which is always solemnized in their houses (never in the Churches)."[14] This was true even though a 1705 act required Barbadians to pay only 5 shillings for a church wedding and 20 shillings for a wedding anywhere else.[15] Perhaps the domestic setting lent itself to convincing the minister to perform the marriage at the couple's pleasure, "never minding Canonicall hours day or night will doe."[16] Domestic marriage was still the rule in 1734, when legislation concerning clandestine marriages affirmed that "it has been customary and usual here to marry in Private-Houses, and not in Churches" and set a £25 fine for any householder who permitted a clandestine wedding to take place "in his or her House, or in any Backside, Yard, Garden, or other place."[17] One rector of Vere in Jamaica alienated his parishioners by "refusing to christen and marry in private houses," though they found the governor could hardly demand the minister desist from following the rubrics and canons of the church. A Jamaican clergyman in 1808 regretted that by "a long established usage funerals, Christenings, & Marriages are attended here at the house of the parties; which renders these a very harassing part of the duty." Most Carolina weddings were celebrated in the manner of John and Elizabeth Basnett, who were "married ye 28 day of Nov.br 1725 Att Mr. John Exhaus in Golden Lane." There was no constant tradition of holding weddings in the bride's home. Carolinians Thomas Elliot Jr. and Mary Bellinger, for instance, were married "at his Father's house at Long Point five Miles from Town."[18] Of the 115 marriages solemnized in the 1758–74 period in St. James's on the Santee, ninety-five were in private homes, eighteen were in the rector's home, five were in the church, and one was in the schoolhouse.[19] Thus the rite that created a new domestic arrangement was, perhaps fittingly, usually celebrated in a domestic space.

There is sadly little detail on the location of the rituals that united those persons of color who were married by ministers of the established church during slavery, especially in the eighteenth century. It seems unlikely, however, that ministers condescended to travel to the homes of free persons of color, requiring them instead to come to the church or rectory. No location was noted in the register of St. Michael's Bridgetown in 1695 when "Peter Simpson & Margaret Dolly, free negroes," were married. It is suggestive that Mary Jones, a free Negro woman, was baptized and then married Charles Cuffee, also a free man, on June 25, 1694, perhaps using the church's font and then moving to the altar step for the wedding service.[20] Edward Reading, a Jamaican minister exceptional in his interest in ministering to plantation slaves in the 1720s, "publickly Married" some recently baptized slaves "in the Church," intending to baptize their children before long.[21] In the 1830s, the first slaves married at St. John's in Barbados were married in the church, the preferred location later shifting to the parson's home and then back to the church.[22]

Besides choosing a location, those marrying also had discretion as to whether they would take out a license from the governor or have the banns of marriage announced in church on three successive Sundays. Though banns were not at all unheard of, there was a general preference for licenses over the decades, more so in certain times and places than others.[23] In South Carolina, custom allowed the minister a fee of 15 shillings for a marriage with banns and £1..10 for one by license. Yet most couples in St. James's Santee used a license, some 97 out of 115 in the 1758–74 period. Very few persons chose banns in St. Philip's parish in Charles Town in the same period. Walduck reported from Barbados that he "never know but one pair asked in ye Churches yet but they all take out licenses Signed by ye Governor he being Ordinary."[24] St. James's parish in Barbados was one of a few that noted the means of marriage with some consistency, with licenses being far more popular in the seventeenth century. Even persons of the most limited means there preferred a license. William Thomas and Ann Jones were married at St. James's via license, even though "she marry'd without cloathes," as a parish official noted.[25] At Christ Church parish in Barbados, marriage by license was far more popular for whites except for a distinct period between 1781 and 1785, when avaricious Governor James Cunningham "laid an exorbitant fee on marriage licenses," to which brides responded by "preferring to be 'asked in church,'" rather than asking their future husbands to pay.[26] Banns announced to the assembled parish community the intention of the affianced to be married, in ways that stimulated local gossip, provoked bawdy talk, or created resistance that couples preferred to avoid. One minister ordered his Carolina congregation that "when Banns are published," they were not to "make it a Matter of Sport." Persons who had been cohabitating for some time in Carolina avoided banns for the public shame they might bring on. When persons sought a quick or quiet marriage, licenses were definitely more discreet and offered greater flexibility.[27] Securing a license made the process of marrying less public, though still fully recorded by public authorities.

Marriage by banns was associated with lower-status persons in the plantation colonies. Prosperous or status-conscious free persons might marry via license, as did Richard Blackman and Jone Siston at St. James's Barbados in 1696. Other free persons of color chose banns because of their lower cost. When Edward Wisehammer and Jane Green, free persons of color, were married in St. Andrew's parish in Jamaica in 1741, they chose banns, which the clerk noted as though it were an exception. The marriage of free persons named David Sarjeant and Sarah Cuffley by banns in 1764 was the only marriage not by license in St. Philip's parish in Barbados that year. Ten of the fourteen marriages contracted across racial lines in St. Elizabeth's parish in Jamaica between 1780 and 1815 were by banns. When large numbers of slaves and apprentices were married in Barbados in the 1830s, it was by banns. Though marriage with banns seems to have been cheaper most of the time, most white couples and some persons of color took the more expensive and seemingly more refined route of securing a license. Persons with fewer resources were thus pushed toward more public and less prestigious rites.[28]

Though the Anglican clergy found their control over marriage much reduced in relation to laypersons, they were often successful in preventing dissenting ministers from conducting marriages. Marriage licenses were not directed to dissenting ministers in the islands, but Carolina clergy found preserving their monopoly more difficult. When the commissary there discovered that licenses were being issued to dissenters, he complained that this was contrary to the laws of the province and to English practice, and "a Dishonour to ye Church & an injury to the Clergy." Earlier the clergy had insisted to the governor they had "the undoubted Right & Priviledge of Marriage," because the "Established Church hath every where been vested by ye Civil Authority with the Sole power of Marriage & its Bishops with the sole Jurisdiction as to the Lawfulness of ye Same, ever since the days of ye first Christian Emperours." One new rector of Prince Frederick parish found that a local dissenting minister had raised his fees for a wedding to the Anglican level during the parish's vacancy, only to cut them by half when the new rector arrived.[29] Francis Le Jau of Goose Creek planned to remarry "conscientious Persons Ignorantly deluded" by dissenting ministers, at least "for the Honour of the Children born of such Marryages," implying to all the illegitimacy of such children.[30] Dissenters in Carolina fought for control over their own marriage rituals. Quakers in Charles Town, for instance, sought to maintain control of marriage among themselves, one recording in 1750 the poor decision of a man "educated in the Profession of Truth, yet not regarding the wholesome discipline of his Friends was married to ye said Mary by a Priest."³¹ Control of the marriage ritual was important to the established church's claim to authority and to dissenters' aspirations to be perceived as legitimate Christian bodies.

Many turned to feasting and conviviality as soon as the ritual was accomplished. In Barbados around 1710, "if the Parties be of any family there is all the Entertainment the country can afford." Even poverty would not prevent a party, for "if they are poor 3 or 4 of their Neighbors will join for they resol'd to be merry once in their lives for a Barbique sport and some find Sugar some Rum (cum multis alis) untill they make up a feast with a Fiddler to be sure. After dinner the parson takes a Bermudas Gigg & Dances Cheger foot with M'dam. Bride all hands gett Drunk, and ye Vinculated couple go to bed in the fear of the Lord."³² Sixty years later on the same island, a recent arrival from England married into an old planter family and later remembered that the day was marked by an assembly of "the several branches of Mr. Wood's [his father-in-law] numerous and extensive family . . . at his house called Harmony Hall." A Jamaican clergyman in Vere parish reported that after age seventeen, the young people of the parish attended every wedding "where there is always fiddlers & Country dancing." In 1751, South Carolinians read in their newspaper a reprinted article from the *Jamaican Courant* that described some island nuptials, "which were very magnificent." "Music instruments of joy" accompanied the wedding festivities of an older couple in the low country in 1743. A Charles Town "widow lady of a good fortune" remarried in 1732, giving "a handsome entertainment . . . to some of their particular friends . . . with abundance of agreeable mirth." Likewise a Beaufort groom "gave an elegant Entertainment, to which those of first Consequence were invited" in 1768. In a manner more or less modest, weddings were marked with displays of domestic hospitality, including food, drink, and dancing in modes that connected these colonial nuptials to English matrimonial customs.³³

Some married couples emerged slowly from the cocoon of family that gathered around them for the marriage liturgy. At William Senhouse's wedding in Barbados, a second and more public day of feasting followed the marriage, as the governor and his wife and other island elites joined the family "and composed a numerous happy and respectable company." Indeed, the "gaiety of our friends was happily and spiritedly kept up for some days," until "the 2nd Sunday after the marriage [when] the Bride and Bridegroom made their appearance in due form at St. Michael's Church," a moment that manifested them as husband and wife to the parish community.³⁴ While residents of the plantation colonies wanted the control of marriage and the marriage liturgy that licenses and domestic liturgies engendered, they also understood the importance of the public manifestations of the new marriage. Banns, licenses, and such formal appearances in public signaled the new legal, social, and economic reality of marriage. Though the desire to marry in semiprivacy was intense, those public moments could not be omitted if marriage was to have its intended social effects.

That manifestation to the wider community signaled that the husband and wife were now full members of the community of responsible white adults and individually of the gendered arenas that men and women inhabited. Though the ritual took place in a private setting, its importance to public life was paramount. For the propertied white elite, the transition from the single to married state could provoke anxiety among relations and other members of the community, for much more than love was at stake. A Barbadian clergyman "omitted going to joyn a Couple when sent for to their house two days before ye Election, the Match being patch'd up by Male-Contents to make a freeholder to vote against the Governours interest."[35] That clerical probity was not found in South Carolina's Brian Hunt. He colluded in the marriage of a minor heiress of considerable means to a man her guardians would not approve. He avoided the interference of the guardians by publishing their banns in a near empty church at holy day services, setting off a firestorm of accusations from the province's political and religious leaders.[36] This was to be expected in a society that recorded marriages in its newspaper largely in terms of the economic repercussions of the match, as when Stephen Bedon married Ruth Nickolls, "an agreeable young Lady, with a large Fortune," or when John Gibbes married Elizabeth Jenys, who had "a very large Fortune."[37]

When clandestine marriages occurred, young women and men could quickly have access to property that their relations and other members of the community were not ready for them to have.[38] By controlling access to the marriage liturgy and insisting that its public manifestation in the publishing of banns or the granting of a license not be omitted, political and social elites in the plantation colonies minimized the disorder that hasty marriages could engender. By 1682, Jamaica law threatened ministers with a £100 fine for marrying any parishioners without thrice-published banns.[39] Barbadian legislators complained that "divers Marriages have been clandestinely consummated in this island, without the knowledge, consent, or approbation of Parents and other Relations, and often to the utter ruin of the Persons thereby running themselves into unsuitable matches." Their act provided that any minister who performed a wedding without banns or license was to be fined £100 and jailed for six months, other penalties being provided for parish sextons or clerks who assisted and for persons who provided their homes for such illicit nuptials. Some brides and grooms used false surnames and claimed residence in other parishes in order to avoid the meddling of their elders. Ministers in Barbados were later forbidden to marry any persons unknown to them if "not in the presence of their Parents, Guardians, or Friends," even with banns or license.[40] One rector of Port Royal in Jamaica married a couple without banns or license and found himself "Oblig'd to Pay the Penalty of one hundred Pounds," and still some members of the Council asked the commissary to prosecute him as a matter of clerical discipline as well. In Carolina, "great care [was] always taken to prevent such irregular marriages," the clergy being cautioned to marry only their own parishioners by license and to keep the commissary informed of their actions.[41] The dangers of these excessively private weddings were keenly felt by the older generations that made law and directed the parish affairs of the plantation colonies. Their control of the rite was essential to the orderly transmission of wealth, property, and racial privilege.

Some ministers were indeed willing to collude in circumventing that control and in ways that brought them into conflict with one another. Not infrequent were the disputes between clergy over the crossing of parish lines for the performance of both weddings and baptisms. One rector of St. Michael's in Bridgetown complained that fellow minister Thomas Warren was supporting himself "by marrying, christening, etc clandestinely; particularly in my parish & by adhering to that Party, that despise government & speak evil of Dignitaries." A minister in Bermuda found his parishioners recruiting another minister for weddings, one willing to take "advantage of my determination to marry my parishioners no where but in the church when the Weather will admit of their comeing there." Bermudians clearly valued their tradition of marriage at home and were willing to foment conflict between ministers to preserve their practice. In Jamaica, the commissary could report to the bishop of London that he had never received a complaint from a layperson at his annual review of the clergy but that there was always a dispute to adjudicate between clergy over the crossing of parish boundaries to marry or baptize.[42]

The self-consciously respectable white residents of the plantation colonies contrasted the ordered, domestic habits they cultivated in marrying with the practices of Africans and common whites. White Jamaicans thought that their slaves "in their Marriages . . . have not Form or Ceremony, but take on another's

Words; and I have known some that never Separated. . . . But in general they often change, when any Quarrel arises." Edward Long explained that Jamaican slaves were "all married (*in their way*) to a husband, or wife, pro tempore" and that their "notions of love are, that it is free and transitory." South Carolina Baptists excommunicated "Madam Bakers Will for unlawfully Seeking after another wife, while his Lawfull one was yet Living." Yet Charles Woodmason described similar conjugal behavior among white residents of the Carolina backcountry in his patronizing tones. In Jamaica, one observer was sure that "the rude and common people seldom marie, according to the Ceremony of ye Church, but are so full of faith as to take one another's words, and soo live together, and beget children, and if they fall out, or disagree, they part friendly by consent."[43] Commenting on such flexible arrangement, those who sought to make up the governing classes of the plantation colonies turned their social inferiors into useful foils.

Clergy required both parties to be baptized before a marriage could be solemnized, meaning that instruction and baptism lay between most slaves and Christian marriage. Edward Reading of Jamaica was one of very few clergymen who followed that course and could say that he had "baptiz'd Sevral & have married some of them." The relatively few slaves who sought Christian marriage also encountered resistance from slave owners. In Goose Creek, though several slaves sought "to be baptised and marryed according to the form of our holy Church," their "Masters are unwilling most of them." Six years later, the same minister reported "many Slaves . . . very Desirous of being Instructed and Baptized. Nay and Marry'd by the Minister of the Parish," suggesting that some slaves recognized that baptism was preliminary to one means of reconstitution of the family through marriage. Clergy who failed to abide by the requirement of baptism before marriage faced discipline, as when the commissary in South Carolina launched an investigation into the actions of a minister accused of marrying an Englishman in Savannah to an unbaptized Indian woman.[44] The disinterest of most Africans and their descendents in the rite and slave owners' reluctance to share these domestic rituals with their slaves means, however, that records of slave marriages in Anglican churches in the colonial period are almost nonexistent.[45]

Free persons of color, generally classified as "Mulatto" or "Negro" in parish registers, were generally baptized, either soon after being born to free parents or as adults if freedom had been recently gained. They were thus eligible for marriage by a minister. The children of white men and black women were often baptized, especially if they were free. They and subsequent generations of free people of color then tended to marry in Christian rites, gaining the social advantages and respectability of the married state. Free people of color were married in St. Philip's parish in Barbados as early as 1676. The marriage rolls of Christ Church in Barbados contain records of the marriages of free people of color by 1700, when Robert Boydon and Sarah Williams, "both free Negroes," were married. A double wedding appears to have been held at St. Andrew's parish in Carolina on September 3, 1738, when Samson and Rebecca and George and Elizabeth, all called free Negroes, were married.[46] A good number of free people of color were married in the parish of St. Andrew's in Jamaica over the course of the eighteenth century, the earliest being recorded in 1741. The grooms' occupations were sometimes recorded: carpenters, saddlers, coopers, and cordwainers were married by the minister of the parish, adding a new element of respectability to their status as honest tradesmen.[47]

Strangely, many whites who commented on the need for converting slaves argued that persistent sexual contact between masters and slave women was an "obstacle towards the Conversion of Negroes; since whilst their Masters are thus minded, it is not to be presum'd that they may ever have the least Thought about the instruction of their Slaves."[48] Instead, it seems clear that sex between Europeans and Africans often broke down the liturgical barriers between the developing races, barriers that many whites were interested in perpetuating. While slave owners prevented the baptism and marriage of their slaves and many slaves expressed little interest in the rites of Christian marriage, the rise of populations of free black persons was the thin edge of a wedge that would slowly make Christian rites available and socially meaningful to nearly all people of color. The social reality of sexual relationships and reproduction across emerging color lines thus led Christian liturgical practice in a new direction. Turning to baptism, a rite that both naturally preceded and followed marriage, provides a further opportunity to consider the social meaning of initiatory ritual in the British plantation colonies.

Baptismal Ways

Europeans in the plantation colonies responded to the birth of their children with much the same ritual attention that marked the birth of children in their cultures of origin.[49] Midwives, neighboring women, and female relatives attended the birth. Mothers spent some time after the birth in seclusion and rest.

In some places, they went to church for their churching some time after their delivery, marking their return to the society of the world generally and their husbands in particular. Yet the ritual most charged with social import after the arrival of a child was baptism. The basic rite of Christian initiation was also an opportunity to name a child, to choose godparents to create or sustain fictive kinship networks, and to celebrate a couple's fecundity with feasting, dancing, and traditional bawdy talk. While the dearth of diarists in the plantation colonies means that we will never recover a full sense of the cultural meaning of baptism in those places, the extant scattered references reveal a rite whose meaning only grew in importance when transferred from the metropole to these slave societies. Operating in a dialectic between "communal ceremony" and "family matter," baptism was also a central location for the creation of American systems of race.[50]

Like marriage, baptism was important to Europeans in the plantation colonies. Anglican parents in Carolina were serious about ensuring that their children were baptized, resorting to dissenting ministers when their own clergy were not available, though pleading that "they themselves were brought up" in "the Orthodox faith." The death of a minister left parishioners in the regrettable position of being "destitute of a Minister, to baptize our Children or bury our dead," two essential ritual moments in the colonial mind. When South Carolina clergyman William Guy visited the Bahamas in 1731, it was in response to "their great Necessity, specially in Christening their Children." Indeed, he baptized "upwards of 130 children" during his brief visit. Soon after Charles Woodmason arrived in the Cheraws, he met a congregation of 500 who presented him some 60 children to baptize, a process of "standing and speaking 6 Hours together" that left him "almost tir'd in baptizing of Children."[51] In the single year of 1767, he baptized 782 persons in Carolina, averaging well more than 2 per day. In eleven years of service in the mid-eighteenth century, a Bermuda minister baptized "near a Thousand Children, Whites and Blacks." Persons not baptized as children sought the rite out as adults. A Barbadian minister of the 1720s reported he "had several Occasions of administering Baptism to Adult Persons both in health, & upon a bed of sickness, some of considerable distinction." He also baptized "a great many children from one to ten years old & upwards." Some irreligious persons may have desired baptism "principally, to become entitled to Christian burial."[52] Perhaps succumbing to the comforts of a national rite of passage, even Quakers in Jamaica's St. Elizabeth's parish permitted their children to be "christen'd by the Minrs of the Church of England."[53] Clearly baptism was a powerful moment for new parents in the plantation colonies, a pious act that also connected their children to the ritual life of the mother country.

In Carolina, however, baptism was also an issue worth fighting about. The colony's high-church attorney general in 1703 complained of being "very Much infested, with the Sect of Anabaptists" and requested a reprint from *Fox's Book of Martyrs* to convince persons "wavering, as to that point of Infant Baptism." Francis Le Jau did theological battle with persons contending for immersion baptism in Goose Creek, claiming to silence them by announcing his willingness to "baptize by dipping when desired." Other Anglican clergy noted occasions on which they dipped catechumens, as when Elizabeth Ladson was "bapt per Dipping" in June 1736 at St. Andrew's parish in Carolina.[54] Le Jau's argument with "a peevish disputing" Baptist failed to convince that disputant but did drive a stander-by to request baptism, which Le Jau dramatically administered on the spot. Welsh Neck Baptists threatened that any who "apostatize from the Truth in which they have been educated by getting themselves sprinkled . . . shall be debarred from our communion."[55] Anglican parents of a more reformed frame of mind sought to have clergy omit making the sign of the cross on their children's foreheads at baptism, continuing a long tradition of objecting to that moment in the Anglican form of the ritual.[56] Carolina Quakers joined them, posting "virulent Libel[s]" that denounced the sign of the cross. Their opposition provoked Anglican clergy in Carolina and elsewhere to celebrate the slow triumph over Quakerism that the baptism of each former member of that group signaled.[57] Amid the greater religious diversity and the larger European population that separated Carolina from the experience of the West Indies, baptism could be an issue of great contention within the European community.[58]

Like the marriage rite that opened the way to licit reproduction among whites, baptism usually took place in the domestic realm of the home, especially in the island colonies. That location worked against the theological content of the prayer book liturgy, strongly suggesting that the baptism of infants was more a ceremony of naming and welcoming into a particular family than one of initiation into the Christian mysteries. Walduck of Barbados explained that while marriage might be "done on a sudden & to serve occasion," baptism was done "with Deliberation and provision, and always in their houses, never in the Churches."[59] The minister of St. James's on that island around the year 1700 found it convenient to baptize several persons at "my house" and also baptized at "Judge Rooks," "at Coll. Farmers," and "at Robt Hill's House."[60] Jamaicans insisted on baptism at home, withholding baptismal fees if the minister obliged them to come to church. In Carolina, the fees for "Christnings in private houses" depended "on the Benevolence of the People whose Generosity is very diffusive."[61] Baptism at home meant that a still-secluded mother might be able to participate, joined by the women who assisted at the delivery. Abigail Martindale, the sister or sister-in-law of Bridgetown shipwright William Martindale, could well remember that she was "present at ye Birth and Baptism" of John Waters Martindale when his baptismal records went missing some thirty-five years after the event.[62] Baptism at home underlined the social meaning of the rite that predominated in the minds of many parents.

As with marriage, conviviality accompanied the baptism of infants and seems to have been integral to many persons' understanding of the rite.[63] A nice meal went well with the sacrament of Christian initiation, as when Joseph Senhouse of Barbados "dined at Carrington Valley & stood sponsor with Genl. and Mrs. Frere for Mr. Carrington's son Paul."[64] Some Barbadian parents postponed the baptism of children "till they have several Children to be Baptized together ... [so] that they may avoid the expence of so many different feasts."[65] For this reason and others, the baptism of siblings at the same time can be found frequently in parish baptismal registers. William and Frances Cudbert's children William, John, and Mary, ages four, two, and three months, were all baptized on November 27, 1698, in St. James's parish. On one December day in 1711, two sets of parents brought two children each to the same parish church for baptism.[66] In St. Michael's parish in Bridgetown, many sets of siblings were baptized together over the eighteenth century, as when Richard and Sarah Bascomb had their three daughters, including infant twins, baptized in 1711.[67]

In Barbados, some parents delayed the baptism of their children until times in the year of "greater plenty & vareity," waiting until the "the good time comes, and the hog is fat." When those good times came, there would be a "Corne Shote & Boviness, a Calipie of Sea Tortoise, a Stude Cofum, and rosted Caberetta & other things baked & barbiqued, with planting, tarts, & yam puddings ... Chegeis Grapes, fat porks, sower sopps and the guavas." These "merry times" also called for abundant drink, including "strong Cowjou, sparkling mobby, Humming pareno, and to crown the feast a lusty bowl of rum punch."[68] Indeed, it was only at "weddings, christenings and birthdays" that some Barbadians might serve wine, otherwise being content with local spirits like falernum, bub, and black-strap.[69] Sometimes guests at baptismal feasts enjoyed these offerings too much. In the mid-1680s, the governor of Barbados investigated accusations that Sir Timothy Thornhill made a blasphemous speech "at a certaine

Christening," which turned up witnesses who could not agree on what exactly Thornhill had said. Those discrepancies led the governor "to apprehend all the Company soe farr gone in drink that none of them could well remember what was sayd." One of the party alleged to metropolitan authorities that Thornhill had wished "himselfe to be the Lord God that he might damn all those that would not be drunk with him."[70] While this sort of behavior was clearly beyond the pale, baptisms were events that gathered communities together for traditional hospitality and were a part of the social fabric that could be taken for granted. Plain people like Barbados Quakers disliked baptismal events, criticizing the "great feasting of late, with fiddling and dancing at the heathenish custom of sprinkling the child."[71]

Christening parties in Tudor and Stuart England called for a modicum of playful sexual banter, at which men were advised to "lard your talk now and then with a little waggery wrapped up in clean linen," and women talked in a similar vein about their husbands and childbirth and childrearing, all of which provided excellent opportunities for the unmatched to evaluate one another.[72] In Jamaica, young men made a habit of attending the christening parties "around the whole Parish" though uninvited, sometimes dancing until midnight and "learning breeding" in the process.[73] A Jamaican resident who had recently married quite well asked his brother, a priest in England, to come to Jamaica to baptize his first child. His wife was "a good & pious Member of the Church of England" and would keep the child "in its proper confinement till that time," so that the christening could be an occasion for the wife to introduce the bachelor clergyman to her youngest sister. Sixteen years old, she was "five foot nine Inches high, black hair, bright black eyes . . . the most beautiful person in the Island." He promised she would be a fine match, "provided this Climate renders you as youthfull as I am."[74] The atmosphere charged with the satisfaction of successful begetting, baptismal festivities were moments in which Europeans could imagine other erotic and marital possibilities.

One could, however, be so dull as to be baptized in church. Churches were invariably furnished with fonts and some persons were baptized in them. One observer overstated the case when he noted that he had "seen founts" in Barbadian churches but "never saw water put in one."[75] Fonts were nonetheless important symbols, and donors presented them to churches with the flourishes typical of early modern generosity. The inscription on the font at Christ Church in Barbados memorialized the generosity of Thomas Lewis and was at pains to note his armigerous status.[76] When John Hothersall gave a "Font of Marble" to St. John's parish in Barbados, the vestry thanked him heartily and ordered it placed to the right of the church's entrance, cutting off the end of the churchwardens' pew to make that possible.[77]

And use was made of them. Fifteen persons were baptized in St. Michael's Church in Bridgetown in 1715, albeit a small number when compared with the ninety-two baptized that year in houses.[78] The 1699 baptism of seventeen-year-old Mary Andrews was in St. James's Church in Barbados, as the baptisms of many older persons likely were.[79] Baptism of older children and adults in church may signal a recognition that while the domestic setting was fitting for infants, older catechumens could find meaning in the symbolically rich atmosphere of the parish church. Poor whites like Barbara Hayman, "a Parish child," and an unnamed "child of Irish Margaret's a poor woman" were also more likely to be baptized in church, as those two children were in Bridgetown in 1712.[80] Without the means or influence to demand that clergy come to their homes, the indigent were obliged to experience the rite in a more public fashion.

Church baptism seems to have been more frequent in Carolina, though some parents clearly resented it. A Huguenot woman and her husband in Carolina precipitated a nasty conflict between a Franco-Anglican priest of St. Denis's parish and the rector of St. Philip's parish when they entreated the former to come into their home in St. Philip's parish to baptize a child privately.[81] The rector of St. Philip's then complained to the bishop of London that he had just brought his "Parish to tolerable good order and conformity in most things," particularly the parishioners' duty "to bring Their Children to Church for publick Baptism," only to be undermined by the other minister's actions. This domestic baptism was contrary to "the known constant Practice in my Parish for several years" and might encourage those who "refuse bringing their Children to Church."[82] One such person was Charles Burnham, who threatened to have his children baptized by a dissenting minister if the rector of St. Philip's would not allow another priest "to Creason my Children at my hows." The rector had insisted on the children being brought to church, since both were in good health, and it was "but 3 qrs of an hours easy riding to the Church, and the weather very fair."[83] Baptismal practice may have been different in the country parishes. Certainly Charles Woodmason's backcountry mission involved "going to different Houses to baptize Children."[84] Though baptismal locations were not often recorded, it appears that some Carolina clergy had greater success in promoting church baptism for whites.

It is likely that the baptism of free people of color often took place in churches, ministers being unlikely to condescend to visit them in their homes. Thus the free couple Joseph and Anne Force were baptized "at a house set apart for the Service and Worship of God" on Harbour Island in the Bahamas in 1727.[85] Though enslaved persons might be baptized at or in their masters' homes, others were baptized in church, as were four slaves in Goose Creek on Advent Sunday in 1710, just after divine service.[86] When Jamaican Christopher Wade brought his three teenage mulatto children for baptism in 1777, he likely judged that the parish church was a more convenient choice due to both the number and size of the candidates and perhaps on account of his and their racial status as well.[87] A Barbadian free woman named Dolly brought her sons Robert, James, and Thomas into St. Philip's Church for their baptisms in November 1772.[88] Anglican ministers' desperate hopes to be identified with the master class likely meant that they summoned people of color to the parish church rather than celebrating these rites in their homes, marking an important difference from the genteel baptism of white infants.[89]

While free persons of color likely had to bring themselves or their children to the parish church, white slave owners could certainly summon ministers to their estates for the baptism of slaves. In Jamaica, it appears likely that some ministers celebrated the baptism of the children of planter fathers and enslaved women at home. In 1740, mulatto children named Frances, Nathaniel, Cleopatra, and Neal were baptized along with their mother Emma, "a black woman . . . at the house of Mr. John Ripley's." Three years later Susannah, another mulatto daughter of Emma, was also "Baptized at Mr. Ripley's." The year before, a mulatto child named Dorcas was baptized at "ye house of Edmd Hyde Esqr." Slave owners might send or allow their slaves, some of whom were their children, to be baptized in the minister's home, such as Jane Adams, a mulatto slave baptized in the rectory at St. James's in Barbados in 1700.[90] When whites were involved in the baptism of persons they enslaved, the location and the ministers' pastoral style likely included a level of deference that corresponded to the owner's station in life.

Anglicans in the plantation colonies preserved the tradition of enlisting friends and relatives as godparents to their children.[91] In Barbados, "the naming of the Child and the Gossips" were done with "great thought and concerne," the people thinking that "a great future may happen from a lucky name." It was more likely that godparents and children's names were carefully chosen to create social networks that could be important to the future of both children and their parents. So important were those relationships that Barbadians took their island's high mortality into account, appointing "3 or 4 Godfathers & Godmothers," knowing that "the Country is sickly & the people apt to Dye."[92] The first son of a prominent customs official in Barbados was named James Lowther Senhouse after his prominent godfather Sir James Lowther, who was joined in that duty by three others.[93] It is likely that many colonial governors were pressed into such service for elite families, as was the governor of the Bahamas in the 1720s.[94] Some parents asked proxies to stand in for godparents in England, forming transatlantic networks of godparenthood. A Senhouse son born in Barbados later in the eighteenth century had a proxy godfather stand in for George Edward Stanley, Fourteenth Earl of Ponsonby.[95] Little Thomas Cheesman, baptized in Barbados on the same day of his birth in 1712, had not a single real godparent present at his baptism, all three being "in London."[96]

Godparents were supposed to be baptized themselves and capable of teaching the growing child "what a solemn vow, promise, and profession *he hath* here made by you," as the baptismal liturgy reminded them. At the font, they were exhorted by the priest to make sure the child learned the Creed, the Lord's Prayer, and the Decalogue and that she or he attended sermons.[97] Clergy sometimes balked at chosen godparents who seemed unlikely to fulfill those duties. The rector of Vere in Jamaica complained that parents withheld baptismal fees if he rejected their chosen godparents. Taking his responsibility for the church's rite of initiation seriously, a conscientious governor of the Bahamas worried greatly about the spiritual status of eleven children baptized by a minister whose orders he doubted. He wrote hand-wringing letters to the bishop of London, wanting to know "what should be done in regard to the Children (to one of which I am Godfather) so irregularly baptiz'd."[98] Dutiful parents could fill in for less attentive godparents, as Carolinian Anne Boughton did when she asked her adult son "to look over your catechism and consider what vows and promises was made for you in your baptisem."[99] A schoolmaster expressed wishes worthy of a godfather to the children of the Stabler family of South Carolina in German verse:

> But is good that the Lord Christ has bought you,
> Because ye have been baptized in Christ's blood.
> Happy is the day and happy is the hour
> In which ye now are righteous in God's covenant of grace.
> Take note of this well and often think of it
> What God has shown to you and done much great good.
> Therefore praise and continue to grow.[100]

For all its social meaning in the plantation world, the theological meaning of baptism was not lost. Though the many thousands of sermons preached in these regions are largely unavailable to us, it is likely that worshippers often heard "a long Discourse, on the Subject of Baptism and Regeneration," such as the one offered by a Carolina clergyman in 1768.[101]

Yet some parents hoped to have their children baptized in the Church of England without godparents, associating that tradition with the Roman Catholic past or hoping to avoid the mutual and potentially costly commitments that godparenting could entail. Clergy in Carolina met parents, "not full Conformists," who desired "to baptize their Children without Godfathers and God Mothers." With some "resolution and steddyness," Carolina clergy found they could get "the better of them" in "the business of Godfathers and Godmothers." French Protestants at one christening in Carolina "began to cry down Godfathers & Mothers," offending the officiating clergyman.[102] Some parents in Goose Creek reported trouble finding godparents, perhaps because they did not want them or perhaps because of a too scrupulous following of the English canons of 1604, which ordered that no person be admitted as a sponsor who was not a communicant.[103] One Carolina minister insisted on that canon "so strictly . . . in his Ministration of Baptism, that he utterly refused to Baptize any of their Children."[104] His persistence, even as senior clergy in the province counseled accommodation to prevailing circumstances, "raised so much Prejudice against him 'mongst his Parishioners, as will require some Time, and obliging Conduct in him, to allay."[105] Clergy on the western edge of the Atlantic world had to steer between the rigorous adherence to the rubrics and canons of the metropolitan church they had promised and the social reality of life in the plantation colonies, where powerful laypersons often had their own ideas. Parishioners were clearly not interested in clerical dictates that interfered with the baptism of their children.

Many parents in the plantation colonies world recorded with care the dates of their children's baptism and the clergyman who officiated, demonstrating the importance of the rite in family memory. William Senhouse noted that his first son "on 26 March was christened by the Revd. Mr. Hebson" and recorded the same details for each of his successive children.[106] The family Bible of the Ellcocks of Barbados records the baptismal dates of their children, all done by Dr. Wharton "3 weeks after" each birth.[107] Sometime Jamaican Curtis Brett wrote a letter to his teenage son, reminding him of the names of his godparents and of the clergyman who officiated at the boy's baptism, even noting the indisposition of the rector.[108] Samuel Peyre of Santee in Carolina took careful note of his first son's baptism, recording the name of the minister and godparents in his commonplace book.[109] These personal records augmented the official baptismal records that were required by the colonial legislation establishing the Church of England in the plantation regions.[110] They also demonstrate the importance Europeans attached to the rite that welcomed their children into the world.

The final step in the ritual process of bringing a child into the world was the new mother's churching, properly the rite for "The Thanksgiving of Women after Child-birth" in the Book of Common Prayer. Like a newly married couple appearing in the parish church for the first time, the churching of women rendered public the rituals of birth and baptism that had been moved into the domestic sphere. There are sadly few records that speak to the frequency with which women sought out this rite, one that was much contested in early modern England. It was not one of the rites recorded in parish registers. It was practiced late in the period in Bermuda, a colony whose Puritan heritage might have suggested its abandonment. A minister there complained of legislation that would reduce his control over chancel seating, perhaps reducing him to the use of a seat "that hath been commonly used by Women coming to return Thanks for safe Deliverance from Child Birth." If churching persisted there, it seems likely that it remained popular in colonies where Puritanism never held sway. The commissary in Jamaica complained about a law providing that fees for churchings and other pastoral liturgies were determined by the vestry, so the rite must have been practiced on that island. His counterpart in South Carolina bemoaned the fact that no more than 20 percent of his people paid the fee for the churching of women. Carolinians of a more reformed frame of mind probably avoided the rite altogether; one minister included the churching of women among the issues about which he contended with "bigoted French Presbyterians."[111] Yet the persistence of the churching ritual in the plantation colonies meant that whites there had access to the full range of rituals that legitimized their sexuality and reproduction and to the comfort those rites brought through the major transitions of marrying, giving birth, and rearing children.

Though some persons of color were regularly baptized in the British plantation colonies, their access to these rites was not guaranteed in the same manner that it was for whites. Complex and cross-cutting issues of ethnicity and race, gender, location of birth, and status as free or enslaved must be contended with in any effort to understand which persons of color were baptized in the plantation colonies and why. Some persons of color had been born in Africa and expressed their identity in terms of various African ethnicities. Others were Creoles but could be the children of Africans or the children of a previous generation of Creoles, leaving them with different senses of the African past and the American present. Some people of color were mulattoes, with varying degrees of African and European heritage and various feelings about those distinct parts of their heritage. Africans, Creoles, and mulattoes could all be either enslaved or free, though freedom was certainly more likely for mulattoes than for Africans. Women and men of color found different theological and social meaning in the rite. All told, free persons of color and elite Creole slaves with some degree of comfort with European culture generally were most likely to seek and be accepted for baptism, a rite Europeans were determined to control.

Age and certainly gender further complicate analysis of the meaning of baptism to people of color in the plantation colonies. The Anglican prayer book provided distinct liturgies for the "Publick Baptism of Infants," the "Ministration of Private Baptism of Children in Houses," and the "Ministration of Baptism to such as are of riper years, and able to answer for themselves." The latter was used for the baptism of adult slaves, whether Creole or African, and required evidence of their Christian belief, giving the rite a different meaning than the baptism of enslaved children. Ministers did not baptize adults who could not articulate their adherence to Christian doctrine, such as a man in Goose Creek who could "hardly Speak, even Comon things, so as to be understood." Some slave owners elected to have children they owned baptized, as did the rector of St. John's in Barbados and his clerk in the 1720s and some parishioners in Goose Creek in 1712. A white woman there presented six youths for baptism in 1716, two speaking for themselves and four being treated as children. Frances, "a little negro girl belonging to Dr. Edwd Ord," was baptized at St. Andrew's in Carolina in 1732.[112] Similarly were three-month-old Samuel, "belonging to Judge Sutton," and seven-year-old Cudjoe, "belonging to Mr. Littler Roe," baptized in 1719 and 1743 respectively in St. James's in Barbados.[113] Few enslaved children were baptized if their parents were present and unbaptized, though certainly some children were enslaved without their parents and were thus fully subject to the religious demands of their owners. While few slave owners sought baptism for their slaves in the plantation colonies, they did frequently baptize those slaves whom they transported to the metropole.[114] Back in England, the inclusive tradition of the parish community reasserted itself in the social and religious practice of slave owners, though those baptized were certainly members of the slave elite.

Barbados established a pattern that associated baptism with freedom and obvious multiracial ancestry and admitted only limited numbers of enslaved persons to the sacrament.[115] While few enslaved persons were baptized, clergy reports suggested that the baptism of slaves was a relatively unremarkable occurrence. The rector of St. Michael's on that island in the 1720s reported that he had baptized "several Negro's of all Ages." Another Barbadian rector "baptiz'd seven Negroes at one time," including three of his own "and four of the Honourable George Gram's."[116] In 1716, twelve slaves of John Bentley were baptized in St. Philip's parish.[117] Numbers increased by the late eighteenth century. On Christmas Day 1784 in St. Joseph's parish in Barbados, some 50 slaves, 45 of them the property of the rector, were baptized.[118] Five years later, under new pressure from metropolitan authorities to baptize slaves, the clergy of Barbados reported that "many are baptized every year, as may be seen by the lists regularly transmitted to the Secretary's office."[119] That "many" was in proportion to the whites being baptized, not the total number of enslaved Africans and their descendents on the island.

In early Jamaica, fewer slaves sought or were offered baptism, and the link between baptism and freedom was underlined by legislation. It was an exceptional minister like Edward Reading who could report being "not without Success" in making converts on a Jamaican plantation, including the baptism of a whole family.[120] James Spenie of St. Mary's parish had "many Infidels, bond, and Some free" in his parish and had baptized "a great many of Both."[121] But most Jamaican clergy spent little time with the enslaved Africans and their descendents in their parishes. The three thousand non-Christian slaves in Kingston in the 1720s were not bothered by the rector, who reported that their masters were recalcitrant and that conversion was rendered impossible by the fact that slaves spoke "a vast Variety of quite different Languages." In St. Catherine's parish in the same period, five thousand slaves were likely content with the neglect that the minister reported of himself, again pleading the resistance of all but a few slave owners to the baptism of slaves. Perhaps the only minister in the early period actually opposed to the baptism of slaves was James White of Vere, who insisted that whites' unwillingness to share Eucharistic fellowship and "freedom of conversation after baptism" with slaves meant that baptized slaves were left to "company with the Heathens as much as ever," an unacceptable condition for Christians.[122] Though confused about many things, White pointed to an essential dynamic for understanding the baptism of slaves in the plantation colonies. Slaves earned little social credit with whites when they were baptized and at the same time risked much in their relationships in the Afro-Jamaican community. The planter class's domestication of baptism ensured that few incentives would attend it in English colonies.

Yet in Jamaica, as in Barbados, twin processes of creolization and metropolitan pressure produced greater numbers of baptisms of enslaved persons of color later in the period. Even by the middle of the century, clergy recognized that "many People . . . have their Slaves christen'd," though some slaves were still wholly "averse to it," declining baptism if not coerced.[123] A decade before, another minister was proud enough of his modest success baptizing slaves to send baptism statistics to London in 1740, including eighteen whites, thirteen mulattoes, and eighty-two Negroes. Late in the century, some eight hundred slaves received baptism at the hands of a rector of Westmoreland parish. He felt that his elimination of baptismal fees had helped, though some slaves argued that "the Christian Obea . . . can be little worth, since obtained at no expence."[124] In the same period, Edward Long concluded that no more than one-third of the baptisms celebrated in St. Catherine's parish were of whites, though his calculation certainly included free persons of color.[125]

Carolina's Church Act of 1706 specifically excepted "Negroes, Mullatoes, & Indian Slaves" from the requirement that records be kept of births, baptisms, marriages, and burials, meaning that records for understanding either the baptism or marriage of enslaved people of color in Carolina are limited.[126] In Carolina, few clergy even thought about the baptism of slaves as much as Francis Le Jau. Early in his ministry in Goose Creek, he reported that "several Negroes have asked me for the Holy Baptism," yet he delayed them to collect "proof of their good life by the Testimony of their Masters." By early the next year, however, he could report that he had "pretty many" in the parish category of "Negroes baptised." This was in the face of planter opposition to his efforts toward "the Salvation, Instruction, and human usage of Slaves and ffree Indians."[127] Those planters perhaps found some comfort in Le Jau's requirement that slave catechumens assent to the following declaration: "You declare in the Presence of God and before this Congregation that you do not ask for the holy baptism out of any design to ffree yourself from the Duty and Obedience you owe to your Master while you live, but merely for the good of Your Soul and to partake of the Grace and Blessings promised to the Members of the Church of Jesus Christ."[128] Though Le Jau was a great exception in his interest in baptizing enslaved persons in Carolina, other ministers could be prevailed upon when masters consented. In St. Andrew's parish above Charles Town, a woman with roots in Barbados sponsored at least twenty-seven slaves for baptism.[129] In the succeeding decades of the 1730s and 1740s, several, like "Cesar, an adult negro man belonging to Mr. Edmund Bellinger," came to the font in St. Andrew's parish.[130] In the 1760s, Charles Woodmason baptized "several Negroes and Mullatoos" at Beaver Creek in Carolina.[131] Yet, as in the islands, they were a tiny percentage of the slave population.

As Robert Olwell has argued for South Carolina, Creole slaves having the greatest comfort with European ways were the most likely candidates for baptism. The rector of St. Philip's in Barbados clearly associated baptism with slave elites, for "in most Families some chief Slaves are instructed & baptis'd," he having "baptis'd some Hundreds" himself. At St. John's in Barbados, the rector "Baptiz'd a very Sensible Negro in my Parish, one of distinction amongst that Colour." Skilled mulatto slaves like Eliza Pinckney's Quash, a carpenter, were likely candidates for baptism; he became John Williams at his baptism in 1749. Thomas Vane, likely a similarly skilled "Mulatto Slave of Mrs. Wade," was baptized in St. James's Church in Barbados in 1699. Whites reported that some Creole slaves in Jamaica desired baptism because it "secured them from *Obeah*," the religious tradition practiced by some African rivals in the slave community. Some persons enslaved in Jewish households likely sought baptism as a means of securing new leverage against their owners, such as Jacob, "belonging to Leah Green a Jew," who was baptized in church in Bridgetown in 1763.[132] Though whites controlled baptism, some slaves like Jacob found unanticipated meaning and power in the rite.

Enslaved women of color involved in sexual relationships with white men were natural candidates for baptism, as were the children conceived in those relationships.[133] Jamaicans' relative lack of discomfort about those relationships shows through in the colony's baptismal records. The rector of Kingston asked for metropolitan advice on the issue of baptizing women who could "give an Account of the Christian Faith" but "have lived in a State of Concubinage with their Masters, or Others, and in all Probability will continue that way of Life."[134] Charles, Robert, and Mary, illegitimate children of "Maria a Molatto of Mr. Fulkers," were baptized at St. Andrew's in Jamaica between 1685 and 1688, the records suggesting Fulker was their father.[135] The experience of Mary, "a quateroon child of Richd Maitland born of the Mulatto Slave of Mrs Laws," or Jane, "the daughter of Phoebe Irving, a Negroe Woman Slave the property of Jeffrey Irving by her said Master," represents that of many mulatto slaves baptized in Jamaica.[136]

The link between baptism and freedom for people of color, particularly mulattoes, became an enduring one in the plantation world, as free people made up the majority of baptisms of persons of color in the period of Anglican hegemony. Sexual contact persistently blurred racial lines, creating a class of persons for whom baptism had a powerful social meaning. A Jamaican clergyman complained of planter resistance to his efforts to evangelize slaves but found success among "some free Negroes and Mulattos," whom he baptized. In Kingston, the rector "baptiz'd Several Free Negroes & Mulattoes," adding to the 106 baptized free people in his parish in 1724.[137] By the middle of the eighteenth century in Jamaica, "the free Mulattoes and Negroes [were] all Christians." Seventeen of the 36 persons baptized in Clarendon parish in Jamaica in 1750 were persons of color, 15 of them labeled "Mulatto."[138] In Spanish Town in 1751, approximately 34 of 61 catechumens were persons of color, the great majority classified as mulatto or quadroon.[139] Similarly in St. Andrew's, 9 of 15 persons baptized in 1751 were persons of color, mostly mulatto. In 1771 in the same parish, 13 of 22 baptisms were of persons of color.[140] By the late 1780s, free "people of colour" in Jamaica were "all anxious to have their Children baptized."[141] Their anxiety grew out of the fact that baptism was legally required for free people in Jamaica who wanted to enjoy certain legal privileges, including access to trial by jury and the ability to give evidence in civil cases involving whites.[142] Free people likely also sought baptism as a binding force for family life in threatening societies committed to white supremacy, as when Abraham Walker, Elizabeth Haywood, and their daughter Mary Clarke were baptized all at once in 1711 in Jamaica.[143] A baptized couple could then be married and have a legal identity in the records of the church, documents that could become powerful if their freedom were ever threatened. Though likely less domestic and more public than the baptism of whites, free persons of color clearly valued baptism.

Similarly in Barbados, baptism was important to free persons of color from an early date. In 1698, Ann Occro, "a free negro woman," and her daughter Diana were both baptized in St. James's parish, cementing their status as free people in the parish register and the parish community. Free persons of color were baptized at St. Michael's in Barbados as early as 1690.[144] By the mid-eighteenth century, the baptismal register for that parish includes a good number of free persons of color, usually classified as "Negro" and "Mulatto," such as Lydia Parsons, "a free Negro woman about 17 years old," and "Jacob Carre a free Mulatto boy about 14 years old." Nineteen of the 46 people of color baptized at St. Michael's in Barbados in 1783 were free, a far larger proportion than the numbers of free people on the island would suggest. The number of persons of color, both slave and free, being baptized in Barbados increased across the eighteenth century, particularly in the urban parish of St. Michael's. In 1714, 6 persons of color and 110 whites were baptized at St. Michael's. By 1763, 15 persons of color and 111 whites were baptized in the parish. In 1783, approximately 46 persons of color and 135 whites were baptized at St. Michael's.[145] Across the eighteenth century, free persons of color recognized the power of baptism in increasing numbers.

Free people in Barbados found that baptism opened the door to marriage in church and attendant improvements in their social position. The Hector family of Bridgetown is a powerful illustration. In March 1704, Charles Hector was baptized, the entry calling him the son of Samuel Hector, "free negro by an Instrument under the hands of Mr. Thoms. Hollard & Mrs. Eliza. his wife." That freedom seems to have been a relatively new development. Indeed, Elizabeth Hollard, Samuel's former owner, was listed among the godmothers. A year later, Samuel's wife Joan, "aged abt 55 yrs," was also baptized, as well as their fifteen-year-old daughter Susan. As if those two baptisms had not been enough for the family that day, Samuel and Joan were then married. On July 31, 1706, Charles's eighteen-year-old fiancée Hannah was baptized, and then she and Charles were married. On the same day, their nine-month-old daughter Joan, named for her grandmother, was also baptized.[146] Between 1704 and 1706, this family of free persons of color consecrated their domestic arrangements and reproduction in ways that established their status as a free family in the Bridgetown parish community.

Though a much smaller group than in the islands, free people of color sought baptism for themselves and for their children in Carolina from an early date. The experience of free people known only as John and Mary demonstrates the relationship between baptism and freedom. "John the son of John and Mary free negroes" was baptized in the parish of St. Andrew in 1730. His parents were the same John and Mary, then "belonging to Mrs. John Godfrey," who had themselves been baptized in 1723. They later brought a son named Thomas to the font in 1741, the register noting that the parents were "formerly belonging to Mr. John Godfrey." While John and Mary's theological understanding of these baptisms is lost to us, clearly they experienced baptism as a prelude to their freedom and sought baptism for their children as a fitting thing in their lives as a free family. In the same parish, "Sampson & Pompey 2 free negroes & their wives" were baptized in 1739, setting those two couples on the same path toward a new mode of family life that baptism could engender.[147] Free persons of color also presented their infants for baptism in the parish of St. Thomas and St. Denis.[148] The very few baptisms of persons of color recorded in St. Philip's in Charles Town included Diana Lampton and Catherine Thorp, "yellow Girls," and Rachel, "a yellow woman," probably all free persons.[149] A smaller free black population in Carolina did mean that fewer persons found this path meaningful in the low country than did so in the islands.

The widespread association of baptism and free people of color sustained long-running white anxieties about the social meaning of the rite. Early in Barbadian history, Richard Ligon encountered the common assumption that the baptism of slaves would make them free, as many early colonists believed that the laws of England forbade the enslavement of Christians.[150] Persistent refutation of that belief from English bishops and the SPG and legislation declaring baptism to be no bar to enslavement assuaged those fears but never eliminated a sense that baptism did change the relationship between master and slave. A minister in Barbados reported a compact between a slave catechumen and his owner to deal with the master's anxiety about that change. For his part, the master "would stand Godfather for his slave when fitted & ye slave promises him ye same service he has hitherto had."[151] A Barbadian act of 1739 amended its slave code to permit slaves to give evidence "against any free Negro, Indian, or Mulatto, whether baptized or not," that evidence being deemed "as good, valid, and effectual in the law, as if the Slave giving evidence or testimony was free, baptized, and not under servitude."[152] While the act attempted to deny it, baptism clearly imparted greater credibility and authority to those who received it, making it far more appropriate for free people of color than slaves in the estimation of whites.

When baptized in the Church of England, persons of color had to have at least two sponsors, though parish records usually failed to record the names of baptismal sponsors. The retention of this godparent tradition meant that individual initiative was not always enough for a black catechumen to achieve baptism; she or he needed already baptized persons to stand as sponsors. The register of St. Michael's in Bridgetown records more names of godparents than any other from these regions, and it notes an exceptional number of occasions of whites serving as sponsors to free and enslaved persons of color.[153] A white woman in Goose Creek in Carolina served as sponsor for one of her female slaves for baptism in 1713, perhaps inspiring a male slave owner to make the same offer for one of his male slaves two years later.[154] Some Jamaican masters tried to stand sponsor for their slaves' baptisms without sufficient preparation, promising to instruct them afterward. Others sought to use the godparent requirement to hinder the baptism of slaves. One foe of the baptism of slave children in Jamaica demanded that the godparent tradition be kept, likely hoping it would be a bar to the baptism of black infants.[155] In Carolina, Le Jau was obliged to hunt up black godparents for enslaved catechumens, "because of the difficulties of prevailing upon the white people to be so charitable."[156] Free persons of color in Barbados (and likely elsewhere) did the godparent duty for one another's children; when Mary Bellarmine's son George and Elizabeth Bellarmine's son James were baptized in 1721, they were each a godmother to the other's child.[157]

This taking up of the tradition of godparentage by free persons of color points toward this chapter's conclusions. Marriage and baptism were powerful rites, conferring legitimacy on the most intimate realities of sexuality and reproduction. On a theological plane, the prayer book and other liturgies for these rites made major claims about ultimate things: that baptism entailed the gift of the Holy Spirit, the remission of sins, and a new birth to everlasting life and that marriage was instituted by God to signify the mystical union between Christ and the church and for the procreation of children. The reassertion of those vast claims at every marriage or baptism, however, did little to disabuse laypersons of the alternative or additional content that they often attached to those rites. Alongside the meaning proclaimed in liturgies printed and performed, residents of the plantation world experienced marriage and baptism as rites rich in social and cultural meaning, indeed, as rites so powerful that they could alter human relationships in an instant.

Whites' determination to control marriage and baptism reveals the tremendous anxiety that their ritual power could engender. The reproduction of metropolitan practices of marriage and baptism was central to sustaining the fiction that the plantation colonies were settler societies that carried the values of the metropole into the wilderness. The celebration of both rites at home kept the power of marriage and baptism under lay control. In the domestic setting, universalizing theological claims ran headlong into the specificity of a small gathering of family and friends. The fiddler tuning his instrument in the corner, the table already spread, and the punch bowl filled rendered the minister's ethereal discourse and actions marginal to the occasion. The Church of England's clergy in the plantation regions were thus constantly reminded that they served very much at the pleasure of their lay masters. The domestication of marriage and baptism reduced clergy control over those rites, further undermining the already limited independence of clergy and any possibility that the English church might find any prophetic stance between slaves and their owners. Moreover, removing these rites from public space made them less accessible to the community in the widest sense. These privatized rites were rendered less available as any sort of model for appropriation by persons of color or poor whites and became moments of boundary maintenance for the plantation elite. Indeed, public baptisms and marriages became lesser events, associated with lower-status whites and persons of color. Domestic rites were thus domesticated as well, evacuated of their spiritual egalitarianism and prophetic potential.

Slave owners followed up on this ritual privatization with a general predisposition to discourage the baptism and marriage of slaves, rites in which few Africans and only a few more Creoles were interested in any event. Though some exceptional whites catechized their slaves, clergy consistently reported planter disinterest in and indeed opposition to the baptism of slaves. With the door to baptism closed, marriage by a minister was not an option either. Whites had no interest in providing slaves with cultural tools for the creation of new marriages, families, and identities. Marriage and baptism could create insoluble bonds that would have contributed to the autonomy of the slave community, legitimizing slaves' sexuality and reproduction and depriving slave owners of the false moral superiority they rhetorically deployed when discussing the sexual lives of the enslaved. The disruption of typical reproductive patterns found among slaves in the plantation colonies served planters' interests better than stable slave families, which were likely to have become the building blocks of an autonomous and eventually rebellious slave community. Whites' consent to some Creole slaves' desire to be baptized was likely motivated by some mixture of commitment to the Christian mission and a realization that a baptized slave elite could be useful.[158]

The actions of free persons of color further reveal what marriage and baptism could mean in the British plantation colonies. They frequently sought out both marriage and baptism for the power those rites lent to their own domestic arrangements and to the birth and rearing of their children, as well as for the distinction from the enslaved that these ritual incorporations gave them. Even in societies dominated by racist white regimes, baptized free people were accorded a greater degree of credibility in legal actions and likely in quotidian interactions as well. Whether they sought baptism as adults or had their newborn children baptized, the free carpenters and cordwainers and free women who became members of the church found in the rite some promise that made it worth seeking. Marriage offered free couples legal and ecclesiastical sanction for their unions, meaningful in societies in which many white males regarded black women as conveniently exploitable sexual objects. The children born to a baptized and married couple were then carried to the font as well, creating a baptismal record and a legal identity that could never be expunged. These were powerful ritual resources in societies that offered few to persons of color.

The social and cultural vitality that surrounded baptism and marriage demonstrates that the notorious irreligion of the British plantation colonies has been much exaggerated by historians and in ways that have distorted our understanding of the entire human community in those places. Clearly baptism and Christian marriage were powerful rites to white residents of the region. They were rites worth controlling, rites best kept private and out of the hands of the enslaved. Indeed, they were rites with which even the clergy could not be trusted. While these regions are not distinguished for any original contribution to the Christian theological tradition, they were places in which the ritual practices of Christianity provided a lively forum for seeking and making meaning in the lives of many people. In the British plantation colonies, the Christian rituals of initiation and matrimony were joined to processes that regulated the diffusion of power throughout the social hierarchy. Thus the meaning of ritual in the plantation colonies is a chapter in the long history of Christian worship and its situation in particular matrices of social power, rather than a chapter concerned with places in which the Christian tradition had no meaning at all. Deep in that tradition was the practice of the Lord's Supper, a rite rich in social meaning that also found its place in the plantation colonies.

CHAPTER 4

The Meanings of the Eucharist in the Plantation World

CERTAIN PASTORAL RITES, especially those closely related to times of life-stage transition, seemed necessary to Christians in the British plantation colonies. Early modern people generally felt that couples needed to be married, babies had to be baptized, and the bodies of the dead had to be buried. Yet those seemingly necessary pastoral rites were not the sum total of ritual practice in the plantation colonies. The sacrament of the Eucharist was celebrated there as well, contrary to the historiographical tradition that suggests that Christian practice in these regions consisted of little more than moralizing sermons on the necessity of obedience and the blessedness of the social hierarchy. This ritual consumption of bread and wine in remembrance of the death of Jesus of Nazareth was emphasized by resident clergy and their metropolitan superiors and proved important to laypeople in both their piety and their understanding of the human community. In addition to its real spiritual import, Europeans experienced this ritual meal as one that created interpersonal mutuality and social cohesion, things often in short supply in the plantation colonies. They also knew from long experience that the sacrament could serve a variety of political, indeed hegemonic, purposes. As translated from England to plantation colonies, the Lord's Supper was a powerful location for the ritual exclusion of most Africans and their descendents from the human community. Re-creating and modifying metropolitan cultural elaborations around the Eucharist was thus essential to establishing the power of the planter regimes of British America.

Metropolitan Precedents and the Political Meaning of the Eucharist

The social importance of the Eucharist in medieval and early modern Europe is difficult to overestimate. In England before the Reformation, the Sunday parish Mass was a powerful moment when the parish community gathered in its ranks to witness the rites of Christ's body and blood. By their gifts of wax, holy bread, and communion linens, parishioners drew near week by week to the altar, even though most only received the host once a year. Rituals associated with the Eucharist emphasized the healing of social ruptures, as parishioners passed and kissed the paxbred, consumed holy bread, and walked in procession together. Yet at the same time, these rites heavily emphasized social hierarchy, for parishioners participated according to their place in the local social order. In the great towns, the guilds processed in elaborate Corpus Christi processions, those of highest status nearest the sacrament as it was carried through the streets, drawing people and precincts together, even as others were excluded. Though these rites of precedence could be divisive, as frequently recorded disputes over them show, in the Eucharist medieval English people articulated a desire for an ordered social cohesion, for an organic unity in the local community. Even the dead were drawn into the Eucharistic community, made present in the reading of the bede roll and as the sacrifice of the Mass was offered for the good of their souls.[1]

After the Reformation, English Protestants' understanding of the Eucharist and the Eucharistic community both maintained medieval precedents and moved in new directions. The contested and haphazard Reformation of the English church meant that the Eucharist itself became a contested rite. In its prayer book form, the Church of England's Eucharistic practice was criticized, denounced, and avoided by both recusants and Puritans, on the one hand for departing too far from medieval precedent and on the other for not going far enough. For the better part of a century, the English debated the proper posture for receiving the Eucharist (kneeling or sitting), the best sort of bread to use (wafers or loaf), and the position and construction of the communion table or altar. The extended argument over these epiphenomena was undergirded by disagreements on the Eucharist as a means of grace, the nature of the sacramental presence and power in it, and the necessity of restricting communion to the gathered saints.

Those disagreements contributed mightily to the onset of a civil war that thoroughly disrupted the Eucharistic practice of the Church of England and of dissenters. After the Restoration, it is clear that in most places the Eucharist was celebrated at Christmas, Easter, Whitsunday (Pentecost), and sometimes at Michaelmas. In a few places, particularly at the cathedrals and in London, monthly and even a few weekly celebrations could be found. But celebrations did not necessarily mean that many people received. Though canon law required parishioners to receive at least three times per year, many received only once a year, at the Easter communion, thus following the medieval practice of a single annual communion. Careful preparation for worthy reception of the Eucharist was demanded by the exhortations of the prayer book and popular devotional manuals on the sacrament.[2] But even if communions were infrequent, the social importance of the Eucharist remained high. Failing to communicate at Easter could result in presentment to church authorities, a presumption of popery (and thus treason) by one's neighbors, or the spread of rumors about one's moral status. Persons in dispute with their neighbors avoided the sacrament.[3] And communion continued to reflect social hierarchy, as great men communed first, "the ordinary sort of people" receiving last, probably much the order in which they were seated.[4]

When compulsory church attendance and communion were abandoned with the Act of Toleration in 1689, the parish Eucharist might have receded in importance as a constituting element for the local and national communities had not the later Stuarts' long flirtation with Roman Catholicism so enflamed the political nation. The 1673 Act "for preventing dangers which may happen from Popish recusants," usually known as the Test Act, made a Protestant understanding of the Eucharist necessary for holding any civil or military office in the realm. In the Court of Chancery, or King's Bench, officeholders were to subscribe to the following: "I, A.B., do declare that I do believe that there is not any transubstantiation in the sacrament of the Lord's Supper, or in the elements of bread and wine, at or after the consecration thereof by any persons whatsoever." While that oath eliminated Catholics from political or military leadership, the act's other provision prevented committed Protestant dissenters from taking those roles as well. Officers were also required to "receive the sacrament of the Lord's Supper according to the usage of the Church of England . . . in some parish church upon the Lord's Day," building on a similar provision in the 1661 Corporation Act that governed municipal officers.[5] Ministers and churchwardens were to prepare certificates of those communions, to be presented in court.[6] Thus the Eucharist became a bright dividing line in England, a ritual practice that marked full citizenship, national loyalty, and political reliability. This departure from the purposes Christians claimed for the sacrament was bemoaned by some, who joined John Oldmixon, an early historian of Anglo-America, in regretting that too many were guilty of "receiving unworthily . . . the Lord's Supper, which is too often prostituted to temporal Concerns."[7]

Given the vitality of metropolitan cultural traditions around the Eucharist, it would be an extraordinary rupture for residents of the plantation colonies to abandon those practices, especially when they were confronted by the difficulties of their colonizing enterprise. Though little attended to by historians, the culture of the Eucharist in the plantation colonies was lively, first in relation to office-holding and the exclusion of Roman Catholics. Barbados and South Carolina, with larger white populations, had room to pass legislation requiring some officeholders to conform to the provisions of the Test Act.[8] Jamaica's difficulty maintaining its white population and finding white officeholders meant that religious tests were not prudent in the face of an overwhelming black majority. One Jamaican clergyman complained that the "great men who rule the Island, Councellours, & Lawyers, may take the Sacrament, or let it alone if they please, Some very few do or have taken it once, but in many years after their entering into Office never do it again." Clergy, however, had to take great care if they desired to "put 'em in mind of ye Statutes on this behalf," for "if they plead at proper times the necessity of them, the Clergy must expect to be call'd Papists, & evil men to all the degrees & denominations that faction can devise." The writer, an eccentric minister of Vere parish, probably endured just that when he sued officers in the militia under an act passed during Lord Hamilton's governorship that required that "every person in the Offices Ecclesiastick, Civil, & Military should qualify themselves by the Sacramental Test according to our manner in England."[9] Even though the act permitted communion in any church tolerated by the laws of England, Hamilton had reported the act to his metropolitan superiors in a critical tone, insisting "it is very little suited to the circumstances of a weake and infant Colony."[10] The island's attorneys general seem to have taken little interest in enforcing that act, reinforcing the idea that Jamaica's plantocracy had no room to deploy Eucharistic practice against other whites.

Oaths against transubstantiation and requirements to communicate were especially popular in the factious political culture of South Carolina, where a larger white population permitted more public political discord. While the island colonies had few dissenters, the Anglican establishment in Carolina served no more than half the white population so that the Eucharist there could serve political purposes similar to those found for it in England. In 1704, the South Carolina Assembly passed an act of exclusion that effectively prohibited the election of dissenters to that body by requiring members to "receive the Sacrament of the Lord's Supper, according to the rites and usages of the Church of England, in some publick Church upon some Lord's Day" or to swear that they were conforming but noncommunicating Anglicans who had not received the sacrament elsewhere in the past year.[11] This act and the act establishing the Church of England in the province that had followed close on its heels were disallowed by the Crown in 1706. A new Church Act was passed in response; it still restricted voters in vestry elections to those who were "of the religion of the Church of England, and that do conform to the same." The vestrymen and churchwardens they elected were subject to the same criteria and were required to "subscribe the test."[12] Like the other plantation colonies, parishes were the only form of local government in South Carolina. Thus parochial officers had important duties: they set tax rates for poor relief, granted the parish's charity, set up schools, and managed elections for the provincial legislature. Rejection of transubstantiation was thus essential to office-holding and conformity to the Anglican rite almost as important.

One can find the oaths throughout the run of colonial vestry minutes for the province. Early in the eighteenth century, the vestry of Christ Church parish took the longer oath against Catholic Eucharistic theology originally found in an English act meant to exclude Catholics from Parliament.[13] Besides the oath against transubstantiation, that oath affirmed that the undersigned believed that "ye sacrifice of ye Mass as ... now Usd in ye Church of Rome ... [is] superstitious & Idolatrous," and that they believed this "in ye plaine and ordinary Sence of the words ... as they are commonly understood by English Protestants."[14] Vestrymen and churchwardens in St. John's parish in Berkeley County took "the State oaths and sign[ed] the following declaration" against transubstantiation every Easter Monday, immediately after the election of officers. Parish officers were still taking the oath in the 1770s, as in the newly organized parish of St. Matthew, near Orangeburg. Indeed, the final entry in the surviving eighteenth-century minutes from St. Philip's parish in Charles Town is a record of the vestrymen's oaths against transubstantiation in 1774.[15] The rejection of Catholic teaching on the Eucharist was thus a boundary for Carolina's political class until the Revolution.

Even when the provisions of the Test Act were ignored, Eucharistic theology was a live issue in the British plantation world. When making converts from the Roman Church, Anglican clergy took special pains to disabuse persons of their belief in transubstantiation. In Jamaica in 1702, Charles Chabrun, raised a Catholic in France, was "made truly Sensible of the Erroneous tenets of the Said Church" and was then particularly directed to "Abhor all the Errors & Corrupt Doctrine of the Same: Such as are Those of Transubstantiation, the Receiving of Communion in one kind, the invocation of Saints."[16] When a former Jesuit, Gregory Ledwich, became an Anglican in Jamaica late in the period, he "read & subscribed the oaths of allegiance, supremacy, & abjuration, & the declaration against transubstantiation & popery; & ... received the Sacrament publicly in the Church of Kingston on Christmas day."[17] Francis Le Jau in Carolina suspected some of his parishioners of being crypto-Catholics, and "if they should present themselves to the Communion, I would do my duty and speak to them of what the world does suspect." He sought abjurations, certainly of transubstantiation, from Catholics desiring to receive the communion in his church, including a slave woman from Guadeloupe and some "Negroe Slaves born & brought up among the Portuguese that are very desirious to Abjure the popish heresy's and be Recd. to the Communion among us."[18] He threatened them with being "sent to Medera again," should they ever "return to the Popish Worship."[19] The rector of St. Philip's in Charles Town preached the same sermon against transubstantiation nine times between 1759 and 1789, calling it "absurd" and "impious" and bemoaning the Roman tradition of communion in one kind.[20] Other Protestants could similarly be incorporated through Eucharistic practice. One Jamaican Anglican celebrated the Anglicanization of Scottish Presbyterians from the failed colony of Darien. Though initially served by Scottish ministers, they became "pretty well reconcil'd to the Church" and began to "frequent it more, yn many of our own people." Two of these were apparently sons of judges of King Charles I, men tainted by regicide who redeemed themselves when they "came frequently to Liguania & rec'd the Sacramt there; so did Harrison (the Son of Coll. Harrison anayr of K: Ch: the 1st judges) & he is buried in the Church of St. Andrews Liguania."[21] While Eucharistic theology seems a minor point to later readers, it was a major cleavage between the nations competing for empires in the Americas.

The conversions of Roman Catholics in the colonies were part and parcel of those persons' efforts to join the British national community by abandoning foreign doctrine. Taking oaths and receiving the sacrament had been the chief components of the English naturalization process since the reign of James I. The Parliament at Westminster sought to extend that link between Eucharistic doctrine and citizenship to the colonies in 1740. *The South Carolina Gazette* carried news of the Parliamentary act for naturalizing foreign Protestants in 1741. It required that "all Persons duely qualifying themselves to be naturalized, (except Quakers or Jews) shall receive the Sacrament of the Lord's Supper in some Protestant Congregation in Great-Britain, or in some of the American Colonies, within three Months next before their taking and subscribing the said Oaths, and Declaration: and shall, at the Time of taking and subscribing the said Oaths, &c, produce a Certificate signed by the Person administering the said Sacrament, and attended by Two credible witnesses, whereof an Entry shall be made in the Secretary's Office of the Colony."[22] One Charles Town jeweler did ask Johann Martin Bolzius "for a testimonial from me that he had received Holy Communion from my colleague in Charlestown and was therefore a Protestant, so as to enable him to be naturalized."[23] In an Atlantic world in which persons of many nationalities washed up on American shores, the English found it useful to continue their long tradition of connecting the Christian ritual meal with the boundaries of the political nation.

English Protestants often coupled the revulsion with which they regarded Catholic Eucharistic doctrine and practice with their similar feelings for African religions in the Americas. They understood both under the heading of idolatry, long the category of religious error regarded as most pernicious in the English national consciousness.[24] A Jamaican correspondent explained one difficulty of converting slaves to Protestantism, noting that slave owners in the Caribbean sometimes sold rebellious slaves "on the French or Spanish Coast," in order to recoup some of their investment before a slave became a runaway and thus a total loss. Thus if "Negros [were] instructed and christen'd, and become Members of the Church of England, there would naturally arise a Scruple in abandoning them to Popery and a new Idolatry."[25] The always provocative and often misinformed Edward Long described the African "*Mocas*, who not only worship, but eat, snakes; now adore, and presently devour, their deity." Yet he found this not so outlandish as it might have been. For they were "not unexampled by some states in Europe," referring to "those pious cannibals, one essential part of whose faith is to believe, that they verily and substantially eat the flesh, and quaff the blood, of their God."[26] English people in the plantation regions understood their reformed doctrine of the Eucharist as a boundary between themselves and the Africans they sought to dominate and between them and their European rivals for empire.

The Social and Pastoral Meanings of the Eucharist

And yet the political meaning of the sacrament was not its only importance, nor were clergy and believers in the plantation colonies straightforwardly Machiavellian in their manipulation of the Eucharist. The frequent celebration of the Eucharistic mysteries was encouraged by colonial clergy and their metropolitan superiors and deeply felt by many colonists. Historical writing on colonial Anglicanism has usually insisted that the Eucharist was celebrated no more than four times per year and that such infrequency suggested a lack of importance. Moreover, scholars have pointed to the wide disparity between the numbers of worshippers in Anglican churches and the much smaller number of persons who received communion as evidence of irreligious attitudes, a serious misunderstanding.[27] General neglect of sacramental worship has also characterized much scholarship. John Woolverton, author of the standard history of colonial Anglicanism in the mainland colonies, thought that only "some city churches in the northern colonies" had monthly celebrations of the Eucharist and included only six references to the rite in his 331 pages.[28] It is quite clear that colonial Anglicans celebrated and received the Eucharist less often than

Anglicans currently do, yet this has too often been taken as evidence of neglect of the rite. Two points thus need to be understood. The Lord's Supper was celebrated more often than four times per year in many places. And even where it was not, infrequency of communion is as likely to be indicative of excessive veneration as it is of disdain.

On the second point first. The 1662 Book of Common Prayer established significant barriers for any person desiring to receive communion. Communicants were required to "signify their names to the Curate, at least some time the day before." Should the minister know of either "malicious and open contention with" a communicant's neighbors or "grave and open sin without repentance," he could refuse the person, preferably in advance but even at the table itself, a potentially humiliating prospect. On the Sunday before a celebration, the minister was to read an exhortation to the congregation, announcing his intention "to administer to all such as shall be religiously and devoutly disposed the most comfortable Sacrament." He reminded them of how "dangerous" it was "to them that will presume to receive it unworthily." Those who failed to examine their lives and conversation, repent of their sins, and make peace with and forgive neighbors "doth nothing more else but increase your damnation." Adulterers and hinderers of God's Word, of whom there were many in the plantation colonies, were specifically warned away from the table, "lest, after the taking of that holy Sacrament, the devil enter into you, as he entered into Judas, and fill you full of all iniquities, and bring you to destruction both of body and soul."[29] If worshippers in the colonies were paying any attention at all, it is no wonder that only a minority regularly communicated. The sacrament was dangerous stuff.

Yet it was regularly available as well, especially in Barbados. In the 1720s, nearly every parish on that island offered the Eucharist once a month in addition to the Christmas, Easter, and Whitsunday celebrations. William Gordon insisted that he "administered the Sacrament monthly to a great number of Communicants," usually about 50, in St. Michael's Church in Bridgetown. His assistant reported that they had "near four times as many at the festival Sacramts." St. Thomas's parish had 12 to 20 communicants at its monthly and festival celebrations, out of 60 to 120 persons usually in attendance. Joseph Holt of St. Joseph's also reported a monthly Eucharist, in addition to those "on the great Solemnities." The rector of St. Philip's reported 20 to 60 communicants at his monthly and festival celebration, "and encreasing." A few years after those figures were submitted, the rector of St. Michael's reported that "my little Church is now fill'd, and the Communion encreases every Month." Three years later, he could still report that "the Number of Communicants increase — Monthly." At midcentury, a clergyman reported that "all things at present are easy & quiet, the Clergy esteemed, the Church frequented, & the Sacrament of the Lords Supper monthly administered."[30] While it might be too strong to describe a sacramental revival in Barbadian Anglicanism, it is clear that a regular and robust Eucharistic practice was present there from the early eighteenth century.

The situation was different in Jamaica in the 1720s, especially in the rural parishes that had small white populations. In general, the plantation colonies conformed to the metropolitan model in having more frequent Eucharistic celebrations in the urban parishes.[31] There was apparently no plan to ever offer the Lord's Supper in rural St. Ann's parish. The rector of Westmoreland parish reported that he could rarely get up the number of communicants required by the canons for celebration of the Eucharist, which was only "four (or three at the least)." Richard Marsden of St. John's, who wandered up and down British America, reported that he "gave warning for the Celebration of ye holy communion in September, but not one person staid to receive," though he had as many as ten communicants at the Easter and Christmas celebrations.[32] The rector of St. Thomas's in the East presided at the table only once a year, at Christmas. Three celebrations a year was the rule in St. Dorothy's, St. Elizabeth's, St. Thomas's in the Vale, and Vere. In Jamaica's urban parishes, celebrations were more frequent. Residents of Port Royal could communicate four times per year, and twenty to thirty persons did so. Up to fifty Kingstonians accepted the seven invitations to the table that they received each year. St. Catherine's in Spanish Town followed the Barbadian model of communion on the first Sunday of every month and on the great festivals.[33] A younger and more fragile colony with a much smaller European population than Barbados, Jamaica apparently found less comfort in and use for the sacrament.

South Carolina had no parishes with so little Eucharistic emphasis as some of those in Jamaica, yet the colony as a whole did not rise to the level of the practice in Barbados. The first English missionary in South Carolina reported that he had "prevailed with many to a carefull preparation for & participate ye Blessed Sacrament of ye Lords Suppr: The first time I administered that Holy Ordinance I could find but 5 communicants but they are Now Increased to ye Number of about 32 and are yet Increasing here being some few young people who Submit to my Instruction in order to their being prepared for ye Blessed Sacramt at Easter next."[34] The cardinal parish of St. Philip's in Charles Town was the only one to report a monthly Eucharist, with as many as 50 communicants. The parish of St. Thomas's had six celebrations per year, with as many as 20 communicants. Every other parish reported four celebrations per year, with small numbers of communicants: 23 at St. Andrew's, 15 in the francophone parish of St. Denis's, 20 at St. James's Goose Creek, 28 at Christ Church. St. James's Santee, a parish with many Huguenot families, reported 65 communicants, more than the Charles Town parish. Little St. George's in Dorchester, perhaps building on the fervor of its New England roots, had a surprising 40 communicants, 17 of them Afro-Carolinians.[35] South Carolina Baptists, whose Eucharistic practice will be discussed below, usually favored quarterly communions, though the Ashley River Church sometimes celebrated eight times per year.[36] In between the practice of Barbados and Jamaica, the Eucharist was nonetheless a reality in the lives of worshippers in Carolina, on levels both social and spiritual.

The celebration of the Eucharist was tied to the extension of the parish's charity. As the rubrics of the prayer book required, monetary offerings for the poor were collected on sacramental Sundays in Anglican churches, giving rise to the category of "Sacrament money" in parish and churchwarden's accounts. Under "Money Recd at the Communion," Prince Frederick parish in South Carolina recorded £9..9..6 at Easter 1744 and £10..7 at Easter 1745, with lesser amounts for the Christmas and Whitsunday celebrations. This money was then applied to parish expenses for maintaining the poor in their own homes and in parish facilities. In 1741, St. Philip's in Charles Town sent a poor man "to the Work house to be maintained out of the Sacrament Money."[37] St. Helena in Carolina paid the "expences of James Smithers, a poor Sick Stranger . . . out of ye Sacramnt.-Money" in the rector's hands. Only in Barbados can one find the widespread early modern practice of feeding the poor on Sundays when the Eucharist was celebrated. St. Michael's vestry ordered "that on every Sacrament day there be bread found and provided in the Church by the Churchwarden . . . to be given to such poor people as will come to the Church for it."[38] Francis Le Jau bargained with his parishioners on the issue. He explained that he "cou'd hardly have prevailed," with more frequent celebrations, "had I not put this condition by way of encouragement that no Offerings shou'd be gather'd but at the three great Festivals." Though thin when compared to the practices of their medieval ancestors, these practices connected a rite confined to the church building to the wider social needs of the parish community.

The Eucharist was also celebrated for the sick, of whom there were many in the plantation colonies. One Barbadian clergyman was exhausted by being "frequently call'd to the most distant Parishes of the Island to visit sick Friends, and administer the Sacrament to them." When a layman in Jamaica was begging forgiveness for having impersonated a priest, he pleaded that at least he never "was prevailed upon either to officiate at the Altar in the Admon of the blessed Sacrament of the Lds Supper or to any Sick pson," suggesting that the sacrament was often offered to the sick. Indeed, sometimes the sick were the only persons who received, as in St. Mary's parish in Jamaica in the 1720s, where James Spenie, having no church, preached in his own home and had no one other than the sick with whom to celebrate the Eucharist. Alexander Garden, rector of St. Philip's in Charles Town, felt sure that the sick should call the clergy to "dispense *Absolution* and the holy *Eucharist*" to them. Clergy negligent in this duty were liable to have trouble, as William Peasely did at St. Helena's in South Carolina. His vestry criticized his "refusing to visit people at the point of Death . . . and suffering them to leave the World without benefit of that spiritual Comfort they so earnestly desired."[39] In celebrating with the sick, clergy extended the Eucharistic community outward from the parish church, connecting even those persons whom illness had severed from the gathering at the table.

Those who received the sacrament were supposed to prepare themselves carefully. Lists of books imported by clergy suggest how seriously they took this part of their duty. A "Catechetical Library" brought to Jamaica in 1724 for the "Instruction of the youth & particularly of the Negroe Children & others" listed Bishop Edmund Gibson's *The Sacrament of the Lord's Supper Explained*, Bishop William Fleetwood's *The Reasonable Communicant*, a book by Theophilus Dorrington on the sacrament, and Archbishop John Tillotson's *A Persuasive to Frequent Communion in the Holy Sacrament of the Lord's Supper*, all under the heading "For the Instruction of the People in that Nature of . . . Baptism & the Lords Supper."[40] Booksellers also made available titles directed toward preparation for communion, including Widow Fisher of Charles Town who offered "Bibles, Testaments, Psalters, Primmers, [and] Mr. Henry on the Sacrament."[41] Individual preparation for first reception of the Eucharist was not unheard of. One Barbadian minister prepared a young woman (whom he had seduced) "for the Table" and "assisted . . . the Easter following, the first time she ever approached it."[42] Carolina Baptists were particularly rigorous in their preparation for the Eucharist, resolving to meet for church discipline and business during the week so that Saturday could be devoted to "a preparation Sermon preacht for the Communion ye Sabbath following."[43] Eating and drinking one's own damnation was a serious concern for many in the plantation colonies.

The limited number of personal papers surviving from the plantation colonies makes recovery of the personal experience of the Eucharist difficult. But hints of its importance in the lives of individuals are not impossible to find. In Carolinian Edward Brailsford's devotional world, the Eucharist was a powerful sign of religious conversion. He called the reader to "give up yourself to God" and then for the "more awful Solemnity of your good Resolution, you would do well to repeat it at the Sacrament."[44] So too a concerned mother in early Carolina "often desired" her adult son to "consider what vows and promises was made for you in your baptisem which it is now high time for you to think of renewing at the lord's table as your sister has don." Becoming a communicant "will still more strictly oblege you to live in the neglect of no known duty, nor commission of any evel," sealing his membership in the community of responsible Christian adults.[45]

The Eucharist thus could bring on feelings of enormous responsibility, indeed of both hope and dread, as it did for William Hutson, a Congregational minister in the low country. He welcomed February 5, 1758, as a "high Day being invited not only to the *House* but also to the *Table* of the Lord." Sometimes the arrival of "Our Sacramental Sabbath" found Hutson "in wt a poor Frame So low & dead & lifeless that I dread entering upon the solemn Work" of leading his congregation in the celebration of the sacrament. Yet even when "waking somewhat low," Hutson could be "edified by Bro. Edmonds's Sermon" and thus have "a very comfortable Season at the Table." He saw some correlation between his comfort and that of his congregation, for he sometimes "heard afterward that this was also a comfortable Sacrament unto many — the Lord's Name be praised."[46] Evan Pugh, a Carolina layman often seized by fear and doubt, recorded in his diary both that he "had Communion a good time" and that he "did not commune" on less auspicious communion days.[47] Dreadful, comfortable, even joyful, the Eucharist challenged early Carolinians to consider the state of their souls in the midst of a social world where interpersonal discord was always possible.

Baptists in early Carolina were particularly inclined to discipline their community through the Lord's Supper. When the Ashley River Church constituted itself separately from the mother church in Charles Town, they directed their minister to "preach Constantly and Administer ye holy ordinances pf Gods house . . . Baptism and ye Supper of ye Lord." Yet they also resolved to gather in Charles Town periodically, "to sit down" together "att ye Lords Table." When church members went astray, they faced being "Suspended . . . from ye Lord's Table," as Mary Shephards was in 1737 for "Railling & evil Speaking agt our Beloved Pastor." So too were slaves like "Madam Baker's Will" made excommunicate "in a Publick manner after Sermon the Ensuing Sabbath being the time of our administering the holy Supper of our Lord."[48] Others were questioned about their failure to be present at the table, as when the church agreed "to admonish Bro. Wm Main for his Neglecting his Place at the Lords Table one time after another" in 1746.[49] By requiring members to communicate, early Baptists created a rigorous Eucharistic discipline in which members could not linger in sin without facing the prospect of public expulsion from table fellowship.

Stress in parish communities was often made manifest in a breakdown of Eucharistic practice. St. Helena's vestry regretted "the animosities and Feuds which has so long subsisted in this Parish, and which are now Swelled to such a Degree as to keep the People from the Church and Communion." This situation was due to an unchaste clergyman, for many had complained "that they cannot Receive the Sacramt. from a man whose Life and Conversation prove him to have little or no Regard for Religion."[50] Thomas Harris, rector of St. Lucy's parish in Barbados, had similar problems. His parishioners were "greatly concerned, if ever the Solemn Offices of Religion shou'd again be performed" by such a character. James White, an eccentric and authoritarian Jamaican minister who spent too much time abusing Roman Catholic doctrine from the pulpit, found that communicants in his parish quickly declined.[51] When conflict arose with their clergy, parishioners signaled their dissent by withdrawing from the Eucharistic community over which the minister presided. Those temporary withdrawals mirrored many parishioners' efforts to exclude persons of color from Eucharistic fellowship.

The social and pastoral meanings of the Eucharist in Carolina can most clearly be seen in the letters of Francis Le Jau, minister of St. James's Goose Creek in the early eighteenth century. Urged by the SPG to increase the frequency of communion, Le Jau was nervous about instituting a monthly Eucharist. "I am sensible that for this present, it were not convenient to require more," he wrote, and he begged not to be ordered otherwise. Lay leaders in his parish apparently had some influence over the frequency of celebrating the sacrament. In a letter of 1709 to the SPG, Le Jau noted that he had "advised with some pious and Worthy persons of this parish and we design to receive the Blessed Sacrament of the Lords Supper in our Church every two Months" and "to improve in time with the Grace of God." Later, he expressed his desire to "bring our holy exercise of receiving the Sacrament to every Sunday rather than every month," though he feared that "we are so scatter'd and meet with so many difficulties that for the present I don't see how I cou'd succeed to urge it further than every two months."[52] Indeed, Le Jau indicated he had already faced some resistance to more frequent celebrations. His parishioners expressed their reluctance to follow the rubric in the communion service that suggested the reception of "Alms for the Poor, and other devotions of the people." Le Jau's people thus permitted more frequent celebration as long as it did not dip into their pockets.

They did dip into their pockets, however, for the construction of the parish church building during Le Jau's tenure of 1706–17. The church has been inactive since the early nineteenth century and remains in remarkable and close to original condition. Its decoration, both interior and exterior, spoke to the importance of

Exterior of St. James's Church, Goose Creek, South Carolina. Courtesy of Suzanne Linder Hurley.

the Eucharist in Le Jau's vision for the Goose Creek community. Early worshippers would have first encountered the entablature over the west door, which featured a pelican piercing her breast with her bill. This image reflects a popular early modern misconception that pelicans fed their young with their own blood. As a result, pelican images had been used since the Middle Ages to symbolize both the Atonement and the mediation of Christ's death to the church through the bread and wine of the Eucharist.[53]

Inside, parishioners were confronted with an imposing altarpiece, inscribed with several Eucharistic texts. Over the central window can be read the first line from the hymn *Gloria in excelsis*, required for use by the 1662 Book of Common Prayer as a hymn of thanksgiving after communion.[54] Below the window are some of the "comfortable words" from Matthew 11, again always read in the Eucharistic liturgy: "Come unto me all ye who labour and are heavy laden, for I am meek and lowly in heart and ye shall find rest unto your souls."[55] On either side of these two texts, worshippers would have seen another pair of Eucharistic texts from the Bible. The first was Acts 8:32, "He was led as a sheep to the slaughter and, like a lamb dumb before his shearer, so opened he not his mouth," a text pregnant with the sacrificial imagery of atonement and Eucharist.[56] On the other side was John 1:29, "Behold the

Meanings of the Eucharist **97**

Reredos of St. James's Church, Goose Creek, South Carolina. Courtesy of Suzanne Linder Hurley.

Lamb of God who takes away the sins of the world," a text used in some prayers of the Eucharist and the basis for the *Agnus Dei*.[57] Painted in bold shades of red and blue and surmounted by the royal arms, the altarpiece made a powerful statement about the importance of the rite that it framed.

St. James's was thus a thoroughly Eucharistic space, perhaps because of the careful attention of Francis Le Jau during the building process. As he negotiated with his parishioners for more-frequent celebrations, he may also have been guiding the craftsmen at work in the church, building an emphasis on the Eucharist into the walls of the church. And just as liturgical theology was used to structure power through the use of oaths and exclusionary acts in South Carolina, Le Jau carefully controlled Africans' access to the Eucharist to further his own social and pastoral goals. He charged baptized slaves with the careful keeping of the Sabbath and monogamous marital relationships, the penalty for failing to do so being excommunication. "They must promise they'l spend no more the Lord's day in idleness, and if they do I'l cut them off from the Comunion," he assured his metropolitan superiors. When some whites resorted to dissenting ministers for their weddings, Le Jau resolved that he would "not give them the Holy Comunion."[58] Admission to communion, the rite so emphasized in the design of the church, was a precious commodity in the economy of grace that Le Jau constructed for lowcountry slaves and whites.

Goose Creek Africans responded by using Le Jau's system for their own purposes. Le Jau encountered some slaves who had practiced Catholicism among the Portuguese, probably in Kongo-Angola. In several letters to London, he commented on the "two poor Negroe Slaves born & brought up among the Portuguese that are very desirous to Abjure the popish heresy's and be Recd to the Communion among us."[59] Even slaves without a Catholic background may have regarded Anglicanism as another potentially useful spiritual tool, its Eucharist as a rite of some spiritual value to be integrated into their established spiritual systems.[60] Others may have sought baptism and communion as a means of ingratiating themselves with powerful whites or of symbolizing spiritual equality with the dominant caste.[61] Though relatively few ever sought admission to communion, it is clear that some slaves quickly understood the ideological power of the Eucharist and sought admission for their own purposes.

All St. James's communicants kneeling to receive the Eucharist would have been at eye level with the inscription just above the altar: "Come unto me all ye who labour and are heavy laden . . . and ye shall find rest unto your souls," another of the comfortable words from the communion liturgy. This text may well have appealed to Afro-Carolinian slaves far more than it did to a white gentry that disdained labor.[62] Evidence suggests that succeeding generations of African American slaves in Goose Creek were drawn to the sacrament in numbers far beyond those of whites. In 1768, one of Le Jau's successors reported twice as many regular black communicants as he did white communicants.[63] Though their reasons are lost to us, it seems likely that those who communed sought both spiritual comfort and the social and political leverage that liturgical culture could provide. The few slaves who read Le Jau and his building may have correctly recognized both an agent and a forum for ameliorating their servitude.

Some white laypersons certainly saw admission to the Eucharist and liturgical culture as problematic forums for African self-assertion. Le Jau had parishioners who resolved "never to come to the Holy Table while slaves are Recd there" and who wondered if they might see their slaves in heaven. The indignation with which Le Jau reported these comments to the SPG was indicative of how differently he understood the Eucharist, as a rite that fully incorporated former dissidents and foreign elements into the social-spiritual body of the parish community of Goose Creek. Just as he proudly related his efforts to incorporate African and European Catholics into the parish communion, Le Jau took great pleasure in reporting that a Quaker woman he had earlier baptized "will soon receive the Blessed Sacrament with us." Le Jau insisted that baptism made slaves dutiful and that the Eucharist made them even better, pointing to "those who are Admitted to our holy Communion . . . [who] behave themselves very well." He was glad that "the most sensible of our Slaves whom I have admitted to the holy Sacrament have solemnly protested to me that if ever they hear of any Ill design of the Slaves I shall know it from them." When Le Jau and his parishioners returned to Goose Creek after the Yemassee War, to their "Great Comfort" they "Received the Holy Communion Twenty of us together the 2d Sunday of the Month."[64] Le Jau saw the disrupted community being gathered again around the Eucharistic table.

The Material Culture of the Eucharist

All who drew near to receive communion in Goose Creek would also have seen the sterling silver Eucharistic vessels given by Ralph Izard in his will of 1706. Now lost, this chalice, paten, and flagon were probably imported from England and engraved with Izard's name.[65] Eucharistic silver was an important investment for colonial parishes. While some vestries decided to purchase silver, many benefited from the munificence of elite donors who presented sets and individual pieces of silver to their parishes. Surviving examples demonstrate a close relationship between the articles of the gentry dining table and those used for the sacred meal.[66] The use of precious materials and a decorative idiom derived from the ruling caste in these liturgical rites marks an effort to identify the plantation colonies' social order with a Christian ideal and to preserve a metropolitan culture of the Eucharist that colonists did not want to abandon. In ornate settings for the Eucharist, colonists also created forums for the ritual celebration of their power over the Afro-American majorities of the plantation world.[67]

While donors drew attention to their own generosity in the process of creating Eucharistic settings, some parishes simply purchased the necessary implements for Eucharistic celebration. The governor of Barbados "mentioned" to the vestry of St. Michael's in 1679 his desire "yt ye Communion Tables be adorned with Plate and Linen, vizt. — 2 Flaggons." They seem to have complied, either purchasing or noting an inventory of "one Table Cloth, one Towell, and Two Napkins of fine linen, Two Silver Flagons, one silver cup, and silver plate," worth £103.[68] Even after silversmiths could be found in Charleston, a parish like Prince Frederick paid a princely £40 for an imported silver cup in 1745.[69] After St. Stephen's parish in Carolina was divided from St. James's Santee, its vestry spent £97 on alms basins, a chalice, and engraving in 1759.⁷⁰ Where such items could not be purchased, colonial Anglicans asked for help from home, as when Governor George Phenney begged the bishop of London from New Providence in the Bahamas in 1723, asking his "Lordship's Assistance in obtaining for us such necessary Ornaments as the decent Worship of God requires."⁷¹

Though Anglicans were particularly interested in furnishing their churches with tasteful silver, they were joined by other Christians who similarly desired to enrich their Eucharistic worship. The leaders of the Independent Church in Charles Town authorized "the Deacons of the Church, to purchase Silver Plate, for the Administration of the blessed Sacrament of the Lord's Supper when Celebrated in this Church."⁷² At a farther end of the theological continuum was the Ashley River Baptist Church in South Carolina, which shared with other Baptists in the early South a robust Eucharistic tradition. They owned a silver tankard and cups, pewter plates, a large bottle, a damask table cloth, and a covered basket for their celebrations.⁷³ The Baptists' intentionally modest mixture of precious and ordinary materials may mark an important difference between their practice of the Lord's Supper and that of the Anglican elite. Across their traditions, Christians in the plantation colonies created a material culture of the Eucharist that has been too often neglected by historians searching for less liturgical manifestations of meaningful Christian practice in the plantation colonies.

The power of this material culture of the Eucharist attracted donors, who furnished Eucharistic silver to colonial churches for reasons both sacred and profane. When Elizabeth Paynter died in Barbados in 1676, she left "two small silver cups gilt . . . for the use of ye parish," a typically pious final act. One might be more suspect of the motives of the lieutenant governor of the island, who gave two silver flagons and large chalice and cover in the late seventeenth century.⁷⁴ A donor presented to St. John's Berkeley County in Carolina "a Silver Cup Gilt" that she claimed was "brought to this Country by the Reverend Mr. Lejou" and had been "used by the Protestants in France before the Persecution."⁷⁵ When the new parish of St. Michael's there was being furnished in the early 1760s, the governor gave two flagons, a chalice and cover, and a large plate engraved in all-caps: "THE GIFT OF HIS EXCELLENCY THOMAS BOONE Esqr. GOVERNOUR OF THIS PROVINCE TO THE CHURCH OF ST. MICHAEL CHARLES TOWN So. CAROLINA 1762."⁷⁶ In 1734, the vestry of St. Helena's in South Carolina thanked Captain John Bull "for his generous donation of 100£ currency" for "the Purchasing of a Piece of Plate for the Use of the Communion Table." They directed the minister to order one from England and that "ye following words be Engraven

Meanings of the Eucharist

upon it, viz: The Gift of Capt John Bull to the Parish of St. Helena."[77] During his term as warden of Charles Town's Lutheran church, a Mr. Timrod "donated to the church a tabernacle [*Hostienschachtel*] made out of silver," for holding communion bread.[78] Receiving the thanks of the parish leadership and seeing their gifts used at holy times were powerful moments in the lives of donors.

These investments in silver had to be cared for, in regular cleaning, occasional repair, and vigilance against theft or loss. In 1742, Kingston paid 17s..6d to repair its church plate, and its minutes are filled with regular payments for cleaning its silver. They likely decided that the silver might tarnish and be dented less often in a better container and paid £4 to John Newson "for Ling & paritiong ye Chest for ye Plate."[79] Departing ministers or churchwardens deposited the articles in their keeping, as in March 1718, when the clerk of Christ Church parish in Carolina noted that he had "received then of the Reverend Mr. Gilbert Jones one silver Chalice and Table Cloth & one napkin all belonging to the communion table of the parish and one large Common Prayer book."[80] At St. Andrew's in Jamaica, "the Honorable Charles Hall Esquire Church Warden produced the Church Plate by him received from the Reverend John Pool late Rector of this Parish on his going off the Island, Consisting a Silver Chalice, Flagon and Waiter, Gilt with Gold, And two plain Silver Waiters — And the Same was delivered to the Reverend John Campbell the present Rector" in 1782.[81] Successive wardens in Charles Town received and turned over the church plate "with a Schedule of the Particulars thereof."[82] The pattern was established as early as 1664 in Barbados, when it was ordered "yt ye old Churchwardens do forthwith deliver ye new Churchwardens ye Parish books and plate, linen and pewter."[83] In 1728, after years of such transfers and monthly use, St. Michael's plate was "very old and battered" and was thus sent to England "to be new fashioned."[84] Such care speaks to the importance of objects that manifested realities both transcendent and mundane in the parishes of the plantation world.

When in use, this silver rested on a variety of imported fabrics used to cover the communion table. Fine church linen could transform simple wooden communion tables into sumptuous altars for the celebration of the Eucharist. Donors were quick to offer these to their parishes as well. At the opening of St. Michael's parish in Charles Town, Edward Fenwick came forward with "Rich Crimson Velvett Covering & Cushions trimmd wth. Gold fringe for use of the Communion Table, Pulpett, and Reading Desk." The vestry expressed to him their thankfulness that "the Places they are Intended for . . . will thereby appear with a Decency becoming the Solemn Purposes they are appointed for."[85] Francis Stuart presented St. Helena's parish with "a handsome large Damask Table Cloth, and two Napkins in one for the use of the Communion Table."[86] Francis LeBrasseur bequeathed "a large Damask Table Cloth, Four Yards in Length and Yards in Wedth . . . for the use of the Communion Table" in St. Philip's Charles Town.[87] Donors could thus draw near to the table through their gifts, even if they did not receive the elements at every celebration. At the same time, ostentatious giving of liturgical accoutrements served as evidence of the donor's gentility and social prominence.

Parishes bought other necessary linens, especially for making surplices, the vestment worn by seventeenth- and eighteenth-century Anglican clergy and some others for the Eucharist. Charles Town's Lutherans demonstrated typical thrift when they directed that an "altar-cloth shall be made from the former white surplice" in 1768.[88] In addition to three new large Books of Common Prayer and an edition of the Church of England's homilies, St. Michael's in Barbados also purchased "two new surplices, and linen for the Communion table" in 1720.[89] Kingston in Jamaica paid 5 shillings to one "Pickering for making Church Linnen" and 2s. 10d. for "6 months washing ditto."[90] It seems likely that some of the men paid for washing linen throughout the vestry minutes of the plantation colonies had recourse to the services of women, some of them enslaved, such as Phibia, who St. Michael's in Charles Town paid for "washing 14 Surpluses."[91] Made of fine Holland linen, church linen was valuable enough that persons unknown did "sacriligiously steal two Surplices" from the vestry room at St. Catherine's in Jamaica, for which the parish offered a dubloon reward.[92] Dull as church laundry may seem, it demonstrates the vitality of the liturgical culture of the plantation colonies.

Eucharistic silver and linens took their places in the chancels of the parish churches of the plantation colonies, areas of the church mostly reserved for the clergy and to which the congregation's visual attention was directed by considerable decorative enhancement. As seen in Le Jau's Goose Creek Church, the altarpiece, consisting of the sculptural, architectural, and textual elements that framed the communion table, was an important location for donors to display their generosity and for parishes to demonstrate their good taste and their cultural and political connections to the metropole. In communion tables and chancel rails, colonial parishes created a symbolically rich environment for the celebration of the Lord's Supper, one that could be viewed even on the many Sundays when the sacrament was not celebrated, thus bringing the rite to mind even in its absence. Elaborate chancels framed the other material elements of Eucharistic celebration, creating a ritual environment that was mostly inhabited by the white elite.[93]

In Jamaica, St. Catherine's communion table was framed by statues of Moses and Aaron that caused consternation for some worshippers. In this elegant church, "the

Statues of Moses, and Aaron on each Side of the altar gave great offense, for Several weak but well meaning people would not approach the altar, for fear of bowing to these images." A writer was glad that "the last Hurricane August 28 1722 flung ym down, & broke yr noses and arms; so they were remov'd into the Vestry room, where it is wisht they may continue. For they were so gaudy, that the occasion'd a great... dissipation of thought in the time of Divine worship, and great animosities among the people."[94] St. Michael's in Barbados authorized its minister to acquire "a new Altar piece and other ornaments for the new Chancel" in 1720.[95] As part of that effort, he ordered communion rails all the way from England. Clergy bemoaned the lack of chancel decorations, as the rector of St. Joseph's in Barbados did when he noted the parish's lack of an altarpiece in the 1720s. They celebrated fine work as well. The rector of St. Philip's in Barbados gave thanks that his chancel was equipped "very well. We have a fine Altar Piece, rich Ornaments, a good sett of double gilt Plate, & good Books." Yet the concern to embellish the chancel was not limited to the clergy. In 1691, John Wright of Port Royal parish gave fifteen pounds "towards procuring Fair Tables of the Ten Commandments in a large and plain Inscription to be set up in the said Church."[96] St. Andrew's in Jamaica accepted the gift of "a Green Curtain & Rod to the Window over the Communion Table" from Wickes Skurray, their clerk for over twenty years.[97] Both clergy and laypersons took an interest in beautifying the Eucharistic space within their parish churches.

Kingston Parish in Jamaica left particularly detailed records of lay efforts to beautify its chancel. In the 1720s, the parish already had "a fine altar piece, with ornaments & Several pieces of plate."[98] But in the mid-eighteenth century, the parish leadership decided to go further in embellishing the chancel. They directed that "the Elevation of the Chancell Ground be 2 Steps or 14 Inches" and "that the ground within the Rails of the Altar be Elevated 3 Steps or 24 Inches." They also returned thanks to Mr. William Lamb for his "offer of presenting an Altar piece for the parish Church." This was to be a fine addition to the chancel. At a subsequent meeting "a grand plan of the Corinthian order" was "laid before the Justices and Vestry by Mr. George Sparks the undertaker amountg to Seven hundred and fifty pounds." They later ordered that the "floor [of] the Altarpeice of the Church" be finished "with Machioneil and Ebony" for £120. They provided a "Ballustrade with two Bannister doors to inclose the Chancell ground of the Church," at a cost of 20 pistoles. After "two pieces of Mahogany Wainscoting one on each side of the Altar" were added, the finishing touch was the decision to "gild the friese of the Altar piece"[99] Enriched with imported varieties of wood and sharing in the classical tastes of Georgian England, the Kingston altarpiece spoke of metropolitan connections and social privilege to those who gathered before it week by week.

A decade later in Charles Town, an altarpiece was being added to the newly constructed St. Michael's parish. There the churchwardens found at least one use for the Francophone refugees that so troubled them by reimbursing Isaac Mayzck £5 for the "Cash paid Two Accadians for Sawing the Marble Slabs for the use of the Altar." These slabs likely ended up as part of the chancel flooring, since they also paid £12 for "laying marble Stones by the Communion Table."[100] The vestry received a proposal from Anthony Forehand for carving the altarpiece in 1762. For a mere £562, he offered "to Doe the Carveing and Imbelishment of the alterpiece of St. Michael's Church," including its "Corinthian Capitals" and "Moddilions." He described how "the ovolo and bead that forms the Tabernacle frame" could be "Inriche'd with Carveing a Cherubim Inriched with fustoons to Stand upon the Pedestal over the Venitian Window."[101] Though this proposal was not accepted, several improvements to the chancel would be made for the next ten years, resulting in a chancel "with four Corinthian Pilasters . . . [t]he usual Tables of the Decalogue, Lord's Prayer, and Apostle's Creed."[102] Like Kingston parish church, Charles Town's new church could boast a rich setting in which the community, largely the white community, could gather for the Eucharist.

Though most free people of color in the plantation colonies were baptized, many were discouraged from communion for much of the eighteenth century. In the 1720s, James White of Jamaica insisted that "not one man or woman Negro baptized since . . . we have been Masters of the Island have ever come to the other Sacrament of Salvation whether bond or free." This was due to the fact that their masters will not come "to the Lord's Table with them." That exclusion continued their general social practice, since "None of the white Xians will admit them to reciprocation of benefits, & freedom of conversation after baptism; so they must company with the Heathens as much as ever," likely the planters' preference in any event.[103] Similarly in early South Carolina, many may have felt as one of Le Jau's parishioners did, resolving "never to come to the Holy Table while slaves are Recd there."[104]

At that holy table, white parishioners found themselves in positions that may well have made them uncomfortable. Though the setting might be ostentatious and the materials luxurious, the rubrics of the prayer book required participants to kneel as they received the elements from the standing minister. This posture of profound humility was not one that prideful planters were accustomed to assuming. As they knelt, the minister offered them a small piece of bread and then a sip of wine from a cup shared by all. Every action required of those communicating signaled penitence and self-abasement, even in a setting that spoke to the wealth and privilege of the planter and merchant class. In a slave society, self-abasement was the very characteristic that whites wanted to see in people of color and not in themselves. To perform in this manner in the company of even a small number of enslaved people or subjugated free people of color must have caused enormous anxiety for white Christians in the plantation colonies. As white uneasiness increased in the black majority colonies, kneeling to share a cup and a humble bit of bread with black Christians seemed a dangerous condescension indeed. For whites, the spiritual comfort of the sacred meal was undermined when the dangerous realities of life in a slave society impinged at the communion rail. It was better to celebrate alone, in the splendid isolation of their elegant churches.

Those readers who encountered an article in an April 1737 issue of the *South Carolina Gazette* were firmly warned away from sharing the Eucharist with people of color. The article explained that in the Antiguan slave conspiracy of 1736 "many of the Heads being capable of Writing and Reading . . . had been taught the Christian Religion conformable to the frequent Admonition of our worthy Diocesan the Bishop of *London*." Thus when it was time to swear "the Multitude in to their Scheme, they swore them and administered the Sacrament to all such as professed themselves Christians according to the Rites of the Bishop's Church, the others they swore according to their several Country Forms; which gives us a Specimen of what may be expected from Converting Negroes."[105] Though this account finds little support in the standard histories of the Antiguan plot of 1736, the story clearly reveals the uneasiness that many whites felt about sharing the sacrament with Africans and their descendents, an anxiety that circulated with news of slave rebellion among the jittery rulers of the plantation world.[106]

Yet white anxiety was matched by black initiative, the creolization and intermingling of the colonial populations, and the persistent demands of metropolitan public opinion. A combination of these factors gradually wore down white colonists' resistance to sharing table fellowship with people of color. Robert Olwell has shown the presence of substantial numbers of black communicants, even black majorities, in St. James's Goose Creek and St. George's parishes in South Carolina at midcentury. His numbers are drawn from reports to the SPG, which did not support parish ministers in Jamaica or Barbados, leaving historians without the insight those records might have provided into similar later developments in the island colonies. It is also to be regretted that succeeding bishops of London abandoned their efforts to supervise colonial clergy in the second half of the eighteenth century, leaving us further bereft of information about participation in the Eucharist. At just the time that evangelicals' missions began to flourish in the British Caribbean and to challenge the established church, the only records of Eucharistic practice for Anglican churches in the colonies peter out.

Loathe as colonialists are to do so, working back from the nineteenth century may offer the best clues for understanding developments in Eucharistic practice in the later eighteenth century. In the nineteenth century, Anglican churches were no less controlled by planter vestries than they had been before, yet most churches were ready to invite some people of color to the table, under tightly controlled conditions and in a manner that sought to reify their secondary status. By 1815, the parish of St. Philip in Charleston owned a growing inventory of Eucharistic metalware that included "two small pewter plates for collecting donations of persons of color on Sacramental days."[107] Farther south, Prince William's parish church commissioned in 1838 a set of communion plate engraved with a reminder that it was intended "for The Colored People."[108] As seating was parceled out along racial lines, it was common for people of color to receive the sacrament together, after all the white communicants had returned to their seats. When a minister in Barbados ignored this custom in presiding at the sacrament, he found himself accused by white parishioners of attempting "to destroy the distinctions which they deem so necessary to their safety," especially by "his disgraceful conduct whilst administering the most holy Sacrament of the Lord's Supper."[109] While this chapter has shown that Anglican liturgical practice consisted of more than dry sermons on obedience, its Eucharistic practice was cozy with hierarchies of all kinds. Whatever increasing hospitality was shown at the table as the nineteenth century drew near, it was offered in the context of increasingly rigidly racialized societies whose norms the church had little success or interest in challenging.[110]

The usefulness of the Eucharist in the construction of these New World societies reveals the general liveliness of religious culture in the plantation colonies. Though home to few spiritually anguished diarists or powerful preachers, the frequent heroes of the historiography of religion in early America, the plantation colonies nonetheless cannot be properly understood without attending to the meaning of Christian ritual in those regions. Colonists there translated a set of English cultural elaborations on the Lord's Supper to the colonies, so as to exclude Roman Catholics and sometimes dissenters from political power. They embellished their parish churches with communion appointments and altarpieces that connected them to the metropole and that normalized a European gentry aesthetic in the most sacred part of the church building. Nearly smothering the rite with their own cultural meaning, whites made it deeply unattractive to most Africans and their descendents. Though many free persons of color and some slaves responded with their own appropriation of the ideological power of the Lord's Supper, whites were very content with the absence of most enslaved persons from the tables they set in these well-appointed ritual spaces. Far from being irrelevant, Christian ritual in the plantation colonies was as socially vital as elsewhere in early America.

Eventually, many people of color responded to these manipulations by leaving the established church's liturgical way for the relative egalitarianism of evangelicalism. Its spirit-filled worship, denounced as enthusiasm by sedate Anglicans, initially offered mutuality without hierarchy and Eucharistic fellowship without second-class status. In relation to other Europeans, some early colonists had success in fashioning political, social, and cultural boundaries around the Eucharist. Their long attempt to do so in relation to Afro-Americans did not go unnoticed and would eventually lead to powerful and separately constituted black churches. At the point in the nineteenth century that whites began to imagine that they understood their slaves (and indeed their mulatto relatives) and could welcome them to the table, many slaves and free people of color arrived at the conclusion that a table of their own was a better choice. While a colored elite persisted in Anglican churches around the plantation world, most people of color began to constitute Eucharistic communities of their own authority. Fusing Christian belief and Afro-American traditions, those black churches incarnated the prophetic promise that centuries of manipulation of the Eucharist and other Christian practices had erased in churches dominated by whites, exposing the hollowness of the spiritual comfort that whites had provided for themselves.[111]

CHAPTER 5

Mortuary Ritual in the British Plantation Colonies

REGULAR WORSHIP, MARRIAGE, BAPTISM, and the Lord's Supper all offered a sense of predictability in the religious life of the plantation colonies. At the same time death constantly disrupted colonists' best-laid plans. One of Jamaica's early historians insisted that "If Death is more busy in this Place than in many others, his Approach is no-where received with a greater Unconcernedness."[1] "Unconcernedness," however, hardly captures the vibrant cultures of death created by colonists in Barbados, Jamaica, and South Carolina. In those tropical and subtropical climates, persons of all ethnicities and social ranks experienced endemic and epidemic mortality at extremely high rates.[2] Besides the disease environment to which all were subject, enslaved Africans faced a brutal work regimen, poor nutrition, and the abuses inherent in slavery, meaning that slave population levels in the colonies could only be sustained by importation until late in the colonial period. Struggling to deal with the death all around them, residents of the plantation colonies maintained the mortuary practices of their cultures of origin and appropriated and rejected practices from other groups. Leveraging and transforming the ritual ways of death from their cultures of origin, residents sought to make meaning of their lives and deaths in the midst of a demographic disaster.

Though widely commented on by contemporaries, the task of quantifying and depicting the scale of that disaster fell to historians in the 1960s and 1970s especially keen to understand the numbers of Africans drawn into the slave trade and to apply demographic analysis to the slave societies of the early South and British Caribbean. Evidence suggests that one-third of Africans arriving in the West Indies died within their first three years in the Caribbean. A simple comparison of Philip Curtin's figures for total importation of Africans to the English islands before 1790 with population estimates for 1790 shows that Barbados, Jamaica, and the Leeward Islands received approximately 1,230,000 slaves but only showed a total enslaved population of about 387,000 persons. Even as the SPG added 450 new slaves to its Codrington plantation in Barbados between 1712 and 1761, the slave population there fell by one-third, as six slaves died for every birth. While conditions may have been more favorable for Africans in the earliest years of colonization, after the 1640s it is likely that sugar culture decreased life expectancy for Africans in Barbados. Mortality patterns for slaves in Jamaica were similarly grim; at no point under the slave regime did the slaves of the well-documented Worthy Park plantation experience natural increase.[3]

The North American colonies were the great demographic exception in the slave regimes of the Americas, for there an initially relatively small number of Africans experienced sustained population growth from natural increase. This was the case in South Carolina from the foundation of the colony in 1670 until the 1720s, when natural increase ended, largely due to the beginning of rice culture and a related influx of male Africans lacking the immunities necessary for survival in Carolina. Natural increase was again possible by the 1760s, but even then, the low country could not match the rate of increase that the slave community experienced in the Chesapeake.[4] Thus, for much of the eighteenth century, the demographic experience of Africans and their descendants in South Carolina was closer to the Caribbean than to Virginia.[5]

Though Europeans were largely responsible for the horrors of life and death in the plantation regions, few escaped from these fertile disease environments unscathed. The register of South Carolina's Christ Church parish (encompassing modern-day Mount Pleasant) shows that of persons both baptized and buried in the parish, 86 out of every 100 died before their 20th birthday. St. Philip's parish in Charles Town recorded 2883 burials and 863 baptisms in the 30 years between 1720 and 1750. Burials thus ran ahead of baptisms by 3.34 to 1, making Carolina's port city nearly as funereal as the 4 to 1 ratio reported for St. Michael's parish in Bridgetown between 1648 and 1694. The similarity between white mortality in Charles Town and Bridgetown is underscored when one considers that Boston, Massachusetts's burial to birth ratio was 1.47 to 1 in the 1704–33 period. The combination of emigration due to land consolidation and a lack of natural increase led the white population of Barbados downward from 22,000 in 1660 to 16,000 in 1713. The 12,000 whites who called Jamaica home in 1680 were reduced to 7000 by 1713. Indeed, Jamaica's white population decreased every year between 1673 and 1730, then rising only 1.2 percent each year between 1730 and 1774.[6] While skewed sex ratios, emigration, and the deaths of transients account for some portion of this population loss and the mortality figures, it remains clear that for both Africans and Europeans, the plantation regions were spectacularly deadly places.

Such high rates of mortality necessarily shaped the rituals of death practiced by inhabitants of the plantation regions. Often more frequently used than they had been in Africa and Europe, mortuary practices were opportunities to re-create the rituals of death practiced in their cultures of origin, a chance to reconnect with the practices of their ancestors, be they in Senegambia or Shropshire. The particular types of care shown for the dead are among the most highly stable features of many cultures, providing "a sensuous arena in which the dead are mourned, social memories are created and (re)asserted, social bonds are renewed, forged, or broken, and individuals make claims for individual identities and group membership." Preserving those ways in the sometimes threatening environment of the British plantation colonies was fundamental to maintaining African and European identities and to any sense of human community in a dramatically new and often threatening situation.[7]

Yet continuity was not the only rule in commemoration. The ritual practices of colonists were also shaped by their interaction with the unfamiliar rites of the hegemonic or subaltern groups they confronted in the plantation regions. While other sorts of rituals could be unintelligible to the opposing group, the presence of a dead body allowed Africans and Europeans to recognize readily and then criticize each other's mortuary rituals. The preservation of African mortuary practices and the rejection of the practices of Europeans by Africans and their descendants both preserved elements of African religions in the Americas and made a powerful statement about African autonomy at a critical personal moment in the midst of the slave regime. For Europeans, criticizing African practices while maintaining Christian practices in the European mode was an essential means of articulating their desire for mastery in the midst of a seemingly overwhelming African majority. Yet much was shared in the African and European ways of death, and more would be shared as life together eroded simultaneously emerging racial lines. Thus in their care for the dead, residents of the colonial world were able to create "faithful replicas of social distinctions among the living" and simultaneously to tie "social memories of the past to the immediate future of the community in mourning."[8] By memorializing their own in their own manner, each distinct community of the plantation world could articulate a vision for the living.[9]

Obscuring Shared Practices

Remarks on the ritual practices of Africans at the time of death was standard fare for European and West Indian observers of black life in the Americas. It was a commonplace for Europeans that Africans had little or no religion, a stunted sense of the divine, and little regard for the notions of family to which Europeans claimed to subscribe. Hans Sloane insisted that Afro-Jamaicans had "no manner of Religion by what I would observe of them. 'Tis true they have several Ceremonies, as Dances, Playing, &c. but these for the most part are so far from being Acts of Adoration of a God, that they are for the most part mixt with a great deal of Bawdry and Lewdness."[10] And yet Europeans, including Sloane, often took note of the distinct mortuary practices of Africans, their expressions of grief, and their abiding commitment to mourning their dead by using these rites. Often meaning to record the curious nonreligious behavior of a people they viewed as barbarous, European observers instead made a record of the tenacity of African religions and their mortuary practices.[11]

Europeans almost universally noted that the burial of Africans in the plantation regions involved more sound than usually accompanied European obsequies. A seventeenth-century resident of Barbados heard mourning Africans "clapping and wringing their hands, and making a doleful sound with their voices."[12] In late seventeenth-century Jamaica, deaths of Africans meant that "their Country people make great lamentations, mournings, and howlings about them expiring." In the middle of the eighteenth century, John Taylor reported that on the way to the grave, Jamaican slaves were known to "sing and Howl in a sorrowfull manner in their own Language," and after the burial they continued "singing in their own Languages very dolefully." Some Jamaican slaves attended the grave with rattles and drums. Little had changed in Jamaica later in the eighteenth century, when clergy still reported that singing was a distinctive feature of Africans' mortuary practice. Edward Long reported that the mourners would join in a "general clamour or song," using musical instruments that made for a "merry dirge." Long reported with some specificity on the meaning of some of their lyrics. At the second funeral practiced by some Africans, mourners sang "a song, purporting, that the deceased is now in the enjoyment of complete felicity; and that they are assembled to rejoice at her state of bliss, and perform the last offices of duty and friendship." After a festive meal at the grave, the ritual concluded with further "vociferation."[13]

Europeans in the islands also took note of the power of African mortuary rituals for the regulation of community life, especially by bearing the corpse through the local community in a postmortem attempt to seek redress of grievances. The bearers would "pretend that the corpse will not proceed to the grave, notwithstanding the exertion of their utmost strength to urge it forwards." Moving through the slave quarters, they would stop at a house "the owner of which, they know, has done some injury to, or even been much disliked by, the deceased in his life-time." After a suitable amount of time at that residence, enough to make the point, the bearers would move on "to the place of repose."[14] Charles Leslie took note of the same practice thirty years before, also in Jamaica. The mourners "sing all the way, and they who bear it on their Shoulders, make a Feint of stopping at every Door they pass, pretending, that if the deceased Person had received any Injury, the Corps moves towards that House, and that they can't avoid letting it fall to the Ground, when before the Door."[15] Europeans realized that Afro-Jamaicans had ritual resources that allowed them to mourn and reinforce communal norms simultaneously.

While Europeans often reported the strangeness of African mortuary behavior, they also unconsciously recorded the many practices that they shared with Africans at graveside. Europeans reported, for instance, that Africans incorporated food into their ritual practice.[16] Arriving at the grave, mourners would gently lay in the "Corps, and with it Casadar bread, Roasted Fowles, Sugar, Rum, Tobacco, & Pipes with fier to light his pipe withal." After this they would fill "up the Grave, and Eat and drink theron."[17] Like other mortuary practices, interment with food and a memorial meal likely depended upon the good will of the community. The deceased must be "one whose Circumstances could allow it, or . . . be generally beloved." If those conditions were met, a hog might be killed "and a kind of soup made, which is brought in a Calabash or Gourd," and placed at the head of the grave, a bottle of rum at the foot.[18] Feasting and food gifts might be part of the second funeral. A month after the death of his wife, Long reported, a man would return to the grave with a fowl that had been dressed at his house and "some messes of good broth." After heaping more earth on the grave, the second funeral concluded with feasting, drinking, and dancing.[19]

Though Europeans remarked on the importance of food in the African way of death as though it was peculiar, many of their own executors spent considerable sums on food and drink for the mourners as well. The executors of Nathaniel Hicks of Jamaica spent part of his £155 funeral expenses on Madeira wine and brandy.[20] One resident of Barbados recorded of whites that "their best feasts are always made at their funerals," for "there is more good Victuall, Wine & Ale devoured that day than all the whole parish eats and drinks in a whole month." Since "a funeral sermon makes them squeamish," someone always "carried to the Church 10 or 12 Gallons of burnt wine or a Pail full or 2 of Rum-Punch," so that "as soon as the Corps are interr'd they sit round the Liquor in the Church porch [and] drinke to the obsequies of the defunct . . . until they are as drunk as Tinkers." One critical island visitor reported that at a merchant's funeral in Bridgetown, "most part of the men were drunk."[21] St. Helena's parish in South Carolina paid £3..11..3 "for Rum Sugar &c at the Burial of Danl Rearden," himself an impoverished tinker.[22] Sometimes funeral drinking was a point of contact between Europeans and Africans, as when planter Thomas Thistlewood of Jamaica recorded that his "Negroes buried poor Chub. I gave them a bottle of rum." Thus Europeans' fondness for "eating and Drinking and Smoken Tobacco . . . at their funerals" was shared with Africans, who similarly nourished the bodies of the living at the burial of the bodies of the dead.[23]

Both groups found evening an auspicious time for burial. Some Africans and their descendents in the plantation colonies preferred to bury their dead at night, either on account of the exigencies of the plantation regime or West African precedent or a combination of both. In seventeenth-century Barbados, Ligon reported that slaves gathered in the evening to inter their dead. One Jamaican clergyman wrote home that Afro-Jamaicans conducted "drunken nocturnal Funerals" for their dead. He regretted that slaves engaged in "singing, dancing, and drinking at them, and all this in the open air, for many hours in the night in an unwholesome tropical climate."[24] Evening or nighttime burial was prevalent enough in mid-eighteenth-century Charles Town that the Assembly treated it in an act for the better government of the city. They decreed "that it shall not be lawful to bury any negro or other slave after sun-set in Charles-Town: And the owner, or in whose care such slave was (buried contrary to the direction of this act) at the time of his decease, shall forfeit *five pounds*."[25] Antiguan elites similarly legislated, likely ineffectually, that slave funerals were to be held during the day.[26] As darkness gathered and a day's work was completed, Africans in the plantation colonies found time and space to care for their dead.

But evening was a popular time for European funerals as well, due to fashion, tropical heat, and the fact that many ministers officiated at more than one funeral a day. The physician-naturalist Hans Sloane noted that since the air in Jamaica was "so hot and brisk as to corrupt and spoil Meat in four hours after 'tis killed, no wonder if a diseased Body must be soon buried. They usually bury twelve hours after death at all times of the day and night." When Alexander Parris died in 1736 in Charles Town, "his Corps was interred on Friday evening in a decent plain manner." The *South Carolina Gazette* recorded that John Baker, an eminent merchant, "was decently interr'd last night, and his Funeral attended by a great Number of Persons." The death of Gabriel Escott, fresh from Barbados, in Charles Town was followed by burial on a "Monday evening." When Scroop Lord Viscount Howe died in the governor's chair in Barbados, his "Corps was carry'd to St. Michael's Church . . . and about 8 o'clock at Night deposited in the Vault belonging to the Coddrington Family." Indeed, these nocturnal rites were frequent enough for St. Philip's in Charles Town to allow no more than three candles to be burned at evening burials in its church. Colonial practice followed an English model here; when Prince Frederick was buried in London in 1751, it was at a fashionable 9:00 at night.[27]

Similar mortuary practices translated from Europe and Africa were the basis for some hybridization in the culture of death, especially for the free persons of color and elite enslaved persons, some of them mulattoes, who were beholden to both ways of death. Francis Le Jau, an early minister at Goose Creek in Carolina, noted his practice of performing obsequies "readily . . . even to poor Baptized Negroes."[28] There are few instances of Christian burial of persons of color in Carolina parish registers, though "William Williams, a Negro," was buried in St. Philip's parish as early as 1723.[29] Since there was a fee for recording funerals and Carolina's Church Act specifically excluded enslaved persons from the record-keeping requirement, it is impossible to know how many were buried using Christian rites. Baptized free persons received Christian burial in St. Michael's parish in Barbados as early as October 13, 1704, when Mary Dally was buried, and baptized slaves were buried by 1717 in St. Philip's parish on the same island.[30] Christian free people like the Hector family of Bridgetown saw to it that members of their family received burial from the church, as when Hannah Hector died in 1743.[31] Certainly by the later eighteenth century, evidence suggests that the burial practices of Europeans and some Afro-Caribbean persons were converging in a limited way. Widespread miscegenation produced a group within the islands' populations of persons beholden to both ways of death. Free persons of color in Jamaica sought Christian burial in increased numbers as the century progressed, though burial records suggest that baptism was far more important to free persons than was the burial liturgy.[32] In 1781, the Kingston vestry found it necessary to require that "the Church Bell be tolled only at funerals, and that, no longer than five Minutes, unless of white persons."[33] While preserving a more impressive tolling for whites, the vestry conceded that solemn tolling would accompany the funerals of persons of color. Elite slaves may have shared free persons' preference for Christian rites; Thomas Thistlewood recorded in his diary that Mulatto Will's last request was "that no Negroes Should Sing &c" when he was buried next to his mother.[34] Long reported that the organist in Spanish Town could expect a good living, "his assistance being generally required at the funeral obsequies even of the free Negroes and Mulattoes buried in this parish."[35] By 1758, twenty-one of ninety-one burials in that parish were persons of color.[36] The curtness of parish records will never tell us if the families and friends of these persons preserved some recognizably African rites in private even as they embraced the public mortuary practices of the master class.

European Continuities, Status, and Race

While they shared more than they admitted with Afro-Americans, whites in the plantation regions did have their own ritual practices for dealing with the death that so often surrounded them. Europeans maintained many of the ways of death used by their ancestors in the British Isles and on the European Continent in ways that were essential to preserving cultural connections to the metropole, seeking to ensure that their colonial enterprise was perceived as a civilizing one, not as a slow descent into the barbarism that Europeans attributed to the aboriginal inhabitants of the Americas and to enslaved Africans. The mortuary practices of Europeans in the plantation regions ensured that the dead bodies of Europeans, even poor ones, were treated with a level of care that marked their superior status in the colonial world. In the midst of tremendous mortality, Europeans in the plantation colonies comforted themselves with rites that articulated values both transcendent and mundane.[37]

The territory of the plantation colonies was divided into parishes, in which qualified white freeholders elected vestrymen at annual elections. These vestrymen and the parish churchwardens took responsibility for raising the parish taxes, relieving the parish poor, constructing and maintaining the parish church, and employing the minister. They also directed, along with the minister, the parish's response to death. For parishioners with means, the vestry established fees for use of the parish liturgical apparatus, including the different grades of palls used to cover coffins. Vestries regulated the location of the burial of the dead, in church yards, in other burying grounds, and in church buildings themselves, again setting fees accordingly. It is from the tedious records of the vestries' deliberations that the mortuary practice of Europeans and the policies they established for others can be recovered.

Poor persons both black and white regularly died on the streets of cities and towns in the British plantation world, as well as in parish poor houses and jails. Parish authorities thus found themselves responsible for interring the remains of persons they did not know. They often buried Afro-Americans who died away from the surveillance of their owners and removed from the care that such decedents might have received from the African communities in their places of residence. In August 1759, the vestry of St. Catherine's parish, in Jamaica's capital city of Spanish Town, paid 10 shillings to bury "A Negro found dead this day at Mendes's House." They did the same in December of that year for another slave "found dead in the Street." This happened frequently enough that the vestry created a procedure for dealing with the death of anonymous black persons in Spanish Town. In October 1760, they ordered the Beadle, a minor parish officer, "to attend the Coroner upon the Inquests of all Bodies of Negroes that are found dead in the Streets of this Town, and the parts adjacent and after the Inquest is over the Beadle for the time being do instantly Cause the said Body to be buried, and that he be paid the Sum of 10 Shillings."[38] While sanitary concerns probably lay behind this order for "instant" burial, it is also true that a quick and efficient burial avoided the possibility of a disruptive gathering of Africans for their funeral rites.

Parishes provided the least possible amount of care for unbaptized dead Afro-Americans, usually no more than the burial that their rudimentary understanding of public health required. There is usually no indication that the minister of the parish officiated at the burial of these unknown Africans, since there was no one to pay his fees. Moreover, Anglican clergy would have been unwilling to use the service for burial in the Book of Common Prayer for unbaptized persons, as these anonymous slaves would have been assumed to be. It is not clear that vestries usually purchased coffins for deceased slaves, as they usually did for poor whites, who were often buried "on the parish." Charles Leslie said that when Afro-Jamaicans buried their own dead, they would use a "Coffin or whatever the Body happens to be wrapt up in," and it is likely that most vestries treated the bodies of Africans and their descendents with a studied indifference.[39] The names of slaves found dead were not recorded, if known, and we can assume that often no more than a shroud covered them in the earth.

Even anonymous poor whites were treated with a level of care that spoke to their emerging racial privilege in the plantation world. In the 1670s, the

"Corroner" of St. Michael's in Bridgetown was to be paid "no more than three hundred pounds [of sugar] for every poor and unknown person that shall be found dead within the precincts of the parish that hath not wherewith to defray the charges." They set their price for coffins for "parish paupers" at 20 shillings in 1717. In 1684, the clerk of St. John's on that island was paid 2 shillings for each grave he dug "for poor people (yt are not able to pay of themselves)." In the 1760s, St. Catherine's parish in Jamaica paid £1..10 for each adult coffin and 15 shillings for each child's coffin for whites and recorded the names of the whites buried in them: Sarah McIntosh and Thomas Francis, for instance. St. Andrew's parish in Jamaica included the burial of dead white people in its enumeration of the sexton's duties when it "ordered that Mr. Wickes Skurray be Sexton of this Parish for the Year 1783 . . . And that he be paid Ten Shillings for burying any White Person who shall be found dead and Shall have had an Inquest taken on the Body." In Kingston, the parish kept a carpenter named Mark Brown on retainer to make "the parish coffins," for the use of poor whites, at 20 shillings each. Port Royal parish similarly set a limit of 20 shillings on the purchase of "parish coffins." In the 1780s, the Kingston vestry inquired into the burial of soldiers, usually classified with paupers in parish records, without attendance by the minister, an omission that clearly violated established practice. Prisoners received similar treatment as when St. Catherine's paid £1..10 "for making a Coffin for a White Man named Humphrey Shuttlesworth died in Gaol." The minutes of Prince Frederick parish in South Carolina are full of approved expenses for the burial of poor whites. Indeed, an entry of April 29–May 1, 1726, for the burials of Roger Mclemorrow, John Fraser, and Eleana Barns in St. Philip's Charles Town's register is entirely typical in its note that "all 3 [were] at ye Charge of ye Parish."[40]

The reign of death in the plantation colonies obliged parishes to employ persons responsible for transporting the dead to their place of burial and for digging their graves. Kingston's vestry paid its "Under Bearers the Sum of Twenty five Pounds ten shillings for carying Fifty One Poor Persons to their Graves" in 1769. St. Catherine's vestry combined the offices of clerk and sexton, paying him 2s..6d for "Tolling the Bell" and 10 shillings for "Digging the Grave 5 Feet deep." Port Royal parish paid sexton Nathaniel Swivany for "Digging the Grave and Ringing the Bell to the Pallisadoes . . . the Sume of Seven Shillings and Six pence and to Green Bay and new Burying Place the Sum of fifteen Shillings." He owned five slaves in 1735, and it is likely that they did much of this work for him.[41] St. Michael's parish in Bridgetown retained one man as "sexton, bellringer, and grave digger." That parish also ensured that its bearers were decently attired for their duties, ordering new gowns for them when the old ones were "worn out" in 1734.[42] The bearers primarily carried the dead poor, especially if the vestry actually received the "hearse and horse" that it ordered the churchwardens to purchase in 1667. A similar arrangement in Charles Town may have moved its vestry to "provide a Bier to be Made to Cary the Corps, for the Benefit of the Poor of the Parish."[43]

Europeans thus also found ways to articulate social distinctions among themselves, as well as distinguishing themselves from Africans and their descendents. They preserved with great enthusiasm in the wealthier parishes of the Americas the use of palls, cloth coverings for coffins. Their use was not required by the rubrics or canons of the Church of England and was in some cases prevented by the fees that parishes required for their use. Palls served to obscure the likely roughness of some coffins, adding a finished look to even the most basic corpse container. They were partially the product of a widespread impulse to soften and decorate plain wooden surfaces with cotton, linen, and velvet. In other areas of the church, fabric coverings were used to draw attention to important liturgical locations and to cover liturgical furniture such as the pulpit, reader's desk, communion table, and the pews of prominent worshippers, such as colonial governors. Coffin palls articulated aspirations to gentility and to some elegance in the colonial way of death.

Some of the earliest surviving vestry minutes for St. Philip's Charles Town record that parish's acquisition in 1732 of "a large Velvet Paul . . . Which cost about One Hundred Pounds of this Currency." The vestry decided to collect a 40 shilling fee to recoup that expense and then to devote that income to poor relief. The new velvet pall likely was meant as an improvement over a "black Cloth Pall" found in a parish inventory from 1740. Though that new pall had been purchased in 1732, the parish was ready to order another new velvet pall by 1744, one that was in need of repair by 1746.[44] The churchwarden's accounts for 1745 record expenses for velvet, fringe, tassels, ribbon, and silk for the making of the new pall and repair of the old one. But money to repair and replace them was easily produced by the fees charged, which amounted to £78 in 1734.[45] Soon after St. Michael's Church in Charles Town opened for divine worship in 1761, its vestry resolved to purchase "a handsome Velvet Pall," demonstrating the importance Charlestonians attached to these objects.[46] Palls were not the exclusive preserve of the Anglican dead. The Independent Church in Charles Town resolved to buy a new pall for funerals in 1754.[47] Even in the midst of the

Revolution, Charleston's German Lutheran congregation resolved to purchase a new pall to match new coverings for the pulpit and altar.[48]

There is ample evidence of a complex use of palls in the principal parishes of Jamaica. The vestry of Kingston in Jamaica "Ordered That the Church Warden do forthwith cause to be made a Black Velvet Pall as also a White Sarsenet Pall for the use of this Parish and that the Old Black Pall be new flownsed" in 1748, considerably enlarging the pall options for that urban parish. In 1750, the vestry laid down its pall practice in the vestry book. They required that the minister "be obliged to take Care of the parish Palls and that he receive from each person that make use of them the following Fees in behalf of the parish." When the new velvet pall was used in the parish, the fee was £2, increased to £3 if the body was buried out of the parish. Nonresidents using the new pall were charged £4. They paid only £1..10 to use the old velvet pall, but when carried out of the parish the fee went up to £3. The white pall cost only £1 when used in the parish. Residents paid an additional 10 shillings to use it out of the parish, and nonresidents an additional £1. There were no variations on the announced fee for the black cloth pall; it was 12s..6d for anyone, anywhere, clearly the option for the most modest of obsequies. St. Catherine's in Spanish Town offered the choice of only the black pall at £1..3..9 or a white one at £ 1.[49] Mourners thus found themselves faced with a choice for their deceased friend or loved ones. How much to spend? What level of ostentation or humility was required for these particular funeral rites?

The much poorer parish of Port Royal in Jamaica charged considerably lower fees for its pall fifteen years before: "the Inhabitants to thereto belonging pay the Sume of ten Shillings for the Use thereof, and all Non Inhabitants to the Sume of One pound three Shillings and Nine pence."[50] It is likely that the generally neglected country parishes of Jamaica made do without palls, a question that their thin records will never answer. Barbados vestry minutes yield surprisingly little information on the use of palls on that island. Yet it seems likely that a people quite willing to import Eucharistic silver, organs, and baptismal fonts from London would have equipped their principal parishes with elegant palls from an early date as well. A pall had likely been in long use at St. Michael's Bridgetown when one was first noted in the vestry minutes of 1741.[51] Thirty years before an island correspondent reported that those with pretensions to gentility insisted on having "a Scuthcheons stuck upon ye pall."[52]

The importance of textiles in West African societies suggests that the use of palls might have been a point of contact between European and African mortuary traditions. In Antigua one observer reported late in the period that the burial of Afro-Antiguans, "particularly such as are of old Creole families, or in esteem among their fellows, are numerously attended. . . . The body is mostly inclosed in a wooden shell or coffin, which during the procession to the grave, is covered with a sheet, by way of a pall." In the 1750s, the Antiguan Assembly had taken note of this practice and created a statute to regulate the "pompous and expensive" funerals held by some slaves. Slaves' bodies were to be buried in nothing other than "a plain Deal-board Coffin, without any Covering or Ornament."[53] The law was reiterated in 1780 and thus seems to have been ineffective. In Antigua at least, the covering of coffins was a refinement of funerary culture that whites sought to reserve to themselves.

Palls became semiprecious possessions for Anglican parishes. It took vestry action for St. Philip's to lend their old pall to the parish of St. John's in Berkeley County in 1748 for the funeral of their minister Daniel Dwight. In 1785, St. Andrew's vestry in Jamaica required "A Good Lock and Key for the Great Chest where the Palls &c are kept." Kingston's vestry required their sexton to accompany any of the palls when taken out of the parish for another fee of 11 shillings.[54] Parishes in the plantation regions thus gradually elaborated their use of palls, adding new palls in finer fabrics while repairing older ones and keeping them clean for more modest rites. They thus presented options to mourners and to testators inclined to offer directions for their own funerals, options that allowed for the replication of social distinctions among the living in the very act of transporting dead bodies to the location of their burial. The locations of those burials were telling as well.

Burial Locations

White Christians in the plantation colonies buried their dead within a rough spatial hierarchy, one that excluded Africans and their descendants from intramural burial and then apportioned burial locations to others partially based on their place in the social system of the living. These practices were largely in keeping with the burial practices in English parishes, where proximity to the communion table or burial in privatized corners of church aisles was reserved to those elite dead persons able to pay the required fees and garner the respect of the parish officials who controlled those spaces. Though Protestants in the plantation colonies had considerable ambivalence about the relative sanctity of any part of the church in comparison to any other, they continued much of the burial practice of their medieval progenitors, practices that stretched back to the late antique Christian preference for *deposito ad sanctos*, burial near the relics of the saints. Augustine insisted that these privileged burials were of "no aid of salvation, but an office of humanity."[55] The Protestants of the plantation world agreed; their privileged interments were largely devoid of soteriological import but full of meaning for human relationships.

Intramural burial was widely practiced in the plantation regions and was often the desired burial location for persons of some standing. In Charles Town, the grave inscription of Robert Tradd proclaimed that this "first male child, born in this town," was "interred/Within the body of this church" when he died in 1731.[56] When Governor Robert Johnson was buried in 1735, it was "in a Vault near the Altar in Charles-Town Church."[57] With considerable pomp, former Lieutenant Governor William Bull "was interred in *Prince William's* Parish Church (which he was the principal Instrument in building, and is esteemed the most elegant and compleatest Country Church in *America*)."[58] The location of his current gravestone in the church's ruins suggests he was buried in the prominent location of the middle aisle, perhaps in front of the altar.[59] Yet even a humble minister such as Francis Le Jau could be interred in front of the altar, as he was in St. James's Goose Creek Church in 1717.[60] St. Helena's parish in Beaufort charged two naval officers £25 each in 1730 "for Breaking Ground in the Chancel" and instituted a fee of £50 for any future intramural interment.[61] When J. F. Bondfield wrote to Carolinian Nathaniel Boughton in 1751 of the latter's son's death in England, he clearly thought it comforting that he had "acted in ye best manner I was able he is Lay close by his Aunt Reaston in the Body of our Trinity Church."[62] Late in the period, the prominent Charleston minister Josiah Smith died in Philadelphia and his son gave thanks that the "Corps was deposited alongside of Two Reverend Divines, Doctor Samuel Finlay, the late President of New Jersey Colledge, and Mr. Gilbert Tennant the founder & Minister for many Years, of said Church, in the Ayle fronting the Pulpit," quite the place for an evangelical preacher.[63]

High fees restricted access to these privileged burial locations. In the middle of the eighteenth century, resident Kingstonians could be buried in the churchyard for only £1, while burial in the church would cost £15. St. Andrew's in Jamaica imposed steep fees that restricted access to the most prominent places of burial, which were likely becoming more scarce by the later eighteenth century. They ordered that "Fees for Burials be without Doors Ten Shillings; Within the Church, Ten pounds; Within the Rails of the Altar Twenty pounds."[64]

Intramural burial was so popular in Spanish Town that the fabric of the church could not sustain it by 1760. Their vestry noted "that the pavement and Pews of the Church are greatly damaged by the Interment of Bodies so as to require a large Sum to repair the same in a Proper manner" and therefore instituted a £20 fee for every such burial. Just four years later, in January 1764, the vestry banned all burials in the church. That ban was not to last, however. The very next month, some inhabitants of Spanish Town, clearly influential persons, convinced the vestry to reconsider the issue. At their meeting in March, the vestry repealed their order and again permitted burial in the church for a £20 fee.[65] Clearly the planters, lawyers, and colonial officials who called Spanish Town home were not ready to abandon their privileged burial places in the parish church.

Prime liturgical spots were popular burial sites in other Jamaica parishes as well, as was revealed when the keeper of St. Andrew's records suddenly began regularly recording the location of burials in the 1760s. The Reverend Gideon Castelfranc died in April 1768 and was "Interred with his family within the Rails of the Altar . . . under the North feet of the Comm[union] table." At least two of his infant children had been buried there some years before. Castelfranc was joined in 1776 by "The Honble Edward Foord Esq," a member of the Council who was also buried in the chancel. A decade later, Rear Admiral Alexander Innes joined them and a naval colleague when he was buried "in the Chancel by Admiral Holmes." Slightly less impressive was the burial of the Hon. Charles Seymour, chief judge of the Court of Common Pleas, "in the Middle Isle." A respectable but prosperous tradesman with no pretension to gentility could hope to rest "in the North Isle," as Jaffray Irving, a carpenter and smith did.[66]

The persons of color mentioned in St. Andrew's burial records were mostly free, some of them mulattoes. There is no record of any person of color being buried in the body of St. Andrew's Church. Instead, their bodies came to rest on private property, in the old churchyard, and, for a privileged few, in the churchyard itself at Halfway Tree. Typical of the domestic burials were Rachel Browne, a "free Negro Woman on Whitehall Plantation," who was buried "on ye Plantn," or "Eleanor Pierce," a "free Black Woman" buried "at Nathl Pierce's Penn," or "Nanny Thomas," an "Old Black Woman," interred "at Pinnocks Negro houses."[67] While Browne and Pierce may have been interred in the burying grounds of white families, Nanny Thomas was clearly laid in a burial ground controlled by the Afro-Jamaican community, where the vast majority of slaves were buried.[68] But some may have been buried in little more than the spot "in

The Church of St. Jago de la Vega, Spanish Town, Jamaica. From *The Gentleman's Magazine*, December 1783. Courtesy of the John Carter Brown Library at Brown University.

her Pasture" found for William Bond, a mulatto man belonging to Dorothy Mohun. Buried in the old churchyard were Elizabeth Strawbridge, a free mulatto woman, Ann Charles, a "free Sambo Woman," and William Wyllis, a "free Quadroon Man." Yet Europeans of modest station were buried in the old churchyard as well, including Michael Obrien, a "Bookkeeper on Mowerleys Estate." And certainly white persons of high status were also buried at home, such as Thomas Burnside, "Lieutenant Coll of the Militia," who was buried "in a Vault at his Penn." There is perhaps no entry more poignant than that for Rebecca Salt, a widow buried "under ye Cashew Tree by her Children."[69]

Thus the old churchyard at Halfway Tree provided a resting place for the dead of various racial backgrounds. Other parishes provided similarly nonsegregated burial spaces, suggesting that class may be as useful as race as a category for analyzing burial location in the West Indies. In 1762, the vestry of St. Catherine's parish ordered "that the Minister of the parish be desired to look out for a proper piece of Ground for a burial place for soldiers, poor people, Mullatoes, and Negroes of a free Condition." White elites were thus comfortable imagining the burial of poor whites and free persons of color in the same consecrated ground. In Bridgetown, the old church yard of St. Michael's became a place where slaves, "free Negroes," mulattoes, and poor whites "buried by the parish," were all interred.[70] These second-tier burying grounds defy any expectation of total racial separation that historians might bring to the subject, at least for nonelites.[71]

Limited space and deepening racism led to increasingly racialized control of burial ground by the middle of the eighteenth century in Jamaica. By 1766, the vestry in Kingston was running out of space and insisted "that the Ground in the Church Yard be not broake to bury any Corps whatsoever for the Term of One Year, excepting Allways such born of White parents, as have families lying there, or such who paid Taxes, being white Inhabitants for four years last past." In the previous decade, a similar order had been entered but without any mention of race.[72] At the same time, the parish took some responsibility for a separate "negro burying ground," at the Spring Path, seeking clarification of ownership of that property in 1752. They moved the gallows there in the same year, allowing slaves to be executed and interred in one location, making burial there quite different from the genteel precincts of the church yard.[73]

Intramural burial was popular in Barbados, the oldest of the colonies in this study. In two wills from the early 1660s, testators requested burial in the chapel-of-ease of Christ Church parish.[74] The practice was carefully regulated from an early date by the vestry of Barbados's principal parish as well. In 1665, St. Michael's vestry ordered that the graves dug in their new church "be full six foote" and the fee "for breaking graves under the new church [be] Three hundred pounds of Muscovado Sugr," the bereaved also being charged with the expense of removing and refitting the pews, charges that effectively limited burial there and any spiritual comfort associated with it to social and economic elites.[75] Local worthies were thus interred inside the church, sometimes in especially appropriate locations, such as when St. Michael's organist Edward Jordan was buried "under the center of the organ in Church" in 1722. William Sharp, instrumental in the building of the same church, was similarly honored with burial "under the Communion Table."[76] Some years later, he was joined by the parish's rector Benjamin Cryer, who was also buried "in ye Communion rails."[77] The Eucharistic leadership of the clergy was often underlined by burial inside the rails, at St. Michael's and elsewhere, as at least two more clergy later joined Cryer in that area.

Some white Barbadians took great care to create familial, semiprivate burial areas in the midst of public burial grounds, sometimes using other facets of liturgical culture as a means of preserving family memory. John Davis accomplished this by substantially enriching the liturgical apparatus of the parish. He was granted a twelve-by-eight-foot space in St. Michael's on the south side of the chancel in 1676 as "a burial place for him and his heirs and relations, the consideration thereof being a purple velvet pulpit cloth and cushion with gold fringe, already by him delivered."[78] In 1694, Captain William Davis complained to the vestry that the plot granted to him twenty years before was now "in the way where the coaches are driven, which the said thinks a prejudice to the said place appointed for the interment of his family." Davis successfully exchanged that spot, profaned by carriage wheels and entirely unsuitable to the status of his family, for a nicer one near the north gate to the church yard.[79]

Some Barbadians sought to construct family pews in close proximity to the intramural graves of their families, joining generations both living and dead when gathered for divine worship. In St. John's parish on the Atlantic coast, Henry Walrond and "his heirs and assignes forever," were granted the north aisle and vault "for Seates and [a] burying place."[80] William Heysham, John Bate, and Thomas Brewster were granted permission "to erect a pew at the West End of the Church for themselves and family near the place where some of their relations are interred" in St. Michael's Church in Bridgetown in 1697. The next year, Thomas Hollord, William Hardinge, Thomas Renholdson, and

Joseph Sheene similarly desired "to erect a pew at the south side of the Church by the great door for themselves and families near unto the place where some of their relations are enterred."[81] Something similar likely happened in Vere parish in Jamaica, where a gravestone proclaimed that "BENEATH THIS MARBLE- IN THIS PEW, LIETH INTERRED THE BODYS OF-THE HONORABLE JOHN MORANT."[82] While the Reformation is widely viewed as having limited the role of the dead in the spiritual world of Protestants, these Barbadian and Jamaican Anglicans sought to be near to their own dead during their Sunday rites.

Still the ultimate in private burial space, perhaps excessively so for some, was burial at home. Sloane reported that Jamaican "planters are very often buried in their Gardens, and have a small Monument erected over them, and yet I never heard of any of them who walk'd after their deaths for being buried out of Consecrated ground." Notes like one found in the register of St. John's in Barbados are typical: "Thomas Davis a Child of Thomas Adamson, interr'd in the family burying place, in Capt. Haynes Land."[83] Carolina clergymen received 9 shillings for burials in the churchyard, 15 for their extra trouble when burials were on plantations.[84] These domestic burials kept the dead close to home, but may have restricted opportunities for more public and socially powerful rites and permanent commemoration. Even if buried at home, the dead could be memorialized in the parish church through an imported memorial plaque, since "a much greater taste for marble monuments" was found in the plantation regions than farther north.[85] For governors and some other elites, burial at home might mean "home" in the colonial sense. The corpse of Jamaica's governor, the duke of Albemarle, was embalmed with pitch in 1688 for its burial in his native soil.[86]

While most vestrymen in the plantation colonies were quite comfortable in their rigidly hierarchical society, family plots and ostentatious grave markers could be a challenge to communal cohesion. Privatizing burial space in church aisles, fencing outdoor burial plots, and erecting tombs to their patriarchs were ways of articulating a family's understanding of its power and preeminence in the community, sometimes in a fashion that other families could resent. That resentment may underlie an order of St. Michael's Bridgetown that "those persons that have built any stone tombs in ye new churchyard do level them with the ground and that notice be given to them to yt end, and if they do not obey the sd. order . . . yt some people be hired to level at ye charge of ye parish." The governor took an interest in this matter as well, instructing the vestry "yt ye tombs in ye Churchyard be leveled" in the same month.[87] Though they remained silent on just what they were, the Lutherans of Charles Town said they had "important reasons [for] a decision [that] was made that no fencing of a grave shall be made without the approval of the Vestry and Wardens."[88] St. Philip's in Charles Town had similar regulations for burials in their churchyard as well. While practical exigencies might have prompted a desire for lower gravestones and no fences, avoiding an arms race in funerary moments probably made good sense to anxious white leaders, intent on preserving the appearance of a united front against their domestic enemies.

The ethnic and confessional diversity among the European residents of the plantation colonies meant that there was some diversity of mortuary practice among them. Carolina Huguenots were buried in their churchyard in Charles Town, using the simpler, even bare, rites of their Calvinist tradition, though they gradually surrendered to prayer book worship.[89] Indeed, the trend was toward convergence in a population that would slowly come to understand its whiteness overcoming different European origins by the end of the colonial period. The "High-German Protestants" who had initially worked to preserve their separation from the Church of England in Charles Town surrendered their own mortuary practices in the 1760s. "It has been customary to read a short resume of the deceased, as part of the funeral service," recorded their clerk, but "the Englishmen among our funeral guests have felt annoyed. They do not even read resumes at the funerals of noblemen." Thus they decided "to leave out the resume in the future, as well as all singing at the grave site."[90] Thus Carolina Lutherans abandoned the funeral singing that may have appeared to the English as something strangely akin to the singing of Afro-Carolinians, a decision that likely served the Germans well in their efforts to join the mainstream of the Carolina elite.

As elsewhere in early America, and perhaps more so, gloves and other favors were distributed to mourners at funerals in the plantation regions. A visiting New Englander "noted that mourning apparel at funerals is greatly in fashion" when he visited Carolina in 1773.[91] At the beginning of the century, a Charles Town minister complained of his own funerary exertions, noting that "all I gett by these is a few rotten Glov's."[92] Distributing gloves and scarves at funerals was common enough for newspaper accounts in Carolina to remark when "no Scarves were given at his funeral, nor . . . was any New Mourning bought." Nor were "Scarves, gloves, or Mourning used" at the funeral of Mr. Solomon Legare, whose relations "thereby conformed to the 8th Article of the Association entered into by the late Congress, in Behalf and on the part of the Colonies."[93]

We will never know how many sons and daughters of Ireland were buried in the manner of Nicholas Cashel, who died in Augusta, Georgia, in 1765, attended by mourners who "wore linen scarfs and cambrick hatbands, agreeable to the laudable custom in Ireland on such occasions."[94] Those mourning for Nathaniel Hicks of Jamaica received gold rings in addition to the standard gloves.[95] Gold rings were distributed when the governor of Barbados died in 1735, one of them being misplaced in Philadelphia by a wandering clergyman.[96] Slaves' appropriation of these practices made whites anxious, resulting in sumptuary laws aimed at funeral attire. The Carolina legislature forbade any "negro to wear a scarf" in its regulation of slave funerals.[97] Among other Antiguan legislative provisions for slave funerals was one that never "shall there be worn any Scarfs or Favours at any of their Funerals."[98] While such cultural transmission made whites nervous, they made little effort to control traditional African rites, which whites found useful in the construction of a rhetoric of slave inferiority.

Thus, Europeans in the plantation colonies did carefully consider their own obsequies and evaluated those of others, often with an eye to the degree to which those rites were in line with the social position of the decedent. The ultimate funerals within their frame of reference were those performed for English royalty, and plantation provincials were provided with both detailed information on royal funerals and with opportunities to mourn for royals.[99] When Queen Caroline died in 1737, the Carolina newspaper reported that "the Musick was extremely grand and solemn." They noted that "ten Bishops walk'd in their Robes in the Procession" and printed the lyrics of Handel's anthem for the event.[100] The death of Frederick, prince of Wales, in 1751, occasioned a full-page description of the funeral. The article explained the separate burial of the prince's bowels "in an urn cover'd with crimson velvet" and of his corpse "covered with a black velvet pall, adorned with 8 escutcheons, & under a canopy of black velvet." The article included a diagram of the funeral procession, listing the thirty different ranks of mourners, from the initial "Knight marshal's men, with black staves" to the final "grooms of the bed-chamber." The movements of the clergy and corpse were carefully described inside Henry VII's chapel inside Westminster Abbey, and the common people were congratulated for showing "the utmost decorum."[101] Colonial cities marked royal deaths with the firing of guns and other public displays of mourning, as in Jamaica in 1768, when news of the death of Princess Louisa Ann prompted the guns of Fort Charles to be fired, one for every year of her age, and the officers of the 36th Regiment to put themselves in mourning.[102] St. Michael's Bridgetown covered its pulpit, reading desk, and governor's pew with "black broad cloth" in 1727 for the death of George I.[103] As consumers of metropolitan funerary news, colonials maintained a connection to the ritual life of the metropole and sought opportunities to recreate that life in their distant locales.

For the funerals they planned, some elite colonists likely reproduced as much of the metropolitan ideal as their finances would allow. When the wealthy Mrs. Mazyck died in Charles Town in 1732, her funeral was conducted "in a very handsome Manner," and the death of Governor Robert Johnson's wife later that year occasioned a funeral "in the most handsome Manner that possibly" could have been.[104] Some in St. James's Goose Creek presumed to follow Barbadian and English gentry precedent and had "a Hatchment sett up in the Church," one of which can still be seen today.[105] At the same time, a funeral more modest than one's station could be considered tasteful, and overreaching rites for humble people could earn censure. A dying governor of Barbados had desired "that his Funeral should not be pompous or expensive . . . none were invited besides the Gentlemen of the Council and Assembly, with the Two Commanders of His Majesty's Ships in the Road," a small but opulent group.[106] Robert Pringle's will, proved in Charles Town in 1777, kept with convention by asking that his body "be interred in a Christian but not very Expensive Manner."[107] Some prominent persons were buried "in a plain decent manner," avoiding the Carolina newspaper's scathing comment that "the most pompous *Funeral-Procession* is but the *Burial of an Ass*." When a promising young man was buried at Peter Manigault's Goose Creek plantation, it was "without any funeral pomp, agreeable to his own request."[108] When young Manigault was in London, he wrote home to his mother about the death of a Quaker relation, somewhat surprised that "she was buried very privately, for nobody besides myself, except the People of the House was at her Funeral."[109] The paper could approve of crowds that attended the probably modest burial of the "honest and industrious" tailor John Rantowle, even though they were greater in numbers of persons of all ranks "than are generally seen at the internment of Persons of the greatest Fortune and highest Distinction." Liturgies such as his reinforced the established order of things in the plantation colonies, where most were buried "in a Manner suitable to his Degree and Character."[110]

Those planning funerals had some consumer choice in the sort of coffin they could select for their particular dead.[111] Thomas Elfe, the famous Charles Town furniture maker, produced for Edward Legg "a Cedar Coffin for his Son plate & Handles," for John Giles "a Cedar Coffin with Plates, Handles, & Nails," while a simple "Cypress Coffin" sufficed "for a Negroe Child." Elfe provided Plowden Weston with "a full Trim'd Cedar Coffin Lined with flannell" for £47.[112] Sometime in the eighteenth century, presumably much earlier, the estate of Richard Bohun Baker paid £10 for "a Mahogany Coffin Trimd," clearly an elegant container made of tropical wood.[113] A Charles Town cabinet and coffin maker advertised his readiness to meet these needs in 1741: "I have now a large Assortment of Coffin Furniture lately imported from London, all Persons in Town and Country who at any Time may be reduced to that melancholy necessity may have coffins of any sorts, made cheaper and better than any ever yet made in this Town."[114] The consumer choice that confronts the bereaved in contemporary society was already present in the colonial way of death.

Sometimes the costs of a funeral in "a Manner suitable" exceeded the ability of the deceased or the family to pay for those rites. The bereaved may have selected the finest pall or a more prestigious burial location and subsequently sought to avoid the parish officials intent on collecting those fees. A 1767 accounting of "Mortuaries Outstanding" in St. Catherine's parish showed some fourteen persons who owed money for the use of the pall, for a total of £36. The vestry faced a similar problem in Kingston at midcentury, where "complaint hath been made to the Justices & Vestry that Severall of the Inhabitants are indebted for Buriall fees; the person impowred to receive them reports he meets with uncommon delay in payment of said fees." Earlier in the year, a parish officer had "presented to the Justices & Vestry a list of Bad Debt for Palls and Burials from 1748 to 1752 amounting to Twenty eight pounds five Shillings," and it was "Ordered that the said Bad Debts be allowed and wrote off." St. Michael's Bridgetown resolved to "take advice of Counsel and proceed accordingly," when Jane Jones refused to pay the fee for her husband's burial in the church.[115] While many wanted the services without the fees, certainly some agreed with the outburst recorded at a funeral in Port Royal, Jamaica, late in the period. "Damn you and Buggar your Prayers," hollered a friend of the deceased at the priest. "We want none of your Prayers I'll be Damn'd if you shall get your Fees."[116]

That last case excepted, these unpaid fees likely mark a desire for unaffordable services rather than evidence of disdain for funeral rites. There is abundant evidence of how great a value Europeans in the plantation colonies put on having the burial office performed by a minister. The leaders of Prince Frederick parish in South Carolina bemoaned their lack of a minister in 1751, complaining that they and neighboring parishes were "destitute of a Minister, to baptize our Children or bury our dead." Clergy in the colonies reported great demand for their mortuary services. One Barbadian clergyman "Bury'd, Marry'd, and Visited at all times of the Night & Day I was call'd on, which in so large a Parish as mine is that has the Misfortune of being visited with pestilential Diseases, will take up two thirds of any Man's Time." If that were not enough, he "was then frequently call'd to the most distant Parishes of the Island to visit sick Friends, and administer the Sacrament to them, and to preach funeral Sermons."[117] The sickly season in the early eighteenth century in Charles Town saw one minister performing "three Funeralls of a day, and some times four are now very usual."[118] Twenty autumns later, another rector of St. Philip's buried "From 5 to 10, and once 11, of a Day . . . [t]he Sick Chamber or Church-yard were my constant Stations."[119] When a Jamaican rector was presented with the bodies of three dead seamen, he intended to make quick work of it "by only one reading of the burial-service," which infuriated the sailors' friends. They "insisted upon three several readings, in honour of their comrades."[120] Funerals became central events in these communities, with visitors consistently reporting the frequency of rites at the grave: "Divers other burials I was at in this Island, which indeed doth prove a grave to many new-comers," noted one visitor to Barbados.[121] With death always at hand, Europeans in the plantation colonies comforted themselves and reinforced their place in the structures of power by avoiding the humiliations of a negligent burial. In 1730, the vestry of St. Helena's in South Carolina sought to prevent the departure of their minister to the Goose Creek parish by reminding the SPG that "if any of us should die while our Parish is unprovided; tho' we are Christians we must be buried like dogs."[122] Burial in the manner of dogs, as the vestry of St. Helena put it, was reserved for slaves in the plantation colonies. And Europeans thought about that as well.

When challenged by enslaved persons, Europeans in these slave societies often responded with a violent suspension of their own mortuary norms and those of the slave community. Rebellious slaves like Quamina, "who was hang'd up alive in the Spring Path," in Kingston in 1746, were usually left unburied as a warning to others. The vestry paid for the set of irons in which he was hanged but incurred no fee for his nonburial.[123] On a ride across Barbados in the later eighteenth century, one could easily encounter "the Head of a Negroe stuck upon a pole"; indeed, four such heads were displayed at one time on Foursquare plantation, severed from black bodies by a vengeful owner.[124] Another visitor to the island encountered "a mastiff dog eating the carcase of a negro man," noting that the "dog had eaten off one of his arms and torn his face and bowels and was eating the fat of his thighs as we came by (a sight very horrible to behold)."[125] In

Jamaica, Thomas Thistlewood put an executed slave's head on a pole as a warning to potential runaways in 1751.[126] In these very intentional postmortem cruelties, whites demonstrated the unlimited power over slaves that they sought to exert and purposefully displayed their disregard for the basic human tendency to care for the dead.[127]

Over time, whites created a body of literary reflections on African mortuary traditions that equaled their description of black sexuality in its crudeness. They described the mortuary practices of Africans as strange and often as threatening, the very opposite of the rites they experienced as comforting and important to their continuing human community. Edward Long explained to his readers that "their funerals are the very reverse of our English ceremony," because "every funeral is a kind of festival; at which the greater part of the company assume an air of joy and unconcern." Long went on to compare Afro-Jamaican rites with those of Highland Scots and the ancient Irish, groups he associated with a childlike barbarism as well. Like Africans, mourning Scots gathered in the evening, and were similarly "attended by bag-pipe and fiddle." Long imagined that Scottish mortuary practice tended toward sexual license, just as that of Africans did. Scots engaged in "such gambols and frolic among the younger part of the company, that the loss which occasioned them is often more than supplied by the consequences of that night." The strange Irish addressed "earnest reproaches and expostulations" to the corpse for his taking leave of the world. All told, there seemed to Long "a striking conformity between this antient rite and that in use among the Negroes," both of which he thought the very reverse of the supposedly civilized practices of the English in the plantation regions.[128]

Long was joined in his derision by a writer in the *South Carolina Gazette*, who touted the virtues of African women as sexual consorts for white planters while mocking the African way of death. "When they are Sick, they are not costly, when dead, their funeral charges are but viz. an old Matt, one Bottle Rum, and a lb. Sugar."[129] Barbados clergy described slave funerals as consisting of "horrid music, howling & dancing about ye Graves of the dead."[130] Governor Charles Pinfold of Barbados called the "great Pomp and Solemnity" that accompanied the burial of executed slave felons "an Outrageous Insult on the Publick Authority," and forbade it in the future.[131] Late in the period, a Jamaican clergyman insisted that Afro-Jamaican funerals must be suppressed, for they furnished slaves "with rebellious Ideas, by contemplating their own strengths in the multitudes that attended, for at many of those funerals [I] have seen above A thousand Negroes collected."[132] Europeans insisted that African mortuary practices were wild, dangerous, and profoundly uncivilized. With death constantly surrounding them, those attitudes toward African mortuary customs were essential in the white effort to understand their slaves as cultural inferiors.

Many Africans and their descendents similarly felt that European ways of caring for the dead were profoundly deficient. The exchange between one potential Afro-Jamaican convert and an Anglican priest in Westmoreland parish was likely repeated thousands of times. The minister complained that "I myself offer'd to baptize a sensible well inclin'd Negro, but he declin'd it, saying, that after that he must go to no more Dances, nor have any of their antic Ceremonies about his Grave, of which these poor ignorant Creatures are fond of to a surprising degree; So that to deprive them of their funeral Rites by burning their dead Bodies, seems to Negroes a greater Punishment than Death itself."[133] Though their practices were shaped by the Europeans whose power predominated, the black majorities of the British plantation colonies cared for their dead as they saw fit, resisting Christian rites they found deficient, and finding in that care an important venue for preserving their cultural autonomy.

Though Africans and their descendents carefully considered the meaning of many European rituals, the European way of death seems to have been the least compelling to them. Recent scholarship has argued that Africans in the Americas explored rituals like Sunday worship, and even baptism and the Eucharist, without "converting" in the wholesale sense that European missionaries demanded.[134] Unlike those ritual moments that might be experienced from some metaphysical distance, the embrace of European and Christian mortuary ways deprived Africans of the comforts of their community as both fellow mourners and future decedents. Africans could add some of the ritual practices of English Christianity to their established spiritual systems without disrupting those systems. Many, like the man in Westmoreland parish, may have done so until they reached the point at which Anglican clergy demanded an end to their participation in slave funerals. Forced to imagine themselves no longer attending those funerals and then unattended on the way to their own grave, it became clear that the costs were simply too high.

A healthy contempt for each other's funeral rites was thus an essential feature of Africans' and Europeans' way of living together during the colonial period. Facing high levels of mortality, both groups were obliged to come to grips with the loss of members of their discrete communities. They shared some very basic practices when facing the grave: sharing food and drink, attending the body to the grave, perhaps a preference for interment as the sun dipped below the western horizon. While they misunderstood much about each other's ritual lives, especially in matters less basic than death and burial, residents of the plantation regions realized that they shared much in their respective responses to death. Followers of these two ways of death were thus even more intent on preserving their differences and understanding the shortcomings of the opposing group's practice. Whites maintained mortuary practices that provided continuity with the practices of their ancestors in Europe, that allowed for the performance of varying degrees of social privilege within the white community, and that proclaimed their racial privilege to the wider community that included persons of color. While Africans and their descendants could not pretend to the social dominance so desired by whites, the maintenance of their way of death was central to resisting the dehumanizing program inherent in slavery and to the creation of new identities in the British plantation colonies. Though beholden to both traditions, persons of biracial ancestry were most likely to explore Europeans' way of death in their efforts to be identified with the master class.[135]

Even as they struggled for power, residents of the plantation colonies had to deal with the death of fellow human beings in ways that preserved them from the genuine trauma possible in the midst of a demographic disaster. Historians interested in the ways that funerary practice articulated understandings of power in the plantation colonies need not deny that real grief was assuaged in rites like the baptism of William, the son of Susanna and John Townsend, who, "born the 13th August 1779, was baptized the same Day over the Mothers Coffin."[136] Could there have been a dry eye in St. Catherine's Church for the second funeral on a December day in 1754 when the infants Lucretia Lewis and Mary-Jane Dehany were "buried in one Coffin" or on a Barbadian April day when William Wilkinson and his daughter Grace similarly disappeared from human sight in a single box?[137] Death was indeed busy in the plantation world, and the humans struggling to make lives there sought to make meaning out of it, ironically making their rituals of death one of the liveliest forums for creating the new societies of early America. The liveliness of that and other liturgical forums, however, would be severely tested by the rising evangelicalisms of the later eighteenth century, which would combine with the convulsions of an age of revolutions to produce a dramatically different religious and political landscape.

CHAPTER 6

Revolution, Evangelicalisms, and the Fragmentation of Anglo-America

SPEAKING TO SOUTH CAROLINA'S GENERAL ASSEMBLY in 1777 in favor of the disestablishment of the Church of England, Congregationalist minister William Tennent dwelled on the colonial government's material support for the worship of the established church. He complained that among the many denominations of early Carolina, the "law knows the Clergy of the One, as Ministers of the Gospel; the law knows not the Clergy of the other Churches, nor will it give them a license to marry their own people." Furthermore, "the law builds superb Churches for the one — it leaves the others to build their own Churches." And yet Tennent made a show of *not* calling for restitution of the public funds expended on the Anglican Church. "Let her be contented with her superb Churches," he insisted, "her spacious burying grounds, her costly parsonages, her numerous glebes, & other Church estates, obtained in a great degree from the public purse."[1] Tennent implied that the emerging Episcopal Church would enter the new religious marketplace with mere material rather than spiritual advantages over other Christian denominations. While its liturgical apparatus dwarfed the resources of South Carolina's evangelical churches, Tennent knew that the Revolution marked the end of liturgical culture as a hegemonic forum.

The preceding chapters have uncovered a vibrant culture of liturgical worship in the plantation colonies. Drawing on a ritual tradition that extended deep into the Christian past of Europe, colonists created a comprehensive ritual environment in sacred time and space. That environment framed their actions for maximum social impact, setting them off as public and important even as it rendered the ritual lives of Afro-Americans private and illegitimate. Colonists privatized other rites, carefully controlling the domestic rites of marriage and baptism that lent legitimacy to their sexuality and reproduction. In their celebrations of the Lord's Supper, colonists sustained theological and national boundaries from the European past even as they explored the Eucharist's social meaning for emerging American systems of race. In a horrific mortality environment, both African and European residents of the plantation colonies found in funerary ritual a lively means for creating identities for life in the Americas. In all these areas, the white minorities of the plantation world sought to maintain cultural connections to the metropole. Yet their studied attempts at continuity were constantly transformed by life in slave societies.

Even before the Revolution, men like Tennent knew that the Church of England was already *not* the church of most white Carolinians. Protestant dissenters had flourished in Carolina from an early date, and since 1730 their numbers had been augmented by immigration from overseas and other colonies. Evangelical theology in the colony was further stimulated by the preaching of George Whitefield in the early 1740s, which created new evangelical energy, especially in the southern parishes of Carolina.[2] Moreover, the Anglican Church failed to extend its liturgical culture into the Carolina backcountry. Besides the colorful ministry of Charles Woodmason and infrequent visits from parochial clergy, there was little meaningful effort on the part of the low country elite to extend the parish system and its worship life to the west and north. Indeed, the settlers from Virginia and the Middle Colonies who populated the midlands and piedmont were hardly attracted to the ritual ways of the low country, schooled as many of them were in Reformed traditions. Presbyterian churches came to dot the backcountry landscape, and Baptists and Methodists would not be far behind. Tennent was right: the leaders of Carolina's manifestation of the Church of England were largely content with their "superb churches" and stately liturgy, and white evangelicals wanted nothing to do with them.[3] The disestablishment of the Anglican Church in South Carolina was a recognition of how much the cultural landscape of the new state would differ from that of the old colony.

Before the Revolution, most in Carolina's black majority shared evangelical whites' distaste for Anglican worship, though for very different reasons. While clergy tended to blame slave owners for preventing missionary work among their slaves, it is clear that most slaves took little interest in the Church of England on its own terms and that clergy failed to appreciate slaves' rejection of their ministrations. With a few notable exceptions, most enslaved persons in Carolina experienced Anglican worship as an alien tradition that hardly connected to

Exterior of St. Michael's Church, Charleston, South Carolina. Courtesy of Suzanne Linder Hurley.

their everyday lives. Anglican liturgy's material idioms, its stress on deference and hierarchy, and its hostility to ecstatic traditions marked it as an unlikely avenue for Afro-Carolinians' incorporation into the Christian tradition.[4] A "combination of fierce hostility and total indifference from planters and slaves alike," directed toward Anglicans' already meager missionary efforts, meant that the wholesale conversion of African Americans would be a project of Tennent's evangelical churches, with their decidedly different mode of worship.[5]

These related failures in the colonial period to offer compelling opportunities for worship to Carolina's black majority and to the burgeoning backcountry were the roots of the social irrelevance of liturgical worship in Carolina after the Revolution. Throughout the early national period, new evangelical churches were established across the South, and the Anglican "gentlefolk [who] seated themselves in the front pews of Anglican chapels" found that increasingly "evangelicals were not present to witness the spectacle."[6] In addition to the rites of an Anglican Sunday, evangelicals eschewed the social rituals of court days and cock fights and embraced "a stark alternative to the region's traditional culture based on conviviality and competition." They substituted the right hand of fellowship, the kiss of peace, and the washing of feet, rites of mutuality rather than deference. Methodist love feasts and Baptists' baptism by immersion signaled alike the rise of a new ritual vocabulary, an earthy vocabulary that entirely displaced that of the traditional leaders of the plantation colonies, at least within evangelical communities. While white evangelicals would back away from some of these rituals and their related racial and gender egalitarianism by 1830, they did so after successfully challenging the older ritual way.[7]

Before southern whites backed away from evangelicalism's revolutionary potential, biracial evangelicalism carried enough prophetic potential to find confirmation in the lives of persons of color. While some enslaved African Americans would worship in biracial evangelical churches until after the Civil War, others created congregations under the discipline of black ministers and elders. The African American churches they created in the lower South were largely the products of black initiative, an unimaginable development under the old ritual regime. Before the end of the eighteenth century, African American Baptists like George Liele created North America's first public Eucharistic and exegetical communities constituted under African American authority along the banks of the Savannah River.[8] Black Charlestonians in turn created an African Methodist church in 1815, one that may have nurtured the Denmark Vesey conspiracy.[9] In the worship of the black church, African American Christians created a vibrant tradition of enormous political power, appropriating the liberating narratives of the Bible for their own struggles and rejecting the manipulations of Christian liturgy long practiced by whites. Evangelicals black and white thus abandoned the liturgical tradition in the era of the early Republic, their absences substantially negating its cultural power. Paradoxically, the political separation that coincided with the disestablishment of Carolina Anglicanism also spread the tradition of independent black churches to the British Caribbean, where African religious practices had been largely unaffected by white missionary activity.

George Liele left Savannah and the First African Church he had founded there during the British evacuation of that city in 1782. Like many Loyalist refugees, he found his way to Jamaica.[10] He called together a Baptist church in Kingston in 1784, one that had 225 members and 350 other adherents by 1791. The spread of Liele's Afro-Baptist faith across Jamaica was aided by other Georgia immigrants, who faced no interference from British Baptist missionaries until 1815.[11] When the first resident Methodist missionary in Jamaica, William Hammett, organized his first class in Kingston in 1791, it consisted of three whites and five free persons of color who had come from the mainland in the 1780s.[12] While missionaries sent from Britain would further the Christianization of Jamaican slaves, they did so on the heels of the free persons of color from the lower South who had first created independent black churches in the British Caribbean.

White West Indians responded with a fury that demonstrated their understanding of the revolutionary power of Christian worship. One angry white Jamaican showed what he thought of George Liele's ministry by demanding that he administer communion to his horse. Rioters attempted to destroy the Wesleyan chapel in Kingston in 1791 and forced its closure in the evenings.[13] The opening of the Wesleyan Church in Bridgetown in 1789 had similarly been met by "large mobs [who] pelted the building with stones and frequently interrupted the prayers with hideous noises."[14] Though often countered by the Colonial Office, the Jamaican Assembly and magistrates persistently attempted to restrict preaching to slaves in the early nineteenth century, shutting down some dissenting churches that served slaves and free people.[15] In 1823, whites, who by then associated all dissenting Protestants with metropolitan abolitionists, destroyed the Wesleyan Church in Bridgetown.[16] Whites were right, of course, in their contention that slaves were experiencing the beginning of their liberation in the worship of these evangelical churches. By 1831, the Baptist churches of the western parishes in Jamaica had nurtured the largest slave revolt in the history of the British Caribbean, to which whites responded with their usual bloodletting and the destruction of chapels all over the west and south of the island.[17]

The displacements of the American Revolution were thus partially responsible for the creation of an Afro-evangelical tradition in the Caribbean that would challenge the foundations of the plantocracy, especially in Jamaica. At the same time, the departure of South Carolina and the other continental colonies with Anglican establishments from the British Empire was part of a general disruption of patterns of trade and cultural exchange that had created a substantially common colonial experience in the British colonies south of the Chesapeake and north of the Spanish Main. White Barbadians and Jamaicans alike found that the Revolution "destroyed the cultural unity of British America," simultaneously isolating West Indians from the rest of Anglo-America and forcing them into a greater dependence on metropolitan Britain.[18] Cut off from the slave states of North America, West Indian slavery looked increasingly anomalous to metropolitan eyes. Metropolitan criticism of slavery in the British Caribbean was joined to a criticism of the West Indian Anglican Church's indifference to slaves, and both led to metropolitan efforts to place that church on a more substantial footing.

The Anglicization of the colonial experience that marked the second half of the eighteenth century in all of British America thus continued in the Caribbean after the Revolution. But the dynamics of that Anglicization switched, as metropolitan pressure for reform replaced colonists' drive to re-create metropolitan culture. While colonists had earlier been eager to import English ways, the British ministries of the 1820s and 1830s increasingly disregarded the wishes of the West Indian lobby as they sought to impose metropolitan mores on the British Caribbean. By the mid-1820s, there were Church of England bishops in Barbados and Jamaica, sent out to prod the clergy into missionary work among the enslaved. The British government's seriousness about reining in the planters was demonstrated by its allocation of £6540 sterling for the creation of the new ecclesial hierarchy in Jamaica. These well-funded bishops and their assisting clergy imposed liturgical standards that challenged venerable West Indian practices. Eucharistic practice was opened up to persons of color, the Barbadian bishop disallowing the pregnant pause that had long been observed between the communion of whites and that of blacks. Whites' preference for marriage at home was discouraged, even as clergy exhorted slaves and the newly freed to be joined together at the altar.¹⁹ The churches in the West Indies would no longer be the ritual bulwark of the plantocracy, though it can hardly be said that they took much of a prophetic stance in the nineteenth century.

Thus a combination of evangelical awakenings and the American Revolution disrupted a pervasive liturgical culture that had united the British plantation colonies. In Carolina and then the American South generally, that liturgical culture was washed away by the waves of evangelical revivals that swept across the region in the nineteenth century, producing dominant evangelical traditions in both the black and white populations. Tainted by its association with the former imperial power and slow to adapt to its sudden status as one among many other voluntary religious associations, the new Episcopal Church in Carolina found its mission largely limited to meeting the spiritual needs of a tiny white elite. That elite and its chaplains maintained their superb buildings, celebrated their rites of passage, and made a modicum of effort in patronizing missionary work among the small number of African Americans who were still willing to give Anglican ritual ways a chance.[20]

Jamaican whites had persistently lagged behind the other plantation colonies in their enthusiasm for the liturgical life throughout the eighteenth century. The colony's already small white population shrank in the nineteenth century, and the Anglican Church in Jamaica struggled to sustain its ministries as metropolitan support waned and as evangelical missionaries from Britain competed successfully for the allegiance of newly freed people. It endured as the worship community of elite and middle-class whites and persons of color.[21] More important than missionary-derived evangelicalism was Afro-Jamaicans' creation of powerful religious traditions that sometimes remained within the limits of a black evangelical Christian experience but that often moved well beyond the theological norms of Christianity, at least as Europeans knew it. In expansive Christianities like that of the Native Baptists, and in Revival, Zion, and Holiness traditions, Afro-Jamaicans embraced African traditions of visions and visitations and experienced new spiritual realities well suited to the struggles of life in postemancipation Jamaica. They did so in a setting increasingly unlike Carolina or Barbados, one in which the cultural power of whites was fast disappearing and in which new indentured immigrants from Africa were reinvigorating some older traditions.[22]

Only in conservative Barbados did something of the older ritual tradition endure on a larger scale. Its larger white population was intent on sustaining that ritual tradition in the postemancipation world. The Barbadian slave population had been majority Creole since sometime in the first half of the eighteenth century, and African ritual ways were thus a more distant memory than in Jamaica.[23] In 1891, 85 percent of all Barbadians were still members of the Church of England, which had been reestablished by the Barbadian legislature after the withdrawal of Colonial Office support in 1868. Its liturgical life remained a lively forum for establishing and contesting white hegemony in a nominally free society. The governing class continued to care deeply about church seating; four times between 1880 and 1890, the legislature passed or amended acts on pews and related behavior in church. White laypersons wrote letters to the editor when they felt their liturgical privilege was threatened, as when the curate of a Bridgetown church required all children to be baptized on Tuesday or Sunday, forcing elite whites into church space and into church records in close proximity to those they considered their racial inferiors. And persons of color continued to worship in Anglican churches, despite ongoing efforts to contain their participation within the confines of whites' preferences. Though sometimes given the rear stall, black men sang in Anglican choirs at St. Michael's and elsewhere. Though refused communion for violating white racial etiquette, black Barbadians continued to come to the altar. Though provided with inferior seating, large numbers of persons of color still came to church, sometimes challenging white ministers' authority over that seating in the midst of divine service.[24] In Barbados, the older ritual way and the contests that played out in its context survived far longer than in the more fluid and confrontational societies of Jamaica and Carolina.

The British plantation colonies of Barbados, Jamaica, and South Carolina shared much at the beginning of the eighteenth century: black majorities, plantation economies, established Anglicanism, and an enthusiasm among whites and some persons of color for exploring the social meaning of English ritual ways. Those ways were invested with new meaning as blacks and whites negotiated power in these evolving slave societies, indeed, as they created American racial systems. Yet existing differences, some subtle, others more overt, would radically distinguish these three colonies from each other in the years during and after the rebellion of the mainland colonies. The plantation colonies drew apart later in the eighteenth century, indeed, so far apart that their importance as a unit of analysis has been lost in later national narratives. Divergent political trajectories fractured the plantation world in a process that also unleashed the power of black evangelicalism into the British Caribbean. As the political and cultural unity of the plantation world was lost, English ritual ways faded in their importance, among both blacks and whites. Indeed, that older ritual way faded to the degree that historians have left it largely unnoticed in the archives, preferring to study the evangelicalism that replaced it. The historiographical neglect of the meanings of liturgical worship in the British plantation colonies that this book has tried to correct finally reveals the totality of evangelicalism's triumph over the vitiated and racialized ritual culture of the earlier period. It is, fittingly, as though the ritual ways of the British plantation world had never been.

NOTES

Abbreviations

BA   Barbados Archives, Black Rock, Barbados
BMHS   Shilstone Library, Barbados Museum and Historical Society, Barbados
CCPL   Charleston County Public Library, Charleston, South Carolina
JA   Jamaica Archives, Spanish Town, Jamaica
NLJ   National Library of Jamaica, Kingston, Jamaica
SCDAH   South Carolina Division of Archives and History, Columbia, South Carolina
SCHS   South Carolina Historical Society, Charleston, South Carolina
SCL   South Caroliniana Library, Columbia, South Carolina

Where necessary, dates have been modernized, to make the year begin on January 1.

Chapter 1. Christian Ritual in British Slave Societies

1. For the founding of Barbados, see Harlow, *History of Barbados*, and Gragg, *Englishmen Transplanted*. Greene, *Imperatives, Behaviors, and Identities*, 73; Dunn, *Sugar and Slaves*, 111–16; but see Roper, *Conceiving Carolina*, for a caution on ascribing too much to Barbadian influence in Carolina. "British plantation colonies" in this book refers to Barbados, Jamaica, and South Carolina. A broader set of plantation colonies would include the Leeward Islands, the Chesapeake, and others.

2. See Berlin, *Many Thousands Gone*, 8–11, quotation at 9. Indians were present as well, as powerful independent groups in Carolina and as slaves early in the history of all three colonies. While the interaction of Native Americans and Europeans is essential to understanding the development of South Carolina, that is not the case for Barbados and Jamaica, and indeed religion was hardly a meaningful point of contact between the two groups in Carolina. Those factors and the comparative goals of this project produce here a focus on slave societies made up of Africans, Europeans, and their descendents.

3. On colonial Anglicanism generally, see Woolverton, *Colonial Anglicanism in North America*; James B. Bell, *Imperial Origins*; Doll, *Revolution, Religion, and National Identity*; Bridenbaugh, *Mitre and Sceptre*.

4. On Jamaica, see S. A. G. Taylor, *Western Design*; Pestana, *English Atlantic*, 93–110;

Kupperman, "Errand to the Indies"; Beasley, "Wars of Religion." On South Carolina, see Edgar, *South Carolina*, 43; Weir, *Colonial South Carolina*, 57. For the Fundamental Constitutions of Carolina, see Wootton, *John Locke*, 210–32. A wider collection of early material related to Locke and Shaftsbury can be found in The South Carolina Historical Society's edition of *The Shaftsbury Papers*. See Collinson, *Religion of Protestants*; Davies, *Caroline Captivity of the Church*; Fincham, *Early Stuart Church*; Russell, *Causes*; Morrill, *Revolt of the Provinces*; Parry, *Arts of the Anglican Counter-Reformation*.

5. Woolverton, *Colonial Anglicanism*, 223, quotation from a letter to Thomas Sherlock, May 27, 1750. The clash between Whig and Tory and high and low churchmen reached an apex in the reign of Queen Anne, 1702–14. On colonial resistance to episcopacy, see Bridenbaugh, *Mitre and Sceptre*; Cross, *Anglican Episcopate*, 88–112; Woolverton, *Colonial Anglicanism*, 220–25; Butler, *Awash*, 197–200. The most recent and sophisticated entry into this literature is Doll, *Revolution, Religion, and National Identity*.

6. On the preponderance of males in emigration to the plantation colonies, see Games, *Migration*; Weir, *Colonial South Carolina*, 206–7.

7. Dunn, *Sugar and Slaves*, 83. But see Menard, *Sweet Negotiations*, for questions about the nature and pace of the conversion to sugar production. A useful introduction to the economic development of the plantation colonies in a comparative perspective is found in Eltis, *Rise of African Slavery*, 193–223.

8. Greene, *Pursuits of Happiness*, 160, 147; Olwell, *Masters, Slaves, and Subjects*, 33–36; Alice Hanson Jones, *Wealth of a Nation*, 377–80; Burnard, "Prodigious Riches." For a helpful comparison of elite experience in the British American colonies, see "Toward a History of Elites in the Eighteenth-Century British Empire," in Burnard, *Creole Gentlemen*, 237–64.

9. See chap. 2 on the liturgical year as one remedy to climatic and seasonal difference. A helpful analysis of white colonists' reflection on the relationship between troubling landscapes and slavery can be found in Edelson, "Nature of Slavery."

10. See Sypher, "West Indian as a Character"; Greene, "Liberty, Slavery, and the Transformation."

11. Burnhard, *Mastery, Tyranny, and Desire*, 16–18; Peter H. Wood, *Black Majority*, 218–21; Greene and Pole, *Colonial British America*, 138.

12. Edgar, *South Carolina*, 54; Weir, *Colonial South Carolina*, 208–9; Pares, *War and Trade*, 229. The Carolina legislature also attempted to require the retention of one white male servant for each ten slaves. Weir, *Colonial South Carolina*, 208.

13. Genovese, *From Rebellion to Revolution*, 35–36; Dunn, *Sugar and Slaves*, 259–62; Mark M. Smith, *Stono*; Dunn, *Sugar and Slaves*, 257–58. Major plots were uncovered in 1675 and 1692, though confessions obtained by torture and probable white paranoia make it impossible to be sure that the plots were real. The debate over the Denmark

Vesey plot in Charleston in 1822 is instructive in that regard. See "The Making of a Slave Conspiracy, Part 1," beginning with Johnson, "Denmark Vesey and his Co-Conspirators," and a subsequent forum, "The Making of a Slave Conspiracy, Part 2."

14. Peter H. Wood, *Black Majority*, 221–24.

15. Klingberg, *Carolina Chronicle*, 81.

16. For the optimistic view of the cultural power of the Anglican Church in the eighteenth century, see Clark, *English Society*, which makes the case that *ancien regime* England was a "confessional state," as well as Gibson, *Achievement of the Anglican Church*. See also Colley, *Britons*, which points to Protestantism generally, if not Anglicanism, as a key to creating British identity.

17. On that defense of the Anglican service book, see Gragg, *Englishmen Transplanted*, 74. On Barbadian religiosity and the problems historians face in describing lay religion, see ibid., 74–86.

18. Handler, "Father Antoine Biet's Visit." For one such citation of Biet, see Greene, *Imperatives, Behaviors, and Identities*, 26.

19. Here I annex Puritanism to a broad understanding of evangelicalism, realizing that both new and old lights would resent the conflation.

20. "Journal of Josiah Quincy," 444; John K. Nelson, *Blessed Company*, 9. On efforts to undermine that evangelical synthesis, see the "Preface to the Updated Edition," in Bonomi, *Under the Cope of Heaven*, xvi–xx. It is infrequently noticed how closely this American evangelical synthesis parallels British historians' reiteration of Non-Conformist, Anglo-Catholic, and evangelical Anglican criticism of the eighteenth-century Church of England in England. See Gregory, "Church of England."

21. Peter H. Wood, *Black Majority*; Dunn, *Sugar and Slaves*; Bridenbaugh and Bridenbaugh, *No Peace Beyond the Line*. For an account stressing the pathology of Jamaica's slave society, see Patterson, *Sociology of Slavery*. A comparison of supposedly more secular Caribbean colonists with more religious New Englanders opens Craton, "Reluctant Creoles."

22. Greene, *Pursuits of Happiness*, 205.

23. Burnard, *Mastery, Tyranny, and Desire*, 245–50. A similar argument for Barbados can be found in Gragg, *Englishmen Transplanted*, and Watson, *Civilised Island Barbados*. All build upon Brathwaite, *Development of Creole Society*.

24. Zaceck, "Death in the Morning."

25. Note, for instance, Greene's promise in *Pursuits of Happiness* to consider "religious, political, and even economic developments only insofar as they have social dimensions" (xiii). Though Anglicization and development are Greene's great themes, religious dimensions are not important in his work. The little attention he pays to religion suggests that it lacked the "social dimensions" he seeks, perhaps because "few people seem to have been compulsively religious" in the southern colonies (149). The suggestion that

socially meaningful religious life must be "compulsive" is clearly a secularized version of the evangelical critique.

26. In addition to Nelson, *Blessed Company*, see Brydon, *Virginia's Mother Church*; Bonomi and Eisenstadt, "Church Adherence"; Bonomi, *Under the Cope of Heaven*, 245–86; Upton, *Holy Things and Profane*; Gundersen, *Anglican Ministry in Virginia*; Bond, *Damned Souls*; Hatfield, *Atlantic Virginia*, 110–36.

27. Population estimates for Virginia and South Carolina can be found in Peter H. Wood, "Changing Population."

28. Berlin, *Many Thousands Gone*, 26. For a comparison of the transition from servants to slaves in Virginia and Barbados, see the classic Edmund S. Morgan, *American Slavery, American Freedom*, 298–304.

29. Berlin, *Many Thousands Gone*, 109; Kulikoff, *Tobacco and Slaves*, 261; Parent, *Foul Means*.

30. Peter H. Wood, "Changing Population," 60, table 1.

31. Absenteeism in Barbados should not be overstated, and it is important to differentiate the Jamaican and Barbadian experience from that of the Leeward Islands. See Greene, *Imperatives, Behaviors, and Identities*, 78–79.

32. Berlin, *Many Thousands Gone*, 64; Philip D. Morgan, *Slave Counterpoint*, 101. See Philip D. Morgan, *Slave Counterpoint*, 35–58, for an introduction to the divergence between the plantation systems of the Tidewater and the low country. Those enslaved on Caribbean islands in this study obviously experienced a plantation system and demographic pattern more akin to Carolina than Virginia.

33. Philip D. Morgan, *Slave Counterpoint*, 95, 394–96, 61, table 10 (quotation at 95). Pages 79–95 offer a useful demographic comparison of the two slave populations. Carolina's percentage of Africans in the slave population was as high as 66 percent in 1740 before falling to 23 percent in 1790. Virginia's African-born slaves were as much as 52 percent of the slave population in 1710, falling to 2 percent by 1790.

34. See Sensbach, "Religion and the Early South."

35. See Bolton *Southern Anglicanism*; Caldecott, *Church in the West Indies*; Minter, *Episcopacy Without Episcopate*; Campbell, *Church in Barbados*.

36. See a call to take up these subjects in Westerkamp, "Religion," 382–83.

37. Little, "Origins of Southern Evangelicalism." Little notes the existence of one church for every 283 whites in Carolina in 1740, a ratio nearly twice that of Virginia, as well as the regular weekly attendance of one-third of white Carolinians in an Anglican church in the 1720s (771, 779–80).

38. John K. Nelson, *Blessed Company*, 8. Here I apply his words about Virginia to points farther south.

39. Rhys Isaac's *Transformation of Virginia* is a notable exception, though hardly departing from the evangelical synthesis. For early modern Europe, see Karant-Nunn,

Reformation of Ritual; Muir, *Ritual in Early Modern Europe*; Duffy, *Stripping of the Altars*; Rubin, *Corpus Christi*; Geertz, *Interpretation of Cultures*; Victor Turner, *Ritual Process*; Catherine Bell, *Ritual Theory, Ritual Practice*; Catherine Bell, *Ritual*.

40. Victor Turner, *Anthropology of Performance*, 158, quoted in Driver, *Liberating Rites*, 189; Todd, *Culture of Protestantism*, 7. One of Hall's calls to the study of ritual is found in David D. Hall, "Religion and Society," 136–38.

41. Though it rebelled, a place like South Carolina was marginalized for its failure to measure up to optimistic national narratives.

42. O'Shaughnessy, *Empire Divided*, xi; Frey and Wood, *Come Shouting to Zion*, xiii.

Chapter 2. Ritual Time and Space in the British Plantation Colonies

1. On ritual, community, and hierarchy, see Driver, *Liberating Rites*, particularly part 3, with chapters on order, community, and transformation. He extends and critiques the classic Victor Turner, *Ritual Process*.

2. Jonathan Z. Smith, *To Take Place*, 94.

3. See Louis P. Nelson, "Building Cross-Wise," and his dissertation "Material Word."

4. On Anglican liturgical space in England, see Addleshaw and Etchells, *Architectural Setting of Anglican Worship*; Basil F. L. Clarke, *Building of the Eighteenth-Century Church*; and Yates, *Buildings, Faith, and Worship*. On pews and church space, three recent articles of Christopher Marsh are helpful: "Sacred Space in England," "Order and Place in England," and "'Common Prayer' in England." See also Dillow, "Social and Ecclesiastical Significance," and Tittler, "Seats of Honor."

5. *American Papers*, 16:83, Samuel Thomas to the Treasurer, May 3, 1704; Fulham Papers, 9:160 (Alexander Garden of St. Philip's); St. Philip's Parish Vestry Minutes, 1732–55, 135, January 9, 1745, South Carolina Division of Archives and History, Columbia, South Carolina, hereafter SCDAH. The figures in this and the following two paragraphs are largely drawn from clergy responses to the queries of the bishop of London, sent out in 1723 and returned in 1724. While clergy could be expected to put a brave face on the state of their parishes when writing to the bishop of London, it is striking how much bad news can be found in the responses, especially in most ministers' admission that they were doing little to evangelize slaves. For careful use of the Fulham Papers and the queries, see also Bonomi and Eisenstadt, "Church Adherence."

6. Circular Church, Registers of the Corporation, vol. 1, 1695–1796, 20, December 18, 1729, South Carolina Historical Society, Charleston, South Carolina, hereafter SCHS; Pinckney, *Letterbook of Eliza Lucas Pinckney*, 40, May 22, 1742, letter to Thomas Lucas, her brother; Fulham Papers, 9:161, William Guy, responses to queries (for St. Andrew's

parish), 9:162–65 (St. Thomas's), 9:170 (Christ Church), 9:168 (St. James's Goose Creek), 9:169 (St. James's Santee). A sense of the small size of the country parishes can be gained from Linder, *Anglican Churches.* Also see Bonomi and Eisenstadt, "Church Adherence," for the conclusion that a mean of 61 percent of white Anglicans were regularly attending church (256–57, table 1).

7. Fulham Papers, 15:206, (W. Gordon, St. Michael's), 15:207 (Joseph Holt, St. Joseph's), 15:209–10 (Charles Irvine, St. Philip's), 15:205, 208 (Alexander Deuchar, St. Thomas's); Oldmixon, *British Empire in America*, 2:99; St. Michael's Parish Register, 1771–94, 253–56, October 10, 1780, Barbados Archives, Black Rock, Barbados, hereafter BA, by John Orderson, Parish Clerk.

8. Fulham Papers, 17:224–25 (William May, Kingston [see Fulham Papers, 17:215–16, for the report of Galpine of Port Royal]); Lewis, "English Commemorative Sculpture in Jamaica," 31; Fulham Papers, 17:230–31 (John Scott, St. Catherine's, Spanish Town), 17:219–20 (John Kelly, St. Elizabeth's), 17:221 (Nicholas McCalman, St. Thomas's in the East), 17:222–23 (Richard Marsden, St. John's), 17:228–29 (Edward Reading, St. Thomas's in the Vale).

9. Circular Church, Registers, vol. 1, 1695–1796, 1, January 25, 1732, SCHS. See Edwards, *History of the Independent or Congregational Church of Charleston.*

10. Circular Church, Registers, vol. 1, 1695–1796, 9, August 8, 1734; 118, August 26, 1759, SCHS.

11. On St. Michael's generally, see Williams, *St. Michael's, Charleston.*

12. St. Michael's Church Records, Pew Applications, 1760, folder 2, August 20, 1760, letter of J. A. Reid (?), SCHS.

13. Ibid., 1759, folder 1, SCHS. See also the letter of William Hopton, St. Michael's Church Records, Pew Applications, 1759, folder 2, SCHS.

14. Circular Church, Registers, vol. 1, 1695–1796, 156–57, November 8, 1772.

15. "Records of the Vestry," *Journal of the Barbados Museum* 20, no. 3 (1953): 139, March 29, 1726. For the gallery addition, see "Records of the Vestry," *Journal of the Barbados Museum* 19, no. 1 (1951): 44, October 16, 1717.

16. St. Michael's Church Records, Pew Applications, 1760, folder 2, August 20, 1760, letter of J. A. Reid (?), SCHS. It has been a common practice for English parishes to assign pews close to the pulpit to the elderly and hard-of-hearing, meaning that persons of limited means sometimes occupied the most prominent pews. See Marsh, "Sacred Space in England," 308.

17. St. Michael's Church Records, Pew Applications, 1760, folder 3, SCHS.

18. On pewing new churches in England, see Basil F. L. Clarke, *Building of the Eighteenth-Century Church*, 214–15.

19. "Records of the Vestry," *Journal of the Barbados Museum* 24, no. 4 (1957): 198, December 16, 1754 (quote); 26, no. 1 (1958): 47–52; 26, no. 2 (1959): 96–97. See also

the refusals of various pews in 1729 in "Records of the Vestry," *Journal of the Barbados Museum* 21, no. 1 (1953): 44–45.

20. Howe and Middleton, *Minutes of St. Michael's Church*, 54, April 21, 1766. They later received complaints about the "Extravagant prices" that resulted.

21. Prince Frederick Parish, Winyah, Vestry Minutes and Registers, 1713–94, 6, March 30, 1730, Charleston County Public Library, hereafter CCPL. See Rogers, *History of Georgetown County*, 79–86.

22. Prince Frederick Parish, Winyah, Vestry Minutes and Registers, 1713–94, 18, October 2, 1734. These prices can be correlated with the numbered plan of the pews published in Pringle, *Register Book*, 80.

23. St. John's Parish, Colleton County, Vestry Minutes, 1738–1817, n.p., 1742–43, SCDAH; Reece and Hunt, *Barbados Diocesan History*, 25; Marsh, "Order and Place in England," 9.

24. "Records of the Vestry," *Journal of the Barbados Museum* 18, nos. 3 and 4 (1951): 178, January 21, 1712; 20, no. 4 (1953): 196, March 23, 1728; 17, nos. 2 and 3 (1950): 137, April 5, 1697. See "Records of the Vestry," *Journal of the Barbados Museum* 17, no. 4 (1950): 194, May 23, 1698, for another such grant. The reverse request for burial near one's traditional seat is discussed in Marsh, "Sacred Space in England," 291.

25. *South Carolina Gazette*, April 6, 1734. A pew is not actually mentioned in the story, but one must have been involved in a church dispute over "their Right of Precedency," even if the issue was the order of departing from different pews.

26. "Records of the Vestry," *Journal of the Barbados Museum* 17, no. 1 (1949): 59. They had ordered in 1711 that "all locks be taken off all the pews except the Governor's and Council's." See "Records of the Vestry," *Journal of the Barbados Museum* 18, nos. 3 and 4 (1951): 170, January 15, 1711.

27. "Records of the Vestry," *Journal of the Barbados Museum* 23, no. 2 (1956): 83, January 20, 1746; 24, no. 2 (1957): 86, February 4, 1751. The vestry determined that she had inherited half the pew from her husband, who had been given it by Skeen.

28. St. Philip's Parish Vestry Minutes, 1732–55, 40, January 9, 1738, SCDAH ("towards the Repairing"); letters of Philip Porcher and Charles Richbourge, August 1768, printed in Porcher, "Minutes of the Vestry," 169.

29. "Records of the Vestry," *Journal of the Barbados Museum* 16, nos. 1 and 2 (1948–49): 60, September 29, 1676. It again ordered the pew relined in 1721. See "Records of the Vestry," *Journal of the Barbados Museum* 19, no. 4 (1952): 178. Ten years later, "Scarlet Cloth, brass nails, and other necessarys" were ordered for relining the pew. See "Records of the Vestry," *Journal of the Barbados Museum* 21, no. 2 (1954): 95. The Council had a pew in St. Michael's as well, "facing the altar." See "Records of the Vestry," *Journal of the Barbados Museum* 18, nos. 1 and 2 (1950–51): 66.

30. St. Catherine's Parish Vestry Minutes, 1759–68, November 6, 1762, Jamaica

Archives, Spanish Town, Jamaica, hereafter JA; Roby, *Monuments of the Cathedral-Church*, 7. On the early modern habit of adding tops to important objects in the tradition of state furniture, see Upton, *Holy Things and Profane*, 135–37.

31. St. Catherine's Parish Vestry Minutes, 1759–68, May 15, 1764, JA; Kingston Vestry Minutes, 1752–54, 548, April 3, 1754, and 550, April 22, 1754, JA; Trott, *Laws*, 35–37, March 1, 1711; "Records of the Vestry," *Journal of the Barbados Museum* 19, no. 1 (1951): 39, June 24, 1715. The governor's pew was one center of visual attention in these churches. When George I died in 1727, the St. Michael's vestry ordered the churchwarden to cover in black broad cloth "the Pulpit and Desks, and the Governour's pew." See "Records of the Vestry," *Journal of the Barbados Museum* 20, no. 3 (1953): 146, August 31, 1727. The pew was also covered in black cloth on the death of governors.

32. French, *History of Col. Parke's Administration*, 64. Compare this with Franciscans in New Mexico hurling their excommunicated governor's pew from the church. See Alan Taylor, *American Colonies*, 87. For more on Parke's administration and murder, see Zacek, "Death in the Morning," 223–43.

33. See Labaree, *Royal Instructions to British Colonial Governors*, 2:482–83.

34. "Records of the Vestry," *Journal of the Barbados Museum* 15, no. 2 (1948): 92, October 29, 1663; 16, no. 3 (1949): 140, May 15, 1682. Various schoolmasters and schoolmistresses kept assigned space for their students in St. Michael's, including "Mr. Hull's Scholars" and "Mrs. Spyre's Scholars" in 1700. See "Records of the Vestry," *Journal of the Barbados Museum* 14, no. 4 (1950): 199, September 2, 1700.

35. "Records of the Vestry," *Journal of the Barbados Museum* 21, no. 2 (1954): 95, July 26, 1731. They decided at this meeting to reserve that pew for the use of strangers and to keep it locked for that purpose. The Lawyer's Pew is mentioned in "Records of the Vestry," *Journal of the Barbados Museum* 23, no. 3 (1956): 142, January 1749.

36. St. Andrew's Parish Vestry Minutes, 1781–87, 168, April 9, 1785, JA. For more on pews in Jamaica, see Minter, *Episcopacy Without Episcopate*, 241–42. There is considerably less detail on pews in Jamaica's vestry minutes than is found in the other plantation colonies. On the parish, see Ryden, "One of the fertilest pleasantest Spotts."

37. St. Catherine's Parish Vestry Minutes, 1759–68, March 1, 1760, JA; Salley, *Minutes of the Vestry*, 9, April 22, 1728. On Beaufort, see Rowland, Moore, and Rogers, *History of Beaufort County*.

38. Circular Church, Registers of the Corporation, vol. 1, 1695–1796, 10, August 8, 1734, SCHS; St. Philip's Parish Vestry Minutes, 1756–74, October 13, 1766, SCDAH.

39. "Records of the Vestry," *Journal of the Barbados Museum* 14, no. 4 (1950): 198, May 1, 1700; 20, no. 3 (1953): 146; 20, no. 4 (1953): 187, September 7, 1727; St. Philip's Parish Vestry Minutes, 1732–55, 13, November 18, 1734, SCDAH. In the 1750s, the pew was still set aside for masters of merchantmen and king's officers and could be opened

to others after the voluntary if empty. See St. Philip's Parish Vestry Minutes, 1756–74, 11, November 9, 1756, SCDAH.

40. Salley, *Minutes of the Vestry*, 108, 1759.

41. St. Philip's Parish Vestry Minutes, 1756–74, October 16, 1766, SCDAH; Webber, "Peter Manigault's Letters," 271–72, February 20, 1750.

42. See the "Act for the Establishment of Religious Worship in this Province, according to the Church of England," printed in Dalcho, *Historical Account*, 447.

43. Fulham Papers, 9:171, Francis Varnod, St. George's. The Skene-Hague family had roots in Barbados.

44. Letters of Le Jau to the Secretary of the SPG, February 1, 1710, and June 13, 1710, quoted in Klingberg, *Appraisal of the Negro*, 16–17; Robert Stone to the Secretary of the SPG, March 22, 1751, quoted in Klingberg, *Appraisal of the Negro*, 93; Thomas Hasell to the Secretary of the SPG, August 18, 1712, quoted in Klingberg, *Appraisal of the Negro*, 31; Olwell, *Masters, Slaves, and Subjects*, 107.

45. On free people in the plantation colonies, see Cohen and Greene, *Neither Slave Nor Free*; Olwell, "Becoming Free."

46. Fulham Papers, 17:219–20 (John Kelly, St. Elizabeth's), 12:222–23 (Richard Marsden, St. John's), 17:230–31 (John Scott, St. Catherine's, Spanish Town), 17:224–25 (William May, Kingston), 18:45–52 (John Venn to Bishop Sherlock, June 15, 1751), 19:65–70 (W. Stafford to Bishop Porteus, Westmoreland, July 22, 1788). Moreover, Stafford reported that "they are remarkably well behaved and attentive, most of them have their Prayer Books and repeat the responses aloud and with propriety, and [I] never yet had occasion to check with Male or Female for any levity of conduct at Service."

47. One can also cautiously read that situation backward from the nineteenth century, using Handler, *Unappropriated People*, 154–71.

48. Morgan Godwyn, *The Negro's and Indians Advocate: Suing for their Admission into the Church* (London, 1680), 105, quoted in Frey and Wood, *Come Shouting to Zion*, 76.

49. Some would own pews in the antebellum period. William Ellison of Stateburg, South Carolina, owned a pew in Holy Cross Episcopal Church, in addition to nine hundred acres of land and sixty-three slaves. See Edgar, *South Carolina*, 309.

50. I would disagree with Sylvia Frey and Betty Wood on their point that blacks were consistently "seated separately." Evidence they offer from Virginia seems to show poor whites and blacks sharing space near the doors. They cite St. Michael's (Charles Town) move of its black worshippers as evidence of established segregated seating, when it seems more likely to be a moment of increasingly racialized thinking late in the period. See page 89 for further discussion of seating developments at St. Michael's.

51. "Records of the Vestry," *Journal of the Barbados Museum* 16, nos. 1 and 2 (1948–49): 62, February 1677. She would later remove a set of gallery stairs near the end of her pew that impeded her ingress.

52. "Records of the Vestry," *Journal of the Barbados Museum* 21, no. 3 (1954): 116, April 25, 1734.

53. Seating with or near their owners was common in Virginia. See Upton, *Holy Things and Profane*, 218.

54. St. Philip's Parish Vestry Minutes, 1756–74, March 22, 1756, SCDAH; "Records of the Vestry," *Journal of the Barbados Museum* 20, no. 4 (1953): 193, February 1, 1728; Klingberg, *Carolina Chronicle of Dr. Francis Le Jau*, 81.

55. Howe and Middleton, *Minutes of St. Michael's Church*, 108.

56. Handler, *Unappropriated People*, 169. The pew rent system remained a matter of controversy in Barbados until late in the nineteenth century. See Davis, "Pew Rents, People, and Parsons," in *Cross and Crown in Barbados*, 54–74.

57. Brathwaite, *Development of Creole Society*, 187; Matthews, *Religion in the Old South*, 205–6.

58. Part of this chapter was published as "Ritual Time in British Plantation Colonies, 1650–1780," *Church History: Studies in Christianity and Culture* 76 (2007): 541–68.

59. Thomas Nairne, *A Letter from South Carolina* (London, 1710), in Greene, *Selling a New World*, 42 ("Heats"); Glen, *Description of South Carolina*, 11; Nairne, *Letter from South Carolina*, 66 ("September"); Weir, *Colonial South Carolina*, 39 ("baked" and "4 months"); ibid., 262, quoting the younger William Bull; Bridenbaugh and Bridenbaugh, *No Peace Beyond the Line*, 124.

60. Mulcahy, *Hurricanes and Society*, 49; Pares, *West-India Fortune*, 114; Mulcahy, *Hurricanes and Society*, 89, 3; Steele, *English Atlantic*, 9, 26.

61. Nairne, *Letter from Carolina*, 39; *Further Observations*, 24 ("never"); John Norris, *Profitable Advice for Rich and Poor* (London, 1712), in Greene, *Selling a New World*, 103 ("Spring"). Norris also advised that to plant new land, a man "begins to prepare for it in the Beginning of Winter, or about *Michaelmas*, if his other Business permits him" (96).

62. Carney, *Black Rice*, 118–19, 121–22; Berlin, *Many Thousands Gone*, 146–47. The South Carolina Commons House of Assembly accommodated planter members by adjourning for a few weeks in planting and harvest seasons. See Sirmans, *Colonial South Carolina*, 241–42.

63. Pares, *A West-India Fortune*, 114.

64. Martin, *Essay on Plantership*, 30.

65. Craton and Walvin, *Jamaican Plantation*, 104–5.

66. Merrens and Terry, "Dying in Paradise," 541; Chaplin, *Anxious Pursuit*, 105 (figures for 1700–1750); Merrens and Terry, "Dying in Paradise," 548, quoting Joseph

Manigault in 1784; Raven, *London Booksellers and American Customers*, 21; Merrens and Terry, "Dying in Paradise," quoting Morrison, *Travels in the Confederation*, 2:172.

67. Weir, *Colonial South Carolina*, 171; Robertson, *Gone is the Ancient Glory*, 59. Indeed, there was a political crisis in 1688 when a member of the Assembly sought to leave the house to race his horse. The Assembly met between October and December. See also Brathwaite, *Development of Creole Society*, 50–51. On a less splendid level, whites like Thomas Thistlewood of Westmoreland parish in Jamaica could expect their service on quarterly court days to be relieved with food, drink, and sometimes raucous male gatherings. See Bernard, *Mastery, Tyranny, and Desire*, 83.

68. Robertson, *Gone is the Ancient Glory*, 109 ("social"); Craton and Walvin, *Jamaican Plantation*, 57, 84 ("sickly stink"); Sirmans, *Colonial South Carolina*, 241; Rogers, *Charleston*, 23, 114; Pearson, "Planters Full of Money," 307; Willis, *Charleston Stage*, 229–31.

69. Book of Common Prayer, in the section "Of Ceremonies, why some be abolished, and some retained."

70. The Conversion of St. Paul, St. Matthias, St. Mark, St. Philip and St. James, St. Barnabas, Nativity of St. John the Baptist, St. Luke, St. Simon and St. Jude, St. Andrew, St. Thomas, St. Stephen, St. John, Holy Innocents.

71. See the calendars in the front of any Book of Common Prayer from the period. I used *The Book of Common Prayer* (Oxford: Printed at the Theatre, 1688) and another printed at Oxford by the university printers in 1698.

72. The calendar and related issues are treated in Cressy, *Bonfires and Bells*. See particularly chap. 12, "The English Calendar in Colonial America," which treats Virginia and New England.

73. See Cressy, *Bonfire and Bells*, 193–96, for an account of the perseverance and weakening of the Anglican calendar in Virginia. On the ritual year in Europe generally, see Muir, *Ritual in Early Modern Europe*, 55–80.

74. On the English Sunday, see Parker, *English Sabbath*. While the town parishes of the plantation colonies had two services every Sunday, it is likely that relatively few of the rural parishes did with any regularity. The vestry of St. Michael in Barbados complained to the governor when their rector stopped preaching during the afternoon service, a duty that some ministers found difficult in the heat. "Records of the Vestry," *Journal of the Barbados Museum* 16, nos. 1 and 2 (1948–49), 59, August 26, 1676. Carolina ministers noted the difficulty of preaching in the heat in Williams, *St. Michael's, Charleston*, 23, and Fulham Papers, 9:160.

75. Trott, *Laws*, 354–55.

76. Ibid., 69–73. Passed 1712.

77. *South Carolina Gazette*, March 9, 1737, January 5, 1747. On Glen, see Robinson, *James Glen*.

78. Leslie, *New History of Jamaica*, 163.

79. Curtis Brett Letters, Summary of & extracts from 1775–80, 47–48, JA; Leslie, *New History of Jamaica*, 34. See also Long, *History of Jamaica*, 2:267.

80. *South Carolina Gazette*, February 19, 1732.

81. Howe and Middleton, *Minutes of St. Michael's Church*, 83, May 28, 1770. In late eighteenth-century Barbados, young men also "congregated in the church porch merely for the gratification" of seeing eligible young women, though "never entering to join in the service." See Orderson, *Creoleana*, 34.

82. Memorial plaque of Thomas Harrison, St. Michael's Church, Bridgetown, Barbados. He died in 1746. Author's visit, October 2005.

83. *Interesting Tracts*, 74. This is from General Venables's narrative of the Western Design. After the failure to take Santo Domingo, he was faulted for many things, including taking "too much state upon me at Barbados." See also the painting *The Governor Going to Church*, ca. 1740s, unsigned, in the collection of the Barbados Museum and Historical Society. It is reproduced in O'Shaughnessy, *Empire Divided*, 116.

84. John Taylor, *Multum in Parvo*, 511. On St. Catherine's parish church in Spanish Town and the colonial capital generally, see Robertson, *Gone is the Ancient Glory*, 69–70.

85. The Council of Barbados carefully guarded its right to control political speech in churches. It ordered that no minister "presume to publish in any church . . . any writing or writings . . . unless it be by order or Command from ye Governor, or Governor & Council." See Minutes of the Council, Lucas Transcripts, Reel 1, 196, February 26, 1656. Public Library of Barbados, hereafter PLB.

86. Richard Hall, *Acts*, 1, March 22, 1666.

87. See "An Act for the good governing of Servants, and ordaining the Rights between Masters and Servants" from 1661. So "that no person may pretend ignorance, in this Act or Statute. . . . It is lastly enacted and ordained . . . That the Minister of every Parish-church within this Island, twice every year, that is to say, the Sunday next before Christmas-day and the Sunday next before the five and twentieth day of June, distinctly read, and publish this Act, in their respective Parish-churches, upon pain of forfeiting five hundred pounds of Sugar." Ibid., 42.

88. Ibid., 112–21, August 8, 1688. By the mid-eighteenth century, the reading of acts in church was not always having its intended effect. "An Act for the better regulating of publishing all Laws and other Papers appointed to be read in Parochial Churches of this Island" allowed for more abbreviated summaries of legislation to be read instead. See ibid., 336–37, December 27,1744. It is also possible that the clerk read legislation.

89. Fulham Papers, 16:56–57. Renunciation of the Roman Church by Christopher Gilmor.

90. See "An Act to keep inviolate, and preserve the freedom of Elections," which directed that "the said Minister shall publish the said Writ or cause the same to be published as in the like cases hath been usual, in the Church of Chapel, of the said Parish, the three next succeeding Sundays." Richard Hall, *Acts*, 257, July 18, 1721. For churchwardens' management of elections in parish churches in Carolina, see Bolton, *Southern Anglicanism*, 148–49, and Olwell, *Masters, Slaves, and Subjects*, 104. See the *South Carolina Gazette*, March 10, 1733, for an Assembly election "on Tuesday the 20th Inst. at 10 o'clock in the Forenoon, in the Parish Church," in Charles Town.

91. See the successive articles of Webber, "Abstracts," *South Carolina Historical and Genealogical Magazine* 26, no. 2 (1925): 124–27; 27, no. 2 (1926): 91–94; 31, no. 1 (1930): 63–66; 31, no. 2 (1930): 154–57. Administrations were to be announced in the churches of St. Michael's, St. Andrew's, and St. Bartholomew's in these records.

92. Trott, *Laws*, 360–61; Leslie, *New History of Jamaica*, 170.

93. Richard Hall, *Acts*, 63–64 (passed in 1668; "many lewd"); John Taylor, *Multum in Parvo*, 517 ("chief day"); *South Carolina Gazette*, October 29, 1737 ("disorders in Punch-houses"); Eaden, *Memoirs of Père Labat*, 124 ("pleasure of watching"). On drinking and Sunday pastimes generally, see Underdown, *Revel, Riot, and Rebellion*.

94. *South Carolina Gazette*, October 29, 1737; Fulham Papers, 9:31–32 (Le Jau to Bishop Compton, May 27, 1712), 17:219–20 (John Kelly, St. Elizabeth's), 17:173–74 (James White, Kingston, March 5, 1724). On Sunday markets in the Leeward Islands, see Goevia, *Slave Society*, 238–39.

95. Port Royal Vestry Minutes, 1735–41, May 3, 1736, JA; Kingston Churchwarden's Accounts, 1722–59, July 21, 1730, JA; Orderson, *Creoleana*, 43. On Afro-Jamaican marketing systems, see Mintz and Hall, "Origins," and Sheridan, *Development of the Plantations*, 43. On black women and marketing in Barbados, see Beckles, *Natural Rebels*, 72–89.

96. Richard Hall, *Acts*, 112–21. From "An Act for the governing of Negroes," August 8, 1688. After a slave conspiracy scare in February 1686, the governor of Barbados had ordered planters to keep a better watch on Sundays, especially. See Craton, *Testing the Chains*, 111.

97. Port Royal Vestry Minutes, 1735–41, May 3, 1736, JA; *South Carolina Gazette*, March 9, 1737, May 1, 1756; Bolzius, "Reliable Answers," 234. Yet the grand jury there presented "the neglect of carrying arms to church and other places of worship, and against the bad custom of delivering their arms to negroes or other slaves to keep while they are at divine worship." *South Carolina Gazette*, May 1, 1756. Fines for "no arms in Church" can be found in Salley, *Minutes of the Vestry*, 89, ca. 1757.

98. Peter H. Wood, *Black Majority*, 313–14. The 1683 plot in Barbados was to have begun on Sunday; see Craton, *Testing the Chains*, 110.

99. Craton, *Testing the Chains*, 123.

100. In celebrating the major feasts and other holy days, some plantation parishes compared favorably with metropolitan practice. See Yates, *Buildings, Faith, and Worship*, 55–65.

101. Kingston Churchwarden's Accounts, 1722–59, April 20, 1725, January 14, 1724, JA. On Kingston's history, see Colin Clarke, *Kingston, Jamaica*.

102. Kingston Churchwarden's Accounts, 1722–59, February 5, 1723, JA; Port Royal Vestry Minutes, 1735–41, February 2, 1736, JA. See Port Royal Churchwarden's Accounts, 1766–93, June 6, 1786, JA, for a 3..9d charge "for Bushes & Bread for the Church," at Whitsuntide; St. Catherine's Vestry Minutes, 1759–68, with minutes of January 28, 1760, JA, for payments "To Dressing the Church at Xtmas." and "To Dressing the Church at Easter & Whitsuntide"; St. Michael's Church Records, Records of the Treasurer, Treasurer's Receipts/Vouchers, 1792, for payments "To Drayage for Christmas bushes & Negro hire" and "For Easter bushes to dress the church."

103. Fulham Papers, 15:206. Gordon of St. Michael's; "Records of the Vestry," *Journal of the Barbados Museum* 21, no. 3 (1954): 111, February 6, 1733. "Ordered that the churchwarden pay to the Rev. Mr. Wm. Johnson £35. current money for accommodating the Lent preachers this ensuing season of Lent." Similar notes can be found throughout the minutes.

104. Fulham Papers, 17:224–25 (William May, Kingston), 9:161, 171. A bad poem for Good Friday appeared in the *South Carolina Gazette* on April 1, 1751, noting that "this is a Week set apart for serious Contemplation."

105. Fulham Papers, 15:203–14.

106. Sloane, *Voyage to the Islands*, 2:lii. On slaves' celebrations at Christmas somewhat later, see Dirks, *Black Saturnalia*, 1–8.

107. Long, *History of Jamaica*, 2:491, note x; John Taylor, *Multum in Parvo*, 542; Fulham Papers, 17:185–88 (James White to Bishop Gibson, Vere parish, April 23, 1724); Craton, *Testing the Chains*, 129, 133. Bussa's Rebellion in Barbados in 1816 also began on Easter Sunday. Planning took place at Sunday dances and at a final dance on Good Friday. Ibid., 261.

108. Gaspar, *Bondmen and Rebels*, 185–86. The 1831 Baptist War in Jamaica was also partially precipitated by attempts to shorten the Christmas holidays. Mullin, *Africa in America*, 254.

109. Minutes of the Council, Lucas Transcripts, Reel 1, 43, August 1, 1654, PLB. On indentured servitude in Barbados, see Beckles, *White Servitude*.

110. Pinckney, *Letterbook of Eliza Lucas Pinckney*, 105, early 1759; *South Carolina Gazette*, May 27, 1751; Salley, "Letter from Dr. Tucker Harris,"; Curtis Brett Letters, Summary of & extracts from 1775–80, 19, JA.

111. Fulham Papers, 15:143–48 (Gordon to Gov. Lowther, April 26, 1717; "every Day"), 15:211 (Joseph Napleton, Gordon's curate at St. Michael's; "every morn"), 16:27–28 (William Johnson to Bishop Gibson, June 17, 1732; "unwilling"), 15:210 (Adam Justice, St. Peter's Parish; "divine Service" and "on Tuesdays"), 9:160 (Alexander Garden, St. Philip's, Charles Town); Hooker, *Carolina Backcountry*, 70–71, from Woodmason's "Account of South Carolina" in the Fulham material, 1766; Fulham Papers, 17:215–16 (Calvin Galpine of Port Royal), 17:224–25 (William May, Kingston), 17:222–23 (Richard Marsden, St. John's; "Chapel in Spanish Town"), 17:230–31 (John Scott, St. Catherine's, Spanish Town). See Leslie, *New History of Jamaica*, 283, for notes on the death of James Hay, chief justice of the island, who never "neglected his Family Devotions." The lack of weekday and holy day services in the rural parishes of the plantation world is similar to contemporary rural English practice, where distance and the nature of agricultural work also resulted in less frequent corporate prayer than was to be found in towns and cities. See Gregory, "Church of England," 237.

112. Fulham Papers, 15:203–14, 15:211 (Joseph Napleton, curate of St. Michael's); Minutes of the Council, Lucas Transcripts, Reel 2, Section 2, 15, Meeting of November 5, 1684, PLB; Fulham Papers, 17:211–35, 9:160–71. St. Michael's in Charles Town would have holy day worship after its opening in 1761.

113. Klingberg, *Carolina Chronicle of Dr. Francis Le Jau*, 86, To the Secretary, February 9, 1711.

114. Amussen, *Caribbean Exchanges*, 116, quoting Lord Francis Russell to Lords of Trade, March 23, 1695, CO 28/2/81, Colonial Office, National Archives of the United Kingdom.

115. Mark M. Smith, "Remembering Mary, Shaping Revolt," 521–30. See also Thornton, "African Dimensions of the Stono Rebellion."

116. Craton, *Testing the Chains*, 121.

117. Hooker, *Carolina Backcountry*, 30, 1767; 33, 1768; 30, 1767.

118. First Consistory Book, St. John the Baptist Lutheran Church, 2, SCHS. This was joined to a recommendation that "the minister should also take care not to refute the Anglican Church in public sermons." Presumably he continued to do so in private. On Lutherans in Carolina and elsewhere, see Roeber, *Palatines, Liberty, and Property*.

119. Kingston Vestry Minutes, 1750–52, 159, January 14, 1750, SCHS; "Records of the Vestry," *Journal of the Barbados Museum* 22, no. 1 (1954), 48, January 17, 1737; St. Philip's Parish Vestry Minutes, 1756–74, 20, 26 July 1746, SCDAH. On church music, see Williams, "Charleston Church Music."

120. *South Carolina Gazette*, January 27, 1733, November 16, 1753.

121. Yorke, *Diary of John Baker*, 79, December 27, 1754.

122. *South Carolina Gazette*, December 25, 1740. For a similar celebration in

Dorchester with sermon and entertainment, see ibid., May 15, 1755. For Beaufort, see ibid., January 10, 1752.

123. "Records of the Vestry," *Journal of the Barbados Museum* 20, no. 3 (1953), 139, March 26, 1726. They were rung on Sunday as well. On festive bell ringing in early modern England, see Cressy, *Bonfires and Bells*, 68–80. For bells in early America, see Rath, *How Early America Sounded*, 43–50.

124. John Taylor, *Multum in Parvo*, 585; St. Michael's Parish Register, 1771–94, 244, July 12, 1780, BA. A similar moment is recorded for the arrival of Edward Hay on June 8, 1773. See ibid., 28, June 8, 1773, BA. Cunningham would be evaluated as decidedly less than righteous by the Barbadian political class.

125. Fulham Papers, 17:207–08. William May's answers as commissary to the bishop's queries. He also noted that his wife "was kill'd in my Arms in the Hurricane."

126. Barham, *Account of Jamaica* 271, West Indies Collection, University of the West Indies, Mona, Jamaica, Reproduction of British Library Sloane MS 3918.

127. Fulham Papers, 17:230–31 (John Scott, St. Catherine's, Spanish Town), 17:221 (Nicholas McCalman, St. Thomas's in the East).

128. Leslie, *New History of Jamaica*, 274. Writing in the 1770s, Edward Long wrote that the June 7 fast "still continues." See Long, *History of Jamaica*, 2:143.

129. Fulham Papers, 9:98–99 (William T. Bull to Robinson, December 19, 1720).

130. *South Carolina Gazette,* June 29, 1738, May 31, 1740, June 29, 1738, May 31, 1740, November 20, 1740, January 20, 1746.

131. Ibid., May 1, 1756. A fast "to implore the Divine Being to send us Rain" was declared in 1733. See ibid., September 1, 1733. Another was declared in 1743 on receiving news of war with France. See ibid., March 14, 1743.

132. William Hutson Diary, 1757–61, SCHS.

133. *Barbados Mercury*, April 19, 1783, PLB. A St. George's Society convened for similar purposes in Charles Town in 1733. See Bowes, *Culture of Early Charleston*, 120.

134. *South Carolina Gazette,* November 29, 1738. Alexander Skene was the president.

135. Ibid., March 13, 1749 (Dumbleton ode); "Records of the Vestry," *Journal of the Barbados Museum* 20, no. 4 (1953), 198, April 11, 1728 (organist pay); Moreton, *West India Customs and Manners*, 34 ("mirth and cheerfulness"). See Jonathan Z. Smith, *To Take Place*, 94–95. Here he cites Stefan Czarnowski's work on the cult of St. Patrick in Ireland, showing that "in the processes of forming a national community, the celebrations of those heroes whose feast days are marked out in time, rather than being distributed in different places, supply the unifying occasions. It is through structures of temporality, as ritualized, that the divisiveness and particularity of space are overcome." Czarnowski, *Le Culte*.

136. Jonathan Z. Smith, *To Take Place*, 94.

137. On the naturalization of the constructed, see Bourdieu, *Outline*, 164–69. For the creation of Carolina's parish boundaries and communities, see Duff, "Designing Carolina."

138. Jonathan Z. Smith, *To Take Place*, 109. Smith also points out that "Ritual gains force where incongruency is perceived and thought about," making it an especially important form of human behavior for elites in a colonial slave society (109).

Chapter 3. Marriage and Baptism in the British Plantation Colonies

1. This was generally less true in South Carolina than in the island colonies, though true for some people some of the time there as well. For Jamaica, see Burnard, "Failed Settler Society."

2. In this school, see Bridenbaugh and Bridenbaugh, *No Peace Beyond the Line*; Dunn, *Sugar and Slaves*; Patterson, *Sociology of Slavery*; Peter H. Wood, *Black Majority*. But compare Gragg, *Englishmen Transplanted*; Greene, *Imperatives, Behaviors, and Identities*, 13–112; and his helpful review "Society and Economy," which deals with some of the above works.

3. A version of this chapter was published as "Domestic Rituals: Marriage and Baptism in the British Plantation Colonies," *Anglican and Episcopal History* 76 (2007): 327–57.

4. "T. Walduck's Letters from Barbados, 1710," 44.

5. See, for instance, the "Journal of Josiah Quincy, Junior," 463, for that New Englander's observation in Carolina that the "enjoyment of a negro or mulatto woman is spoken of as quite a common thing."

6. On marriage and reproduction in England, see Stone, *Family, Sex, and Marriage*, and Cressy, *Birth, Marriage, and Baptism*. For marriage ritual generally, see Stevenson, *Nuptial Blessing*, and Muir, *Ritual in Early Modern Europe*, 31–44.

7. Fulham Papers, 17:238–41 (Calvin Galpine of Port Royal, Jamaica, to Bishop Gibson, September 29, 1725; "Journey"), 9:108–9 (John Barnwell to Governor Nicholson, including petitions from the wardens and vestry of St. Helena's parish), 10:209–22 (a document on the backcountry by Charles Woodmason; "marry people . . . as they please"), 10:168–85 (a remonstrance submitted to the Assembly in 1767, perhaps also written by him; "vilest Abominations"); Hooker, *Carolina Backcountry*, 15, 56, journal entries of January 25, 1767, and August 12, 1768 ("numbers accepted").

8. The 1662 Book of Common Prayer's "Form of Solemnization of Matrimony" directed that "the Persons to be married shall come into the body of the Church with their friends and neighbors." Moreover, the Canons of 1604 required marriage in church. See Cardwell, *Synodalia*, 282, canon 62.

9. Stone, *Uncertain Unions*, 4, 13. Matters concerning marriage, sex, and separation were tried by diocesan consistory courts, using the canon law inherited from the medieval church. Chancery courts had jurisdiction in matters related to marriage settlements and trusts (13).

10. See Richard Hall, *Acts*, 241–42, for "An Act to quiet the minds of the Inhabitants of this Island, against the terrors and apprehensions they are under of a Spiritual Court; and to provide that no Ecclesiastical Law or Jurisdiction, shall have power to enforce, confirm or establish any penal mulct or Punishment in any case whatsoever, within this Island," legislation that alleged that such a court would "clash with the municipal laws of this Island, embarrass the Government, vex and torment the Gentry, depauperate the substantial Freeholders, and ruin the common People." For context, see Findling, "Lowther-Gordon Controversy." For the Jamaican legislation, see *Laws of Jamaica*, 337–39, for a law prohibiting the bishop of London from gaining any "juridical authority or coercion, either spiritual or temporal, over the lay inhabitants of this island." On colonial governors' ecclesiastical authority and commissarial courts' unpopularity in the thirteen colonies, see James B. Bell, *Imperial Origins*, 26–57, 65–71.

11. For instance, see Fulham Papers, 17:219–20 (John Kelly, St. Elizabeth's parish in Jamaica, response to queries). He complained that the lack of an "Ecclesiastical Law" left the clergy like "soldiers going to war without weapons."

12. St. John Vestry Minutes, 1649–99, 114, May 13, 1692, Shilstone Library, Barbados Museum and Historical Society, Barbados, hereafter BMHS. From the vestry's resolution to find a house for the minister closer to the parish church.

13. Cressy, *Birth, Marriage, and Baptism*, 190.

14. "T. Walduck's Letters from Barbados, 1710," 43–44.

15. "An Act for the Better Encouragement of the Clergy," in Richard Hall, *Acts*, 161–62. While the 5 shilling fee for a church wedding was unchanged in 1764, the fee for other places had risen to £1, strongly suggesting that few persons were being married in church. See Richard Hall, *Abridgement of the Acts*, 25. This is bound with Hall's *Acts* in the copy at the Barbados Archives in Black Rock.

16. "T. Walduck's Letters from Barbados, 1710," 43–44. The Canons of 1604 permitted marriage "between the hours of eight and twelve in the forenoon." See Cardwell, *Synodalia*, 282, canon 62.

17. "An Act for Preventing Clandestine Marriages," in Richard Hall, *Acts*, 299–300. Clandestine marriages were those solemnized without due notification of parents and members of the community, either by omitting the publication of banns, obtaining a fraudulent license, or simply convincing a clergyman to conduct the service without either.

18. Fulham Papers, 18:228–33 (Account of "The State of the Church in Jamaica," ca. 1722), 18:151–52 (Alexander Campbell of Kingston, April 23, 1808); "Historical Notes,"

173, from "Records of the Burden Family," noted in their Bible and printed in that section of the journal; Webber, "Journal of Robert Pringle," 101.

19. See the parish register edited by Mabel L. Webber and printed in Bridges and Williams, *St. James Santee Plantation Parish*, 351–80. This register is one of few church records that consistently noted the location of weddings and thus permits meaningful counting.

20. St. Michael's Parish Register, 1648–1702, 483–84, BA.

21. Fulham Papers, 17:159–60 (Edward Reading to Mr. Dean, February 13, 1723). This letter is not calendared in Manross, *Fulham Papers in the Lambeth Palace Library*.

22. St. John's Parish Register, Marriages, 1657–1848, BA. The very late eighteenth century may have seen a shift back toward weddings in church in Barbados, perhaps as much for whites as for persons of color. See St. Philip's Parish Register, Marriages, 1672–1848, 54, ca. 1778, BA. Here the clerk temporarily recorded the location of a dozen weddings, ten of which were in the church. The records for this parish in the 1820s reveal a majority of weddings in the church, then in the rectory, and then in the church by the end of the 1830s. It is inadvisable to generalize on this limited evidence, however.

23. A general analysis of the frequency of marriage by banns or license is not possible, since many parish registers only inconsistently took note of either that choice or the location of the nuptials. In England after the Restoration, "virtually all the middling sort and above were married by license, but the cost put it out of reach of the lower classes." Stone, *Uncertain Unions*, 22.

24. Fulham Papers, 10:153–54 (Notes attributed to Charles Martyn, April 11, 1762); St. James's Santee Parish Register in Bridges and Williams, *St. James Santee Plantation Parish*, 351–80; Smith and Salley, *Register of St. Philip's Parish*; "T. Walduck's Letters from Barbados, 1710," 43. The term "Ordinary" refers to the official holding some of the powers of a diocesan bishop.

25. St. James's Parish Register, 1693–1825, 8, March 3, 1696, BA.

26. Christ Church Parish Register, Marriages, 1643–1848, BA. At St. John's in Barbados, the clerk only noted banns or license in 1790, in which six of seven marriages were by license. The quotation on brides' response to the higher license fee is found in Orderson, *Creoleana*, 29–30. In the preface to this novel, Orderson insists that "his materials are all (with the exception of one incident) drawn from facts, which are as closely adhered to as the nature of the subject would admit" (20). See also Schomburgk, *History of Barbados*, 339.

27. Hooker, *Carolina Backcountry*, 89; Klingberg, *Carolina Chronicle of Dr. Francis La Jau*, 175, To the Secretary, March 19, 1716. See ibid., 150–52, To the Secretary, March 12, 1715, for complaints about three marriages solemnized by other clergy by license in Le Jau's parish. The matches were of a man to his brother's widow (not permitted by the Church of England), of a young man and a fourteen-year-old orphan girl whose guard-

ian did not approve, and a local woman to a young man already married to a woman in Barbados.

28. St. James's Parish Register, 1693–1825, 11, November 28, 1696, BA; St. Andrew's Parish Register, Marriages, 1666–1806, 31, January 16, 1741, BA; St. Philip's Parish Register, Marriages, 1672–1848, 46, August 29, 1764, BA; Brathwaite, *Development of Creole Society*, 188–89. J. W Orderson of Barbados recorded the (perhaps apocryphal) story of a minister publishing the banns of marriage between a young widow and suitor who had been courting in church, neither of whom had requested such publication and both of whom were embarrassed by it. When they angrily questioned him about it, he replied that if they did not "like to wait for three publications," they should "procure the license . . . and then the whole matter may be settled as soon as to-morrow." See Orderson, *Creoleana*, 149–50.

29. Fulham Papers, 9:92–93 (William Tredwell Bull to Thomas Mangey, May 12, 1730), 9:102 (Petition of the Clergy of South Carolina to Governor Nicholson, January 10, 1722), 10:139–40 (Michael Smith to Bishop Sherlock, May 13, 1753).

30. Klingberg, *Carolina Chronicle of Dr. Francis Le Jau*, 143, To the Secretary, July 4, 1714.

31. Webber, "Records of the Quakers," 192. A peculiar poem in the *South Carolina Gazette*, May 13, 1732, dwelt on the efficacy of a dissenting minister's officiating at weddings, arguing that "the long *Surplice*" and the "short *Cloak*" were "effectual alike in the conjugal yoke," transforming "the chaste blushing *Maid*" into "a virtuous *Mother*." The writer affirmed that both Anglican and dissenting ministers could "induce the *gravely precise* / To believe a *brisk girl* 'tween the Sheets, is no vice." Thus the same happiness could be expected, "to which ever of *these* w' apply to befriend us."

32. "T. Walduck's Letters from Barbados, 1710," 44.

33. "Autobiographical Manuscript of William Senhouse," *Journal of the Barbados Museum* 2, no. 3 (1935): 120; Fulham Papers, 17:185–88 (James White to Bishop Gibson, April 23, 1724); *South Carolina Gazette,* July 15, 1751; Salley, *Marriage Notices*, 9, September 5, 1743 (the wedding of Elizabeth Street and John Goodwin), 5, April 29, 1732, and 11, May 10, 1768 (wedding of Nicholas Slidell and Polly Hyeth). Readers of colonial newspapers could follow the ritual lives of English royalty from afar. The *South Carolina Gazette* for December 1, 1737, covered in detail the lavish baptism of the Princess Augusta, a royal granddaughter, noting that the font and flagons were brought from the Tower. The August 4, 1739 edition corrected mistakes in the report of the baptism of Prince Edward Augustus. Both articles listed godparents and noted the lateness of the hour, at 8:00 and 9:00 in the evening respectively.

34. "Autobiographical Manuscript of William Senhouse," *Journal of the Barbados Museum* 2, no. 3 (1935): 120.

35. Fulham Papers, 15:292–93 (Arthur Holt to Bishop Gibson, November 17, 1730).

36. See Laing, "Very Immoral and Offensive Man." See various letters on the matter in Fulham Papers, 9: 206–13, 216–17.

37. *South Carolina Gazette*, August 15, 1743. See Burnard, "Inheritance and Independence."

38. On clandestine marriage in England, see Stone, *Uncertain Unions*, 22–30.

39. Trott, *Laws*, 413, "An Act for the Maintenance of Ministers, and the Poor, and Erecting and Repairing of Churches," ca. 1682. See Long, *History of Jamaica*, 2:237–38, for a general discussion of the Jamaican law of marriage.

40. Richard Hall, *Acts*, 299–300, "An Act for Preventing Clandestine Marriages," 1734; 320–21, "An Additional Act for Preventing Clandestine Marriages," 1739.

41. Fulham Papers, 17:272–73 (William May to Bishop Gibson, May 30, 1737), 9:216–17 (W. T. Bull to Bishop Gibson, May 13, 1728), 9:67–68 (Bishop Robinson's instructions).

42. Fulham Papers, 16:27–28 (William Johnson to Bishop Gibson, June 17, 1732; "by marrying"), 17:33 (Thomas Lyttleton to Governor La Bruere, October 8, 1771; "advantage"), 17:53–54 (William May to Bishop Sherlock, July 21, 1751).

43. Knight, *History of Jamaica c. 1743*, 29; Long, *History of Jamaica*, 2:414–15 (emphasis in original); Ashley River Baptist Church, Records, 1736–69, September 10, 1739, Baptist Historical Collection, Furman University; John Taylor, *Multum in Parvo*, 504.

44. Fulham Papers, 17:193–94 (Edward Reading to Bishop Gibson, from Sixteen Mile Walk, May 26, 1724); Klingberg, *Carolina Chronicle of Dr. Francis Le Jau*, 55, To the Secretary, March 22, 1709, and 149–50, To the Secretary, March 12, 1715; Fulham Papers, 10:28–31 (Alexander Garden to the Bishop of London, June 4, 1736). One pair of Roman Catholics in St. Andrew's parish in Jamaica were required to abjure the tenets of their faith in 1704 before the minister of that parish was willing to marry them. See the marriage section of the St. Andrew's Parish Register, 23–24, JA.

45. Slave marriages in the Church of England became much more common in the West Indies during the period of amelioration. See Minter, *Episcopacy Without Episcopate*, 154–55.

46. St. Philip's Parish Register, Marriages, 1672–1848, 2, October 19, 1676, BA, "George Street and Mary Parr Negroes"; Christ Church Parish, Marriages, 1643–1848, 87, August 4, 1700, BA; St. Andrew's Parish Register, 1709–1856, 63, September 3, 1738, transcript, SCDAH. On free persons of color in Carolina before 1790, see Olwell, "Becoming Free."

47. St. Andrew's Parish Register, Marriages, 1666–1806. In the period before 1780, the marriages of persons of color were recorded on April 7, 1698, January 16, 1741, October 11, 1747, December 24, 1749, January 21, 1753, August 12, 1753, April 20, 1765,

October 18, 1770, January 1, 1771, October 28, 1779, December 19, 1779, and January 9, 1780.

48. Fulham Papers, 17:248–57 (G. [Marquis] Duquesne to [Henry] Newman, May 15, 1728). In the same volume, see James White's letter at 246–47, in which he suggests that sex between masters and slave women made the baptism of slaves impossible.

49. On baptism in early modern Europe, see Muir, *Ritual in Early Modern Europe*, 20–27.

50. Coster, *Baptism and Spiritual Kinship*, 74.

51. Fulham Papers, 9:108–9 (John Barnwell of Beaufort to Governor Nicholson, March 16, 1723), 10:138 (Churchwardens and Vestry of Prince Frederick Parish to Bishop Sherlock, October 23, 1751), 15:74–75 (Alexander Garden to Bishop Gibson, July 24, 1731); Hooker, *Carolina Backcountry*, 13, journal entry of January 25, 1767. On other occasions, he baptized twenty-seven and sixty children at one time. See ibid., 17, 22.

52. Hooker, *Carolina Backcountry*, 25; Fulham Papers, 17:27–28 (Alexander Richardson to Bishop Terrick, June 23, 1766; "near a Thousand"), 15:237–38 (Arthur Holt to Bishop Gibson, April 5, 1726; "had several Occasions" and "a great many children"); Duke, *Course of Plain and Familiar Lectures*, 83 ("Christian burial"). The author, a rector of St. Thomas's parish in Barbados, attributed this sentiment to "many ignorant Christians."

53. Fulham Papers, 18:228–33 (Account of "The State of the Church in Jamaica," ca. 1722). On the importance of baptism in early New England, see Hall and Brown, "Family Strategies and Religious Practice."

54. Fulham Papers, 9:1–2 (Nicholas Trott to Archbishop Tenison, February 17, 1703); Klingberg, *Carolina Chronicle of Dr. Francis Le Jau*, 58, To the Secretary of the SPG, August 5, 1709; St. Andrew's Parish Register, 1709–1856, 34, June 22, 1736, transcript, SCDAH. See the latter source for the baptism of Elizabeth Butler, "(Per Dipping)," 40, February 29, 1743.

55. Klingberg, *Carolina Chronicle of Dr. Francis Le Jau*, 98–99, September 5, 1711; Records of the Welsh Neck Baptist Church, 1737–1935, 9, April 4, 1761, South Caroliniana Library, hereafter SCL. They were surprisingly less demanding of former paedobaptists, admitting them to Eucharistic fellowship without adult immersion baptism "upon their signing such a covenant as shall be thought proper by the Church."

56. Klingberg, *Carolina Chronicle*, 28. Johnston to the Bishop of Salisbury, September 20, 1708. On the English controversy over the sign of the cross, see Cressy, *Birth, Marriage, and Death*, 124–38.

57. Hooker, *Carolina Backcountry*, 46, 1768; Klingberg, *Carolina Chronicle of Dr. Francis Le Jau*, 37. Here Le Jau celebrates his baptism of "several Quakers" in a letter to the Secretary of the SPG, March 13, 1708.

58. Perhaps challenged by some, William Duke apparently justified the use of the

sign of the cross to his congregation in Barbados. See Duke, *A Course of Plain and Familiar Lectures*, 70–71.

59. "T. Walduck's Letters from Barbados, 1710," 44. This is an overstatement.

60. St. James's Parish Register, Baptisms, 1693–1825, BA. Baptisms noted at "my house" occurred on September 17, 1699, October 1, 1699, October 15, 1699 (an infant and an adult), January 9, 1700, and December 1, 1700. Baptisms at the three other locations occurred on September 19, 1699, April 1, 1699, and April 28, 1711.

61. Fulham Papers, 17:185–88 (James White to Bishop Gibson, April 23, 1724), 10:153–54 (Notes attributed to Charles Martyn, April 11, 1762).

62. St. Michael's Parish Register, 1771–94, 347, July 1, 1783, BA. See the reminder from one Barbadian minister of the better practice, in his mind, of baptizing in church; "no other place is so proper for the purpose as the church," in Duke, *A Course of Plain and Familiar Lectures*, 2.

63. On baptismal parties in England, see Heal, *Hospitality in Early Modern England*, 80–81, 367–68.

64. Brandow, "Diary of Joseph Senhouse," *Journal of the Barbados Museum* 37, no. 4 (1986): 381, entry of January 15, 1777.

65. Fulham Papers, 15:215–16 (Arthur Holt to Bishop Gibson, April 30, 1725).

66. St. James's Parish Register, Baptisms, 1693–1825, 16, November 27, 1698, and 41, December 11, 1711, BA.

67. St. Michael's Parish Register, 1702–39, 87, January 1, 1711, BA.

68. "T. Walduck's Letters from Barbados, 1710," 44.

69. Orderson, *Creoleana*, 25. The wife of an early nineteenth-century governor of Jamaica served wine and cake after the baptisms of both slaves and her own children. See Wright, *Lady Nugent's Journal*, 38, 126.

70. Minutes of the Council, Lucas Transcripts, 211–13, ca. May 1686, PLB.

71. Campbell, *Church in Barbados*, 156.

72. See Cressy, *Birth, Marriage, and Death*, 164–72. The quotation is at 171 and comes from Ward, *London-Spy*, 393–412.

73. Fulham Papers, 17:185–88 (James White to Bishop Gibson, April 23, 1724).

74. Letter from John Wigan to George Wigan, October 20, 1739, JA.

75. "T. Walduck's Letters from Barbados, 1710," 44.

76. The inscription reads "Baptiserium hoc Ecclesiae Christi in Insula Barbados honoratissimus Dus. D. Thomas Lewis J. S. Armiger Regis Majestatais Secretionibus Concilys in praedicta insa D.D.D. a partu Christi. MDCLIV." See Farrar, "Christ Church," 143.

77. St. John's Parish, Vestry Minutes, 1649–99, 83, November 11, 1685, BMHS. Other Barbados fonts worth note include that at St. Lucy's in Barbados, inscribed with the name of Susana Haggatt, its donor in 1747, and that of St. Peter in Speightstown,

in marble, a "gift of John Sober, Esq., to the parish of St. Peter, 1767." See Reece and Clark-Hunt, *Barbados Diocesan History*, 101, 98. The font in St. James is inscribed "Dedit Ricardus Walter to the church of St. Iames Anno 1684." Oliver, *Monumental Inscriptions*, 136.

78. St. Michael's Parish Register, 1702–39, 1715, BA.

79. St. James's Parish Register, Baptisms, 1693–1825, 19, September 3, 1699, BA. In the same parish, in the brief period in which baptismal locations were noted, white infants were baptized in church on March 29, 1700, and January 21, 1711.

80. St. Michael's Parish Register, 1702–39, 98, July 26, 1712; 100, October 22, 1712, BA. See also the baptisms of Elizabeth Brown and Mary Ball, "Poor Children at Church," and an unnamed "poor Girl at Church," at 175, April 24 and May 25, 1719.

81. Fulham Papers, 9:178–79 (John LaPierre to Bishop Gibson, January 1, 1726).

82. Williams, "Letters to the Bishop," 127–28, Alexander Garden, May 24, 1725.

83. Klingberg, *Carolina Chronicle*, 163–64. Both Johnston's letter to London and a letter from Burnham to Johnston are printed here.

84. Hooker, *Carolina Backcountry*, April 21, 1767.

85. Fulham Papers, 15:47–48. A baptismal certificate signed by the residents of Harbour Island, October 20, 1727. This was accomplished with "Exhortations Suitable to be given to Such Converts."

86. Klingberg, *Carolina Chronicle of Dr. Francis Le Jau*, 86, To the Secretary, February 9, 1711.

87. St. Andrew's Parish Register, Baptisms, 1666–1807, 92–93, 1777, JA.

88. St. Philip's Parish Register, Baptisms, 1648–1835, 174, November 8, 1772, BA.

89. On the social pretensions of colonial clergy, see Laing, "All Things to All Men."

90. St. Andrew's Parish Register, Baptisms 1666–1807, 61–63, 1740–43, and 60–61, 1739, JA; St. James's Parish Register, Baptisms, 1693–1825, 24, December 1, 1700, BA.

91. For godparenthood in England, see Coster, *Baptism and Spiritual Kinship*, 79–97, and Bailey, *Sponsors at Baptism and Confirmation*.

92. "T. Walduck's Letters from Barbados, 1710," 44. This is a somewhat peculiar comment, three being a very typical number of godparents.

93. "Autobiographical Manuscript of William Senhouse," *Journal of the Barbados Museum* 2, no. 3 (1935): 120. Three of the child's grandparents filled out the group.

94. Fulham Papers, 15:33–34 (G. Phenney to Gibson, April 14, 1725).

95. Brandow, "Diary of Joseph Senhouse," *Journal of the Barbados Museum* 37, no. 4 (1986): 384.

96. St. Michael's Parish Register, 1702–39, 297, October 10, 1727, BA. On patronage and clientage in baptism, see Coster, *Baptism and Spiritual Kinship*, 144–55.

97. For a typical explanation of the duties and importance of godparents, see Duke, *Course of Plain and Familiar Lectures*, 66–69.

98. Fulham Papers, 17:185–88 (James White to Bishop Gibson, April 23, 1724), 15:33–34 (G. Phenney to Bishop Gibson, April 14, 1725). The bishop seems to have replied with an assurance that emergency baptism by laypeople was valid. See ibid., 15:43–44.

99. D. E. Huger Smith, ed., "Broughton Letters," 175, a letter of December 5, 1716.

100. Salley, "Quaint Record," 298. This is a translation from the German of a document owned by a member of the Stabler family in Calhoun County, South Carolina. It is related to the immediate family of Gottlieb Stabler, born in 1732. It also includes a "Thanksgiving for a Baptism Received."

101. Hooker, *Carolina Backcountry*, 36. At other times, he read to the congregation from Samuel Bradford's *Discourse Concerning Baptismal and Spiritual Regeneration* (London, 1709). Hooker, *Carolina Backcountry*, 56. See also Duke, *Course of Plain and Familiar Lectures*.

102. Klingberg, *Carolina Chronicle*, 28, Johnston to the bishop of Salisbury, September 20, 1708, and 56, Johnston to the Secretary of the SPG, July 5, 1710; Fulham Papers, 9:206 (Brian Hunt to Bishop Gibson, February 20, 1728). On French Calvinists in Carolina and elsewhere, see Butler, *Huguenots in America*.

103. Klingberg, *Carolina Chronicle of Dr. Francis Le Jau*, 54–55, To the Secretary, March 22, 1709. Some reported "difficulty" when they sought "to find Sureties to present and answer for them." For the canons, see Cardwell, *Synodalia*, 260, canon 29.

104. Williams, "Letters to the Bishop," 138, Alexander Garden, April 20, 1731.

105. Ibid., 144, February 25, 1732.

106. "Autobiographical Manuscript of William Senhouse," *Journal of the Barbados Museum* 2, no. 3 (1935): 120.

107. Entries in the Ellcock Family Bible, 1755–1846, BMHS.

108. Curtis Brett Letters, 1775–80, JA.

109. Samuel Peyre Commonplace Book, 1740–1818, SCHS. Peyre was born in 1715. His descendents later in the eighteenth century added information on other baptisms in the family, including a girl born in 1777 and baptized "without a name," on account of her evident weakness.

110. See the acts establishing the Church of England. In Barbados, no act seems to specify the necessity of recording baptisms but see the order of the Council of Barbados in 1685 that ministers do a more complete job of reporting baptisms and burials to the lieutenant governor every year, in Minutes of the Council, Lucas Transcripts, 134, December 15, 1685, PLB. Their basic establishment law is "An Act or Order for the Publication and Execution of the Acts concerning the uniformity of Common Prayer," in Richard Hall, *Acts*. For Jamaica, see "An Act for the Maintenance of Ministers and the Poor, and Erecting and Repairing of Churches," in *Laws of Jamaica*, 20–25; for South Carolina, see the "Act for the Establishment of Religious

Worship in this Province, according to the Church of England," printed in Dalcho, *Historical Account*, 437–54.

111. Fulham Papers, 17:39 (Thomas Lyttleton to Bishop Terrick, June 27, 1775; "Thanks for safe Deliverance"), 17:207–8 (William May's answers to commissary queries); Klingberg, *Carolina Chronicle*, 67, Johnston to the Secretary of the SPG, January 27, 1711; Fulham Papers, 9:237–38 (Brian Hunt to Bishop Gibson, September 8, 1729).

112. Klingberg, *Carolina Chronicle of Dr. Francis Le Jau*, 150, To the Secretary, March 12, 1715 ("hardly speak"); Fulham Papers, 15:259 (A. Holt to Bishop Gibson, December 21, 1727); Klingberg, *Carolina Chronicle of Dr. Francis Le Jau*, 112, Le Jau to the Secretary, May 26, 1712; ibid., 173, To the Secretary, March 19, 1716; St. Andrew's Parish Register, 1709–1856, 29, June 30, 1732, transcript, SCDAH ("a little negro girl").

113. St. James's Parish Register, Baptisms, 1693–1825, 54, November 29, 1719; 99, July 17, 1734, BA ("Mr. Littler Roe").

114. Amussen, *Caribbean Exchanges*, 5.

115. Larry Gragg has found records of 135 blacks baptized in the surviving seventeenth-century parish registers of Barbados. See Gragg, *Englishmen Transplanted*, 164. On the free people of Barbados, see Handler, *Unappropriated People*. Chap. 7, "The Religious System: Churches and Christianity," is helpful in showing how free persons identified with the Church of England more than any other denomination.

116. Fulham Papers, 15:215–16 (Arthur Holt to Bishop Gibson, April 30, 1725), 15:292–93 (A. Holt to Bishop Gibson, November 17, 1730).

117. St. Philip's Parish Register, Baptisms, 1648–1835, 94, May 20, 1716. They were John Quaco, Robert, Robin, James, Jeremeach, Francis, Richard, Christian, Catharine, Silvia, Elizabeth, and Charles.

118. St. Joseph's Parish Register, Baptisms, 1718–1836, 63, December 25, 1784, BA.

119. Fulham Papers, 16:174–75 (Clergy of Barbados to Bishop Porteus, September 26, 1788). Similarly in Bermuda in the 1780s, though resistance by whites to the public baptism of slaves was still a reality, one clergyman claimed to have baptized two thousand slaves during his ministry on that small Atlantic island. See ibid., 17:45–46 (Alexander Richardson to Bishop Porteus, May 13, 1789).

120. Ibid., 17:159–60 (Edward Reading to Mr. Dean, February 13, 1723). This letter is not calendared in the otherwise helpful Manross collection. He later reported that he had "baptiz'd Sevral." See ibid., 17:193–94 (Edward Reading to Bishop Gibson, May 26, 1724).

121. Ibid., 17:232–33 (James Spenie, answers to queries). He had also done so in the parishes of St. Ann's and St. George's.

122. Ibid., 17:224–25 (William May, answers to queries; "vast Variety"), 17:230–31 (John Scott, answers to queries), 17:234–35 (James White, answers to queries).

123. Ibid., 18:45–52 (John Venn to Bishop Sherlock, June 15, 1751). He had slaves

of his own who had refused offers of baptism, "who therefore are not christen'd to this Day."

124. Ibid., 18:1–2 (Lewis de Bomeval to Bishop Gibson, May 28, 1740), 18:65–70 (W. Stafford to Bishop Porteus, 22 July 1788). Edward Long put baptismal fees at £1..3..9. See Long, *History of Jamaica*, 2:429.

125. Ibid., 2:28.

126. See the Church Act of 1706 in Dalcho, *Historical Account*, 447.

127. Klingberg, *Carolina Chronicle of Dr. Francis Le Jau*, 48, To the Secretary, November 15, 1708, and 50, To the Secretary, February 18, 1709.

128. Ibid., 60, To the Secretary, October 20, 1709.

129. Klingberg, *Appraisal of the Negro*, 40; Bolton, *Southern Anglicanism*, 110.

130. Also baptized were Robert, slave to Thomas Drayton; Judith, slave to Richard Fuller, and her seven children; Joseph, a slave of Mrs. Perry; Herculus Peter Clark, slave of Mr. Greenland; and William, slave to the minister Charles Martyn; and others. The majority of the people of color baptized in this parish were identified as "Negro" and were enslaved. See St. Andrew's Parish Register, 1709–1856, transcript, SCDAH.

131. Hooker, *Carolina Backcountry*, 23, July 2, 1767.

132. Fulham Papers, 15:209 (Charles Irwine, St. Philip's parish, Response to queries), 15:259 (A. Holt to Bishop Gibson, December 21, 1727); Pinckney, *Letterbook of Eliza Lucas Pinckney*, 57–58n73; St. James's Parish Register, Baptisms, 1693–1825, 19, August 20, 1699, BA; Long, *History of Jamaica*, 2:416, 2:428; St. Michael's Parish Register, 1756–71, 223, July 18, 1763, BA. See also the baptism of a mulatto girl named Elizabeth, the property of a Jewish woman named Hannah Frances, 116, January 9, 1760.

133. On sexual relationships between white males and enslaved women, see Beckles, *Natural Rebels*, 141–51. See also his *Centering Women*, 125–39. On enslaved women in the Caribbean, see Bush, *Slave Women in Caribbean Society*.

134. Fulham Papers, 17:236–37 (William May to Bishop Gibson, April 3, 1725).

135. St. Andrew's Parish Register, Baptisms, 1666–1807, 27–31, JA. Baptisms on August 17, 1685, and December 26, 1688. Two of the children were baptized on the latter occasion. At the first, Maria was referred to as "Fulkers Molatto Woman."

136. St. Andrew's Parish Register, Baptisms, 1666–1807, 61–62, 1740; 90, 1775, JA.

137. Fulham Papers, 17:221 (Nicholas McCalman, St. Thomas's in the East, answers to queries), 17:224–25 (William May, answers to queries).

138. Clarendon Parish Register, Baptisms, 1666–1804, 63b–65b, 1750, JA. The register is silent as to their labor status. Most had "Negro" mothers with only first names given and fathers without any racial designation.

139. St. Catherine's Parish Register, Baptisms, 1750–58, 3–6, covers new-style 1751, JA.

140. St. Andrew's Parish Register, Baptisms, 1666–1806, 68–69, 1751, 86–87, 1771, JA.

141. Fulham Papers, 18:65–70 (W. Stafford to Bishop Porteus, July 22, 1788).

142. Long, *History of Jamaica*, 2:320–21; Brathwaite, *Development of Creole Society*, 170.

143. St. Andrew's Parish Register, Baptisms, 1666–1806, November 27, 1711, JA.

144. St. James's Parish Register, Baptisms, 1693–1825, 11, November 20, 1696, BA; St. Michael's Parish Register, 1648–1702, 403, September 19, 1690, BA. That is the baptism of Robert Overton, a free Negro man. Free Negroes named Mary Edy and William Sambo were baptized in November of the same year.

145. St. Michael's Parish Register, 1771–94, 1783; 1702–39, 1714; 1756–71, 1763; 1771–94, 1783, BA.

146. Ibid., 1702–39, 29, March 9, 1704; 1702–39, 42, March 6, 1705; 1702–39, 55, July 31, 1706, BA.

147. St. Andrew's Parish Register, 21, April 12, 1723; 21, April 12, 1723; 38, November 1, 1741; 36, September 9, 1739, transcript, SCDAH.

148. Such as Isaac Hammond, the son of Isaac Hammond and his wife in 1755. St. Thomas and St. Denis Parish Register, 1693–1778, 112, September 21, 1755, SCDAH.

149. Smith and Salley, *Register of St. Philip's Parish*, 102, November 6 and 8, 1782.

150. Speaking of a slave for whom Ligon sought baptism, a planter assured him that "being once a Christian, he could no more account him a slave, and so lose the hold they had of them as Slaves, by making them Christians; and by that means should open such a gap, as all the Planters in the Island would curse him. So I was struck mute, and poor Sambo kept out of the Church." Ligon, *True & exact history*, 50.

151. Fulham Papers, 15:249–50 (Thomas Wilkie to Bishop Gibson, March 7, 1727). This suggests that baptism would convert their relationship from one of slave and owner to one of client and patron. On patronage and clientage in baptism, see Coster, *Baptism and Spiritual Kinship*, 144–55.

152. Richard Hall, *Acts*, 323–25, "An Act for Amending an Act of this Island, entitled 'An Act for the Governing of Negroes,'" February 27, 1739.

153. See especially the nicely detailed volume covering the earlier eighteenth century, St. Michael's Parish Register, 1702–39, BA.

154. Klingberg, *Carolina Chronicle of Dr. Francis Le Jau*, 126, To the Secretary, February 23, 1713; 150, To the Secretary, March 12, 1715. When David Wilson, "an Adult Negro was baptized the 12th Septr 1756," his witnesses were Daniel Lesesne, William Elliot, and Amey Garden. See St. Thomas and St. Denis Parish Register, 1693–1778, September 12, 1756, SCDAH.

155. Fulham Papers, 17:244–45 (William May to Bishop Gibson, October 19, 1725), 17:246–47 (James White to Bishop Gibson, June 3, 1726).

156. Klingberg, *Carolina Chronicle of Dr. Francis Le Jau*, 112, To the Secretary, May 26, 1712.

157. St. Michael's Parish Register, 1702–39, 194, October 29, 1721, BA. See also the baptism of the free child John Matt (259, October 23, 1725), for whom Elizabeth Moore was a godmother. A free woman of the same name had two children baptized in 1716 (142, October 3, 1716).

158. On this point, see Olwell, *Masters, Slaves, and Subjects*, 126, 138–39. While Olwell's chapter "Communion and Community: Slavery and the Established Church" is enormously helpful, he neglects the experience of African slaves that may have been attracted to Anglican worship because of their Catholic roots as well free persons of color. For a useful corrective on the first point, see Laing, "Heathens and Infidels?"

Chapter 4. The Meanings of the Eucharist in the Plantation World

1. Much of this draws on Duffy, *Stripping of the Altars*, 123–30. See also Elwood, *Body Broken*, 12–26; Rubin, *Corpus Christi*; Bossy, "Mass as a Social Institution"; Mervyn James, "Ritual, Drama, and the Social Body."
2. Spurr, *Restoration Church of England*, 344–53, 360–69.
3. Hunt, "Lord's Supper," 47–49. See also Stevenson, *Covenant of Grace Renewed*.
4. Hunt, "Lord's Supper," 49.
5. For the Corporation Act, see Kenyon, *Stuart Constitution*, 351–53.
6. For the Test Act, see ibid., 385–86.
7. Oldmixon, *British Empire in America*, 2:130. On the use of the Eucharist in judicial ordeals and royal agreements in the Middle Ages, see Rubin, *Corpus Christi*, 336.
8. For the Barbados act, see "An Act for the more effectual putting in Execution a Statute of England, intitled, 'An Act for preventing dangers which may happen from Popish Recusants'" in Richard Hall, *Acts,*, 103–4; the relevant legislation in South Carolina is the Church Act, discussed below. In Barbados, the provisions of the act were applied only to members of the Council and other high positions. See ibid., 103–4. "An Act for the more effectual putting in Execution a Statute of England, intitled, 'An Act for preventing dangers which may happen from Popish Recusants,'" February 19, 1679. Copy at the Barbados Archives, Black Rock. In Barbados, the Council took these oaths well into the nineteenth century.
9. Fulham Papers, 17:173–74 (James White to Bishop Gibson, Kingston, March 5, 1724), 18:175–85 (James White to Edmund Kelly, attorney-general of Jamaica). Undated but likely from the 1720s, the time of White's dated letters. In 1730, the Jamaican legislature repealed an act from the previous year entitled "An Act to prevent dangers that may arise from disguised as well as declared papists," noting that it did not help with the problem that "the number of white inhabitants are few, [which] may be of very bad con-

sequence to the welfare and safety thereof." See *Laws of Jamaica*, 189. The late eighteenth century saw efforts to remove the civil disabilities of Roman Catholics in the Leeward Islands, as "race was becoming . . . almost the sole factor defining eligibility for membership of the ruling class." Goveia, *Slave Society in the British Leeward Islands*, 93.

10. Governor Lord A. Hamilton to the Council of Trade and Plantations, March 5, 1716, Item 78, vol. 29 (1716–17), 42–45, *Calendar of State Papers, Colonial Series, America and West Indies*, 1574–1739, CD-ROM (London: Routledge, published in association with the Public Record Office, 2000).

11. Sirmans, *Colonial South Carolina*, 87. The quotation from the exclusionary act is from the printing in Salley, *Narratives of Early Carolina*, 254. The dissenters' petition to the House of Lords concerning this act is in Johnson and Sloan, *South Carolina*, 57–60.

12. The Church Act of 1706 is printed in Dalcho, *Historical Account*, 437–56. The relevant portion is 446–48.

13. 30 Car. II, st. 2, c.I, printed in Kenyon, *Stuart Constitution*, 386.

14. Christ Church Parish Vestry Minutes, 1708–59, 6, transcript, SCDAH.

15. St. John's Parish, Berkeley County, Vestry Minutes, 1731–1911, SCDAH; St. Matthew's Parish Vestry Minutes, 1767–78, transcript, CCPL; St. Philip's Vestry Minutes, 1756–74, n.p., SCDAH.

16. St. Andrew's Parish Register, Marriages, 24, June 2, 1704, JA.

17. Fulham Papers, 18:71–72 (Thomas Rees, John Campbell, and R. S. Woodham, to Bishop Porteus, January 13, 1792). See also the abjuration of Christopher Gilmor in Barbados, ibid., 16:56–57. He expressed his rejection of transubstantiation, the invocation of saints, the use of images and relics, and prayer for the dead in a document read in St. Michael's Church in 1734.

18. Klingberg, *Carolina Chronicle of Dr. Francis Le Jau*, 102, To the Secretary of the SPG, September 18, 1711, 133, To the Secretary, April 10, 1713; 102, To the Secretary, September 18, 1711. Enslaved persons like these may fit within Ira Berlin's category of Atlantic Creoles. See Berlin, "From Creole to African," 251–88.

19. Klingberg, *Carolina Chronicle of Dr. Francis Le Jau*, 77, To the Secretary, June 13, 1710.

20. Sermon of Robert Smith, Smith Family Papers: Writings and Sermons of Bishop Robert Smith, SCHS.

21. Fulham Papers, 18:228–33 (Account of "The State of the Church in Jamaica," ca. 1722).

22. *South Carolina Gazette*, September 12, 1741. For the complete text of this "Act for naturalizing such foreign Protestants, and others therein mentioned, as are settled, or shall settle, in any of His Majesty's Colonies in America," (13 George II c. 7), see Cay, *Statutes at Large*, 5:216–17. The Jacobean act was 7 James I c. 2.

23. See Bolzius, "Reliable Answers," 254–55, for the request of a Charles Town jeweler "for a testimonial from me that he had received Holy Communion from my colleague in Charlestown and was therefore a Protestant, so as to enable him to be naturalized."

24. See Aston, *England's Iconoclasts*. On the interaction of English and Spanish colonizers regarding Christian imagery, see Beasley, "Wars of Religion."

25. Fulham Papers, 17:248–57 (G. [Marquis] Duquesne to [Henry] Newman, May 15, 1728).

26. Long, *History of Jamaica*, 2:379. Samuel Martin of Antigua also insisted that slavery in America had the positive effect of drawing Africans "from the vilest idolatry of *Snakes* and other reptiles." Samuel Martin Sr., *A Short Treatise on the Slavery of Negroes in the British Colonies* (Antigua, 1775), quoted in Greene, "Liberty, Slavery, and the Transformation," 16.

27. One example is in Bridenbaugh, *Myths and Realities*, 97.

28. Woolverton, *Colonial Anglicanism in North America*, 33.

29. "The Exhortation in the Communion Service," *The Book of Common Prayer and Administration of the Sacraments and Other Rites and Ceremonies of the Church According to the Use of the Church of England* (London, 1763).

30. Fulham Papers, 15:143–48 (William Gordon to Governor Lowther, April 26, 1717), 15:206 (William Gordon's answers to the bishop of London's queries), 15:211 (Joseph Napleton, curate at St. Michael's), 15:205 (Alexander Deuchar, St. Thomas's), 15:207 (Joseph Holt, St. Joseph's), 15:209 (Charles Irvine, St. Philip's), 15:259 (Arthur Holt, St. Michael's, to Bishop Gibson, December 21, 1727), 15:276–77 (Arthur Holt, St. Michael's, to Bishop Gibson, May 28, 1730), 16:81–82 (Thomas Barnard to Bishop Sherlock, February 14, 1749).

31. See Gregory, "Church of England," 237.

32. Fulham Papers, 17:226–27 (Roger Price, St. Ann's), 17:211–14 (John Dickson, Westmoreland, quotation from the rubrics at the end of the communion service in the Book of Common Prayer), 17:222–23 (Richard Marsden, St. John's). This would have been the Michaelmas celebration, a newer practice. See Fleming H. James, "Richard Marsden, Wayward Clergyman." He spent time in Maryland, North Carolina, Virginia, Carolina, Barbados, and Jamaica.

33. Fulham Papers, 17:221 (Nicholas McCalman, St. Thomas's in the East), 17:215–16 (Calvin Galpine, Port Royal), 17:224–25 (William May, Kingston), 17:230–31 (John Scott, St. Catherine's). It is to be regretted that the response from St. Andrew's parish seems not to have survived.

34. *American Papers*, 16:81–82, Samuel Thomas's report to the Society, March 10, 1704.

35. For frequency and figures, see the summaries in Manross, *Fulham Papers in the Lambeth Palace Library*, 137–39.

36. Ashley River Baptist Church, Records, 1736–69, March 14–15, 1741. Furman University. "At our Church Meeting March 14 & 15 It was concluded by the Church that the holy ordinance of ye Lord's Supper Should be administered not only at every Quarter as usual but also in the middle of each quarter."

37. Prince Frederick Parish, Winyah, Vestry Minutes and Registers, 1713–94, transcript, I:38, CCPL; St. Philip's Parish Vestry Minutes, 1732–55, 96, April 17, 1741, SCDAH. See another example in the same collection at 112.

38. Salley, *Minutes of the Vestry*, 23, December 26, 1734; "Records of the Vestry," *Journal of the Barbados Museum* 17, no. 4 (1950): 195, September 22, 1699.

39. Fulham Papers, 15:143–48 (William Gordon to Governor Robert Lowther, April 26, 1717; "distant Parishes"), 17:103–4 (John Mitchell to the Archbishop of Dublin, July 3, 1711; " Altar in the Admon"), 17:232–33 (James Spenie, St. Mary's); Garden, *Doctrine of Justification*, 55; Salley, *Minutes of the Vestry*, 83, from a letter of November 5, 1756.

40. Fulham Papers, 17:175–80 (Catalogue of books brought to Jamaica by one Barrett, April 1, 1724). The books included Edmund Gibson, *The Sacrament of the Lord's Supper Explained* (London, 1705); an earlier edition of William Fleetwood, *The Reasonable Communicant; or An Explanation of the Doctrine of the Sacrament of the Lord's Supper*, 16th ed. (London, 1748); John Tillotson, *A Persuasive to Frequent Communion in the Holy Sacrament of the Lord's Supper* (London, 1705). All ran to many editions.

41. *South Carolina Gazette*, August 31, 1738.

42. Fulham Papers, 16:179–80 (F. Fitchatt to Governor Ricketts, October 12, 1796). She was eighteen years old. The complaint comes from her stepfather. See Gilmore, "Manners, Marriages, and Morals." For a Barbadian sermon on preparation for the Eucharist, see Duke, *Course of Plain and Familiar Lectures*, 139–41.

43. Ashley River Baptist Church Records, 1736–69, November 3, 1750. Furman University. See also the minutes of May 22, 1738. For similar Saturday preparation, see the Cashaway Baptist Church Record Book, 1756–78, also in the Furman collection. On December 22, 1764, their church meeting concluded "that the preparation days for the communion to be quarterly and on the Saturday preceding the Communion."

44. Edward Brailsford, Devotions, 1710–44, SCL.

45. D. E. Huger Smith, "Broughton Letters," 175. Anne Broughton to her son Nathaniel Broughton, December 5, 1716.

46. William Hutson Diary, 1757–61, entries of April 3, 1757, February 5, 1758, and April 2, 1758, SCHS.

47. Evan Pugh Papers, 1762–1801, Diary entries of November 7 and February 7, SCHS. He seems to have worshipped in a church with frequent celebrations.

48. Ashley River Baptist Church Records, 1736–69, May 8, 1736, May 22, 1738,

September 10, 1739, Furman University. His violation was "unlawfully Seeking after another wife, while his Lawfull one was yet Living."

49. Ashley River Baptist Church Records, June 14, 1746, Furman University. One can also see the practice of discipline via the Eucharist in the records of the Welsh Neck Baptist Church, 1737–1935, SCL.

50. Salley, *Minutes of the Vestry*, 74, Vestry to William Peasely, ca. June 1756; Vestry to Alexander Garden, June 24, 1756.

51. Fulham Papers, 16:97–98 (Petition to the Governor, 1765), 17:234–35 (James White, Vere parish, to Bishop Gibson).

52. Klingberg, *Carolina Chronicle of Dr. Francis Le Jau*, 69, To the Secretary, February 1, 1710, and 74, To the Secretary, February 19, 1710.

53. For notes on pelican iconography, see Livingstone, *Oxford Dictionary of the Christian Church*, 1249. Until the Reformation, the reserve sacrament in Durham Cathedral was kept in a pelican-shaped tabernacle suspended over the high altar. John Evelyn took note of "a pelican with her young at her breast just over the altar" in the new Church of St. James, Picadilly in London. Noted in Spurr, *Restoration Church of England*, 369. There were at least three such pelicans in the commemorative sculptures in St. Catherine's parish church in Jamaica. See Roby, *Monuments of the Cathedral-Church*, iii.

54. Marshall, *Prayer Book Parallels*, 374; Hatchett, *Commentary on the American Prayer Book*, 321–22.

55. Marshall, *Prayer Book Parallels*, 350. The text as inscribed reproduces neither the version in the 1662 prayer book nor that found in the authorized version of the Bible. It conflates material from verses 28 and 29 but would have still been readily recognizable.

56. Acts 8:32 as inscribed: "He was led as a sheep to the slaughter and, like a lamb dumb before his shearer, so opened he not his mouth." The text is originally from Isaiah 53:7 and appears in Acts when the disciple Philip encounters an Ethiopian eunuch reading it on the road from Jerusalem to Gaza. After studying the text together, the Ethiopian asks Philip for baptism. Clearly the text may have been suggestive in a black majority situation, even beyond its sacrificial and Eucharistic connotations.

57. Particularly in the Liturgy of St. James and in a more familiar form in the Roman Mass as the *Agnus Dei*.

58. Klingberg, *Carolina Chronicle of Dr. Francis Le Jau*, 61, To the Secretary, October 20, 1709, and 143, To the Secretary, July 4, 1714.

59. Klingberg, *Carolina Chronicle*, 103, To the Secretary, January 4, 1712. Elsewhere he noted "a few Negroe Slaves and were born and baptised among the Portuguese, but speak very good English, they come to Church and are well instructed so as to express a great desire to receive the H. Communion amongst us" (69). On Kongo Catholicism, see Thornton, "Development of an African Catholic Church." On the significance of

African Christianity for slaves in North America, see Laing, "Heathens and Infidels?" and Bonomi, *Under the Cope of Heaven*, vii–viii.

60. See Laing, "Heathens and Infidels?" 197–228.

61. See Olwell, *Masters, Slaves, and Subjects*, 103–40.

62. Note that Le Jau was promoting literacy among the enslaved in his parish. See Klingberg, *Carolina Chronicle of Dr. Francis Le Jau*, 70, for notes on the "best Scholar of all the Negroes in my parish," who was particularly drawn to apocalyptic texts.

63. James Harrison to the Secretary of the SPG, October 18, 1768, quoted in Klingberg, *Appraisal of the Negro*, 98. See also Olwell, *Masters, Slaves, and Subjects*, 133.

64. Klingberg, *Carolina Chronicle of Dr. Francis Le Jau*, 102, To the Secretary, September 18, 1711; 37, To the Secretary, March 13, 1708; 125, To the Secretary, December 11, 1712; 137, To the Secretary, January 22, 1714; 169, To the Secretary, November 28, 1715. Similarly a Jamaican minister reported that Admiral Vernon, after a successful raid on Spanish Porto Bello, "came and Receiv'd the Sacrament at my Church." Fulham Papers, 17:279–80 (William May to Bishop Gibson, Kingston, January 31, 1739).

65. Dalcho, *Historical Account*, 252.

66. See Olwell, *Masters, Slaves, and Subjects*, 132, as well as Upton, *Holy Things and Profane*, 153–58. On English and Anglo-American Eucharistic silver generally, see Oman, *English Church Plate*; Jones, *Old Silver of American Churches*; Peterson, "Puritans and Refinement." The 1711 chalice of St. Thomas's parish in Carolina can be seen in *Palmetto Silver*, 6. More light will be shed on the material culture of South Carolina Anglicanism with the publication of Louis P. Nelson, *Beauty of Holiness*.

67. On the refinement of American liturgical space in the eighteenth century, see Butler, *Awash*, 113–16; Bushman, *Refinement of America*, 169–80.

68. "Records of the Vestry," *Journal of the Barbados Museum* 16, no. 3 (1949): 132, January 19, 1680, January 26, 1680. On Eucharistic silver in Barbados, see Connell, "Church Plate in Barbados," which includes good images.

69. Prince Frederick Parish, Winyah, Vestry Minutes and Registers, 1713–94, transcript, 1:39, 43, CCPL.

70. Porcher, "Minutes of the Vestry," purchase noted at 160.

71. Fulham Papers, 15:19–20 (Governor George Phenney to Bishop Gibson, December 24, 1723).

72. Circular Church, Registers of the Corporation, vol. 1, 1695–1796, 113, SCHS. No date. Silver ordered by that congregation in 1799 can be seen in *Palmetto Silver*, 29.

73. Ashley River Baptist Church, Records, 1736–69, Furman University.

74. "Records of the Vestry," *Journal of the Barbados Museum* 16, nos. 1 and 2 (1948–49): 59, August 26, 1676; 17, no. 1 (1949): 50. Also recorded there is John Mills's gift of a silver basin weighing 44.5 ounces.

75. St. John's Parish, Berkeley County, Vestry Minutes, sometime after July 7, 1748, SCDAH.

76. Howe and Middleton, *Minutes of St. Michael's Church*, 14–15. For a photograph of the silver, see Williams, *St. Michael's, Charleston*, 244.

77. Salley, *Minutes of the Vestry*, 22–23. From minutes of October 1, 1734.

78. St. John the Baptist Lutheran Church, First Consistory Book, 20, June 22, 1769, SCHS.

79. Kingston Churchwarden's Accounts, 1722–59, April 9, 1742, October 11, 1746, JA.

80. Christ Church Parish Vestry Minutes, 1708–59, March 1718, transcript, SCDAH.

81. St. Andrew's Vestry Minutes, 1781–87, 78, June 29, 1782, JA.

82. St. Philip's Vestry Minutes, 1732–55, 27, 1735, SCDAH.

83. "Records of the Vestry," *Journal of the Barbados Museum* 15, no. 2 (1948): 94, Minutes from 1664. See also periodic inventories, such as that of October 25, 1688, which included four cups or chalices, four patens, and two flagons, in "Records of the Vestry," *Journal of the Barbados Museum* 17, no. 1 (1949): 50.

84. Records of the Vestry," *Journal of the Barbados Museum* 22, no. 3 (1955): 140, July 19, 1738.

85. Howe and Middleton, *Minutes of St. Michael's Church*, 23.

86. Salley, *Minutes of the Vestry*, 90, August 1, 1757.

87. St. Philip's Vestry Minutes, 1732–55, 40, February 27, 1738, SCDAH.

88. St. John the Baptist Lutheran Church, First Consistory Book, 16, November 14, 1768, SCHS.

89. "Records of the Vestry," *Journal of the Barbados Museum* 19, no. 2 (1952): 91, April 22, 1720. Poorer parishes were sometimes slow to acquire the required linen. Joseph Holt of St. Joseph's parish in Barbados complained that the parish lacked "a decent Cloth and Cushion for ye Pulpit, & Communion Table." See Fulham Papers, 15:207. Rural parishes in Jamaica were slow to provide surplices and other linens.

90. Kingston Churchwarden's Accounts, 1722–59, June 13, 1723, JA.

91. St. Michael's Church Records, Records of the Treasurer, Treasurer's Receipts/Vouchers, 1792, SCHS.

92. St. Catherine's Vestry Minutes, 1759–68, January 11, 1766, JA.

93. On English altarpieces in the eighteenth century, see Basil F. L. Clarke, *Building of the Eighteenth-Century Church*, 163–68; Yates, *Buildings, Faith, and Worship*, 41–43.

94. Fulham Papers, 18:228–33 (Account of "The State of the Church in Jamaica," ca. 1722).

95. "Records of the Vestry," *Journal of the Barbados Museum* 19, no. 3 (1952): 137.

96. Fulham Papers, 15:206 (William Gordon, St. Michael's), 15:207 (Joseph Holt,

St. Joseph's), 15:209 (Charles Irvine, St. Philip's); Port Royal Vestry Minutes, 1735–41, JA. After the minutes for August 2, 1737, there are extracts from wills with bequests to the parish.

97. St. Andrew's Vestry Minutes, 1781–87, 115, October 2, 1783, JA.

98. Fulham Papers, 18:228–33 (Account of "The State of the Church in Jamaica," ca. 1722).

99. Kingston Vestry Minutes, 1750–52, 144, October 24, 1750; 151, November 21, 1750; 290, May 11, 1752; 320, August 17, 1753; 1752–54, 419, March 29, 1753, JA.

100. St. Michael's Church Records, Commissioners' Accounts and Receipts, 1761, SCHS. For St. Michael's building and alterations, see Williams, *St. Michael's, Charleston*.

101. St. Michael's Church Records, Commissioners' Correspondence, 1762, SCHS.

102. Dalcho, *Historical Account*, 184.

103. Fulham Papers, 17:185–88 (James White to Bishop Gibson, April 23, 1724), 17:234–35 (James White, Vere parish).

104. Klingberg, *Carolina Chronicle of Dr. Francis Le Jau*, 102.

105. *South Carolina Gazette*, April 16, 1737.

106. Gaspar, *Bondmen and Rebels*, as well as Craton, *Testing the Chains*, 115–24.

107. Porcher and Rutledge, *Silver of St. Philip's Church*, 7. From vestry minutes of 1815.

108. See a photograph of the set in *Palmetto Silver*, 30.

109. Quotation from an 1827 resolution of the inhabitants of St. Lucy's parish in Barbados, printed in Schomburgk, *History of Barbados*, 427.

110. For more on the segregated sacrament in nineteenth-century Barbados, see Handler, *Unappropriated People*, 167.

111. For this theme, see Matthews, *Religion in the Old South*, and Raboteau, *Slave Religion*.

Chapter 5. Mortuary Ritual in the British Plantation Colonies

1. Charles Leslie, *A New History of Jamaica* (London: J. Hodges, 1740), 2.

2. Social historians have shown that it was primarily the potent intersection of pathogens originating in African, American, and European populations that made the plantation regions such deadly places. See Coclanis, *Shadow of a Dream*, 38–42.

3. Ibid., 44; Dunn, *Sugar and Slaves*, 314, 324; Craton, *Searching for the Invisible Man*, 85.

4. Coclanis, *Shadow of a Dream*, 43–44. See also Peter H. Wood, *Black Majority*, 144–45.

5. Coclanis, *Shadow of a Dream*, 45. See also the demographic comparison in Philip D. Morgan, *Slave Counterpoint*, 79–101.

6. Dunn, *Sugar and Slaves*, 314; ibid., 312; Burnard, "Not a Place for Whites?" 79. See also his "Countrie Continues Sicklie."

7. Peter Brown, *Cult of the Saints*, 24; Chesson, "Social Memory, Identity, and Death: An Introduction," in *Social Memory, Identity, and Death*, 1. See also Metcalf and Huntington, *Celebrations of Death*; on the changing mortuary practice of Puritan New Englanders, see Stannard, *Puritan Way of Death*.

8. See Peter Brown, *Cult of the Saints*, 31, for a similar dynamic in the funerary practices of Christians in late antiquity; Chesson, "Social Memory, Identity, and Death," 6.

9. For approaches to death and commemoration, see Douglas J. Davies, *Death, Ritual, and Belief*; Hallam and Hockey, *Death, Memory and Material Culture*; Koslofsky, *Reformation of the Dead*; Gittings, *Death, Burial, and the Individual*; Muir, *Ritual in Early Modern Europe*, 44–52.

10. Sloane, *Voyage to the Islands*, 1:lvi.

11. On the ways of death practiced by Africans and their descendents in the Americas, see Philip D. Morgan, *Slave Counterpoint*, 640–44; Mullin, *Africa in America*, 63–66, 137; Brathwaite, *Development of Creole Society*, 216–18.

12. Ligon, *True & exact history*, 50. An archaeological treatment of slave mortuary practices in rural Barbados can be found in Handler and Lange, *Plantation Slavery in Barbados*, 171–215.

13. Sloane, *Voyage to the Islands*, xlviii; John Taylor, *Multum in Parvo*, 544; Leslie, *New History of Jamaica*, 309; Fulham Papers, 18:65–70 (W. Stafford to Bishop Porteus, July 22, 1788); Long, *History of Jamaica*, 2:421.

14. Long, *History of Jamaica*, 2:421.

15. Leslie, *New History of Jamaica*, 309.

16. On food and mortuary rituals, see Douglas J. Davies, *Death, Ritual, and Belief*, 40–42.

17. John Taylor, *Multum in Parvo*, 544.

18. Leslie, *New History of Jamaica*, 309. On double funerals, see Philip D. Morgan, *Slave Counterpoint*, 643–44. Morgan attributes the practice to both West African precedent and the need to wait for the freedom of a Sunday for the second set of rites.

19. Long, *History of Jamaica*, 2:421–22.

20. Dunn, *Sugar and Slaves*, 329.

21. "T. Walduck's Letters from Barbados, 1710," 44–45; Creswell, *Journal of Nicholas Creswell*, 40 (September 1774).

22. Salley, *Minutes of the Vestry*, 88, ca. 1757. Susanna Rearden, tinker's wife, was relieved by the parish around the same time.

23. Burnard, *Mastery, Tyranny, and Desire*, 129; "T. Walduck's Letters from Barbados, 1710," 44. One Barbadian writer who lived into the nineteenth century celebrated the waning of funeral conviviality, as a more Victorian sensibility of death settled over the

island. He noted with "Christian satisfaction" that "the *solemnity* of these occasions has become more decorous now than it was at that time, and the hilarity which formerly amounted to little less than revelry and debauch, created by the profuse introduction or 'burnt wine' and 'sangaree,' is happily exploded." Orderson, *Creoleana*, 87.

24. Fulham Papers, 18:65–70 (W. Stafford to Bishop Porteus, Westmoreland Parish, July 22, 1788).

25. Supplement to the *South Carolina Gazette*, July 2, 1750.

26. Gaspar, *Bondmen and Rebels*, 145.

27. Sloane, *Voyage to the Islands*, xlviii; Salley and Webber, *Death Notices*, 10, 11, 18; Fulham Papers, vol. 15 (excerpt from the *Barbados Gazette*, March 26, 1735, printed after 266–67); St. Philip's Parish Vestry Minutes, 1732–55, 114, December 8, 1742, SCDAH; *South Carolina Gazette*, July 29, 1751.

28. Klingberg, *Carolina Chronicle of Dr. Francis Le Jau*, 143, To the Secretary, July 4, 1711.

29. Salley, *Register of St. Philip's Parish*, 226.

30. St. Michael's Parish Register, 1702–39, 37, October 13, 1704, BA; St. Philip's Parish Register, Burials, 1673–1848, 31, December 22, 1717, BA, "Martin, a Negro Slave." Free and enslaved people were buried in Christ Church parish in Barbados from at least 1701. See the Christ Church Parish Register, Burials, 1643–1848, BA.

31. St. Michael's Parish Register, 1739–56, 72, December 22, 1743, BA. There are many examples of funerals for free persons in this volume.

32. The St. Andrew's (Jamaica) parish register shows in increase in the numbers of persons of color being buried as the eighteenth century passed, but the increase was not dramatic. It seems telling that burial was less popular than baptism. In 1768, four of twenty-one burials were of persons of color, while nine of eighteen baptisms were of persons of color. See St. Andrew's Parish Register, 1666–1807, JA. When John Thistlewood, the son of Thomas Thistlewood and his Afro-Jamaican mistress Phibbah, drowned, he was buried with the Anglican funeral rite. See Mullin, *Africa in America*, 64.

33. Kingston Vestry Minutes, 1781–88, January 17, 1781, JA.

34. Mullin, *Africa in America*, 65.

35. Long, *History of Jamaica*, 2:5.

36. St. Catherine's Parish Register, Burials, 1754–62, JA.

37. On English mortuary practice, see Houlbrook, *Death, Religion, and the Family*, and Gittings, *Death, Burial, and the Individual*.

38. St. Catherine's Vestry Minutes, 1759–68, entries of August 5, 1759, December 29, 1759, and October 15, 1760, JA.

39. Leslie, *New History of Jamaica*, 309.

40. "Records of the Vestry," *Journal of the Barbados Museum* 15, no. 4 (1948): 208, March 13, 1671; 19, no. 1 (1951): 44, October 16, 1717; St. John's Parish Vestry Minutes,

1649–99, 80, December 1, 1684, BMHS; St. Catherine's Parish Vestry Minutes, 1759–68, Account from 1764, in minutes after September 28, 1765, JA; St. Andrew's Parish Vestry Minutes, 1781–87, 90, January 16, 1783, JA; Kingston Parish Vestry Minutes, 1750–52, 161, JA; Port Royal Parish Vestry Minutes, 1735–41, January 18, 1737, JA; Kingston Parish Vestry Minutes, 1781–88, March 28, 1781, JA; St. Catherine's Parish Vestry Minutes, 1759–68, March 13, 1760, JA; Prince Frederick Parish, Winyah, Vestry Minutes and Registers, 1713–94, transcript, CCPL; Salley, *Register of St. Philip's Parish*, 231.

41. Kingston Parish Vestry Minutes, 1768–70, 257, January 10, 1771, JA; St. Catherine's Parish Vestry Minutes, 1759–68, June 28, 1765, JA; Port Royal Parish Vestry Minutes, 1735–41, February 2, 1736, JA. See parish tax roll in this same volume for records of his human property.

42. "Records of the Vestry," *Journal of the Barbados Museum* 22, no. 1 (1954): 37, August 24, 1734; 19, no. 2 (1952): 86, October 11, 1718. The bearers demanded fees for carrying the dead in 1723 but were flatly refused by the vestry, which argued that the provision of gowns was compensation enough and that "no fees be allowed the bearers by the parish for any person buryed by the parish charge." "Records of the Vestry," *Journal of the Barbados Museum* 19, no. 4 (1952): 188, August 20, 1723.

43. "Records of the Vestry," *Journal of the Barbados Museum* 15, no. 3 (1948): 126, April 15, 1667; St. Philip's Parish Vestry Minutes, 1732–55, 49, September 25, 1738, SCDAH.

44. St. Philip's Parish Vestry Minutes, 1732–55, 3, July 17, 1732; 69, April 29, 1740;, 130, April 23, 1744, SCDAH. For repair, 149, December 23, 1746, SCDAH.

45. St. Philip's Churchwarden's Account Book, 1725–52, Accounts of 1745, July 24, 1734, SCDAH.

46. Howe and Middleton, *Minutes of St. Michael's Church*, 37, May 27, 1764.

47. Circular Church, Registers of the Corporation, vol. 1, 1695–1796, May 19, 1754, SCHS.

48. St. John the Baptist Lutheran Church, First Consistory Book, 41, October 10, 1781, SCHS.

49. Kingston Parish Vestry Minutes, 1744–49, October 24, 1748; 159, January 14, 1750, JA; St. Catherine's Parish Vestry Minutes, 1759–68, June 28, 1765, JA. In the later 1750s, an accurate count of pall choices can be made. In 1757, there were 9 uses of the black pall and 6 of the white pall. In 1758, 30 black and 20 white. In 1759, 15 black, 12 white.

50. Port Royal Parish Vestry Minutes, 1735–41, February 2, 1736, JA.

51. "Records of the Vestry," *Journal of the Barbados Museum* 22, no. 4 (1955): 200, June 10, 1741.

52. "T. Walduck's Letters from Barbados, 1710," *Journal of the Barbados Museum* 15 (1947): 45.

53. Gaspar, *Bondmen and Rebels*, 145.

54. St. Philip's Parish Vestry Minutes, 1732–55, 161, March 28, 1748, SCDAH; St. Andrew's Parish Vestry Minutes, 1781–87, April 9, 1785, 168, JA; Kingston Parish Vestry Minutes, 1750–52, 159, January 14, 1750, JA.

55. Augustine of Hippo, "On Care to be Had," 539–51, quotation at 550. See also Peter Brown, *Cult of the Saints*.

56. Webber, "Inscriptions," 57. One wonders if he was only the first white male child.

57. Salley and Webber, *Death Notices*, 8. On Bull, see Bull, *Oligarchs*.

58. *South Carolina Gazette*, March 27, 1755.

59. My visit to the ruins of Sheldon Church in July 2005.

60. My visit to the church in July 2003.

61. Salley, *Minutes of the Vestry*, 16, April 7, 1728.

62. D. E. Huger Smith, "Broughton Letters," 187.

63. Webber, "Josiah Smith's Diary," 70–71.

64. Kingston Parish Vestry Minutes, 1750–52, 160, January 14, 1750, JA; St. Andrew's Parish Vestry Minutes, 1781–87, 26, January 29, 1781, JA. A helpful examination of intramural burial in post-Reformation Scotland is Spicer, "Defyle not Christ's kirk."

65. St. Catherine's Parish Vestry Minutes, 1759–68, January 9, 1760, January 10, 1764, February 6, 1764, March 5, 1764, JA.

66. St. Andrew's Parish Register, 1666–1807, 53, 1768; 59, 1776; 69, 1786; 59, 1776; 59, 1776, JA.

67. Ibid., 59, 1776; 63, 1780; 69, 1786; JA.

68. For an examination of slave burials on plantations, see Armstrong, *Old Village*.

69. St. Andrew's Parish Register, 1666–1807, 69, 1786; 65, 1782; 61, 1778; 69, 1786, JA.

70. St. Catherine's Parish Vestry Minutes, 1759–68, November 6, 1762, JA; St. Michael's Parish Register, Burials, 1756–71, BA. See 212, March 23, 1756, and following for examples.

71. But see Goveia, *Slave Society*, 214–15, for more rigidly racialized burial practices in Antigua.

72. Kingston Parish Vestry Minutes, 1763–67, 115, January 14, 1766, JA. See the minute book of 1752–54 for the earlier order, ibid., 1752–54, JA.

73. Ibid., 1750–52, 313, June 16, 1752; 319, August 12, 1752, JA.

74. Campbell, *Church in Barbados in the Seventeenth Century*, 41.

75. "Records of the Vestry," *Journal of the Barbados Museum* 15, no. 2 (1948): 100, November 4, 1665. This fee had been changed to £3 by 1723. See "Records of the Vestry," *Journal of the Barbados Museum* 20, no. 1 (1952): 47, for "cash recd. for breaking open ye ground in ye church from Majr. Fred. Feake for burying his wife."

76. Oliver, *Monumental Inscriptions*, 5 (quoting the parish register for December 29, 1722), 9 (quoting the parish register for April 25, 1683).

77. St. Michael's Parish Register, 1702–39, 45, May 10, 1705, BA.

78. "Records of the Vestry," *Journal of the Barbados Museum* 16, nos. 1 and 2 (1948–49): 59, September 1676. These minutes also include a note "that in consideration of the above said pulpit cloth etc. the sd John Davis Esq. have credit given him for six hundred pounds of sugar and John Smith, merchant, have credit for Twelve hundred pounds of sugar, being for the burial of their children in the ground granted to sd Davis." This seems to suggest the children were already buried there or elsewhere in the church.

79. "Records of the Vestry," *Journal of the Barbados Museum* 17, nos. 2 and 3 (1950): 129, November 30, 1694.

80. "St. John's Vestry Minutes," *Journal of the Barbados Museum* 37, no. 2 (1984), 169, Minutes of July 23, 1677.

81. "Records of the Vestry," *Journal of the Barbados Museum* 17, nos. 2 and 3 (1950): 137, April 5, 1697; no. 4 (1950): 194, May 23, 1698.

82. Lawrence-Archer, *Monumental Inscriptions*.

83. Sloane, *Voyage to the Islands*, xlviii; St. John's Parish Register, Burials, 1657–1848, 38, June 15, after 1752, BA.

84. Fulham Papers, 10:153–54 (Notes attributed to Charles Martyn, April 11, 1762).

85. "Journal of Josiah Quincy, Junior," 444. Quincy's impression can be confirmed through a visit to many of the surviving churches. See also the collections that record details of these monuments, including Roby, *Monuments of the Cathedral-Church*; Lawrence-Archer, *Monumental Inscriptions*; Lewis, "English Commemorative Sculpture in Jamaica"; Wright, *Monumental Inscriptions of Jamaica*.

86. Amussen, *Caribbean Exchanges*, 217.

87. "Records of the Vestry," *Journal of the Barbados Museum* 16, no. 3 (1949): 135, January 26, 1680; 132, January 19, 1680. There is also an order in 1686 that "for time to come no tombstones in ye Churchyard be raised higher than ye level of ye Ground." See "Records of the Vestry," *Journal of the Barbados Museum* 16, no. 4 (1949): 205, May 21, 1686.

88. St. John the Baptist Lutheran Church, First Consistory Book, 14, n.d., SCHS.

89. See Roussel, "Ensevelir les corps"; Luria, "Cemeteries."

90. St. John the Baptist Lutheran Church, First Consistory Book, 4, n.d., SCHS. On Lutheran funeral biographies, see Moore, "Magdeburg Cathedral Pastor Siegfried Saccus."

91. "Journal of Josiah Quincy, Junior, " 444.

92. Klingberg, *Carolina Chronicle*, 99, November 16, 1711.

93. Salley and Webber, *Death Notices*, 10, 29. In the second section. On funeral gloves and consumer culture in early America, see Breen, "Baubles of Britain," 95–96.

94. Salley and Webber, *Death Notices*, 33. For mortuary ritual in early modern Ireland, see Tait, *Death, Burial, and Commemoration*.

95. Dunn, *Sugar and Slaves*, 329.

96. Dallett, "Griffith Hughes Dissected," 12. Hughes advertised in *The American Weekly Mercury* for its return. He was the author of *The Natural History of Barbados* (London, 1750).

97. Supplement to the *South Carolina Gazette*, July 2, 1750.

98. Gaspar, *Bondmen and Rebels*, 145.

99. On royal funerals, see Fritz, "Trade in Death," 291–316.

100. *South Carolina Gazette*, May 4, 1738, April 27, 1738.

101. Ibid., July 29, 1751.

102. Roger Hope Elletson Letter Book, 76. National Library of Jamaica, Kingston, Jamaica. See the *South Carolina Gazette*, March 16, 1738, for details of similar firing for the death of Queen Caroline.

103. "Records of the Vestry," *Journal of the Barbados Museum* 20, no. 3 (1953): 146, August 31, 1727.

104. Salley and Webber, *Death Notices*, 5, 6.

105. See "T. Walduck's Letters from Barbados, 1710," 45. Walduck alleged that fanciful hatchments were common among social climbers in Barbados. The hatchment of the Izard family can still be seen in the Goose Creek church. See Linder, *Anglican Churches*, 23.

106. Fulham Papers, vol. 15, excerpt from the *Barbados Gazette*, March 26, 1735, inserted after 266–67.

107. Will of Robert Pringle, Pringle-Garden Family Papers, SCHS.

108. Salley and Webber, *Death Notices*, 10, 16, 34. So too was Mary Wragg, "agreeable to her request, interred without any funeral pomp." Salley and Webber, *Death Notices*, 5 (second section).

109. "Six Letters of Peter Manigault," 113–23, July 4, 1750.

110. Salley and Webber, *Death Notices*, 24 (second section), 18 (from the account of Henry Selwin's funeral, 1742).

111. On the commercialization of the culture of death in England, see Fritz, "Undertaking Trade in England."

112. Webber, "Thomas Elfe Account Book."

113. "Eighteenth Century Receipts."

114. *South Carolina Gazette*, April 9, 1741.

115. St. Catherine's Parish Vestry Minutes, 1759–68, June 28, 1765, JA; Kingston Parish Vestry Minutes, 1752–54, 546, March 29, 1754; 402, January 9, 1754, JA; "Records of the Vestry of St. Michael," *Journal of the Barbados Museum* 22, no. 1 (1954): 40, June 28, 1735.

116. Fulham Papers, 18:78–81 (John Barton to Bishop Porteus, May 21, 1796).

117. Ibid., 10:138 (Wardens and Vestry of Prince Frederick Parish to Bishop Sherlock, October 23, 1751), 15:143–48 (William Gordon to Governor Lowther, April 26, 1717).

118. Klingberg, *Carolina Chronicle*, 99, November 16, 1711.

119. Williams, "Letters to the Bishop," 146, November 8, 1732.

120. Long, *History of Jamaica*, 2:238–39. This story does have an apocryphal ring.

121. Cadbury, "Quaker Account of Barbados," 122.

122. Churchwardens and Vestry of St. Helena's Parish to the Society, June 8, 1730, quoted in Bradford J. Wood, "Constant Attendance on God's Alter," 215. See also Thomas Thistlewood's remark soon after his arrival in Jamaica that "Mimber, a Fine Negro Woman, was buried today . . . like a Dog!" Burnard, *Mastery, Tyranny, and Desire*, 129. Burnard argues that Thistlewood's initial shock at ways of death in Jamaica evolved into a general indifference to the death of many of those around him.

123. Kingston Parish Vestry Minutes, 1744–49, January 26, 1746, JA.

124. Brandow, "Diary of Joseph Senhouse," *Journal of the Barbados Museum* 38, no. 2 (1988): 182, January 8, 1778.

125. Cadbury, "Quaker Account of Barbados," 123.

126. Burnard, *Mastery, Tyranny, and Desire*, 150.

127. See Vincent Brown, "Spiritual Terror," and *The Reaper's Garden*.

128. Long, *History of Jamaica*, 2:421, 422.

129. *South Carolina Gazette*, July 10, 1736.

130. Fulham Papers, 15:266–67 (Arthur Holt to Bishop Gibson, March 7, 1729). Largely illegible.

131. Welch, *Slave Society in the City*, 147.

132. Fulham Papers, 18:65–70 (W. Stafford to Bishop Porteus, July 22, 1788).

133. Ibid.

134. Laing, "Heathens and Infidels?" 199–201.

135. Berlin, *Many Thousands Gone*, 324.

136. St. Andrew's Parish Register, August 13, 1779, JA.

137. St. Catherine's Parish Register, Burials, 1754–62, 42, December 13, 1753, JA; St. Philip's Parish Register, Burials, 1673–1848, 30, April 17, 1716, BA.

Chapter 6. Revolution, Evangelicalisms, and the Fragmentation of Anglo-America

1. William Tennent Letter Album, 111, 120, SCL. On disestablishment in South Carolina, see Brinsfield, *Religion and Politics*; Bolton, *Southern Anglicanism*, 83–84.

2. Gallay, *Formation of a Planter Elite*; Rowland, Moore, and Rogers, *History of Beaufort County*, 128–38.

3. Bolton, *Southern Anglicanism*, 63–70.

4. On the creation of an Anglican ethic of slave ownership, one that stressed absolute obedience, see Butler, *Awash*, 135–51.

5. Frey and Wood, *Come Shouting to Zion*, 63. Here I rely on their third chapter in general. On conversion and ecstatic experiences, see Matthews, *Religion in the Old South*, 190–92.

6. Heyrman, *Southern Cross*, 17; Isaac, *Transformation of Virginia*, 161–77.

7. Heyrman, *Southern Cross*, 18–19 (quote), 20–22, 26–27; Matthews, *Religion in the Old South*, 66–80; Klein, *Unification of a Slave State*, 44, 269–302. Klein suggests that white Carolina evangelicalism was always more comfortable with slavery and less egalitarian than other places in the early South (notes 4 and 5, 271–72).

8. Matthews, *Religion in the Old South*, 197–200; Frey and Wood, *Come Shouting to Zion*, 114–17. In Silver Bluff, South Carolina, and Savannah and Augusta, Georgia.

9. Raboteau, *Slave Religion*, 205.

10. Brathwaite, *Development of Creole Society*, 88–92.

11. Frey and Wood, *Come Shouting to Zion*, 131; Mary Turner, *Slaves and Missionaries*, 11.

12. Frey and Wood, *Come Shouting to Zion*, 134. On precedents for this development in the Danish West Indies, see Sensbach, *Rebecca's Revival*.

13. Mary Turner, *Slaves and Missionaries*, 11, 13.

14. Schomburgk, *History of Barbados*, 96.

15. Mary Turner, *Slaves and Missionaries*, 16–17.

16. Schomburgk, *History of Barbados*, 96.

17. Mary Turner, *Slaves and Missionaries*, 148–67.

18. Brathwaite, *Development of Creole Society*, 245.

19. Caldecott, *Church in the West Indies*, 89–92, 91, 107.

20. See Joyner, *Down By the Riverside*, 154–71.

21. Gordon, *Our Cause for His Glory*, 96.

22. Gordon, "Jamaican Christian Groups," in *Our Cause for His Glory*, 69–85; Dianne M. Stewart, *Three Eyes for the Journey*; Robert J. Stewart, *Religion and Society*.

23. Watson, *Civilised Island*, 69–70. Watson notes that by 1817, Africans composed only 7 percent of Barbados's enslaved population, while Africans formed 36 percent of that population in Jamaica in the same year.

24. Davis, *Church and Crown in Barbados*, 26–31, 58–67, 73, 70–71, 71, 61.

BIBLIOGRAPHY

Primary Sources: Archival

BARBADOS

Barbados Archives, Black Rock
Parish Registers of Baptisms, Marriages, and Burials: St. Michael's Parish Register, 1648–1702. RL 1/1; St. Michael's Parish Register, 1702–39. RL 1/2; St. Michael's Parish Register, 1739–56. RL 1/3; St. Michael's Parish Register, 1756–71. RL 1/4; St. Michael's Parish Register, 1771–94. RL 1/5; St. Philip's Parish Register, Baptisms, 1648–1835. RL 1/22; St. Philip's Parish Register, Marriages, 1672–1848. RL 1/24; St. Philip's Parish Register, Burials, 1673–1848. RL 1/25; Christ Church Parish Register, Marriages, 1643–1848. RL 1/20; Christ Church Parish Register, Burials, 1643–1825. RL 1/21; St. John's Parish Register, Marriages, 1657–1794. RL 1/28; St. John's Parish Register, Burials, 1657–1800. RL 1/28; St. James's Parish Register, Baptisms, Marriages, and Burials, 1693–1825. RL 1/46; St. Joseph's Parish Register, Baptisms, 1718–1835. RL 1/30.

Public Library of Barbados, Bridgetown
The Barbados Mercury, April 19, 1783.
Minutes of the Council, Lucas Transcripts.

Shilstone Library, Barbados Museum and Historical Society, St. Ann's Garrison
Entries in the Ellcock Family Bible, 1755–1846. Transcript.
St. John's Parish Vestry Minutes, 1649–99.

JAMAICA

National Library of Jamaica, Kingston
Roger Hope Elletson Letter Book, 1766–80. 2 vols. MS 29.
Taylor, John. *Multum in Parvo or Taylor's Historie of his Life and Travells in America*. 3 vols. 1688. MS 105.

Jamaica Archives, Spanish Town
Curtis Brett Letters, Summary of & extracts from, 1775–80. 7/15/1.
Letter, John Wigan to George Wigan, October 20, 1739. 7/5.

Parish Registers of Baptisms, Marriages, and Burials, 1B/11: St. Andrew's Parish Register, Baptisms and Marriages, 1666–1806, Burials, 1666–1807; St. Catherine's Parish Register, Burials, 1754–62; St. Catherine's Parish Register, Baptisms, 1750–58; Clarendon Parish Register, Baptisms, 1666–1804.

Vestry Minutes and Parish Accounts: Kingston Vestry Minutes, 1744–49. 2/6/1; Kingston Vestry Minutes, Part 1, 1750–52. 2/6/2; Kingston Vestry Minutes, Part 2, 1752–54. 2/6/3; Kingston Vestry Minutes, 1763–67. 2/6/4; Kingston Vestry Minutes, 1768–70. 2/6/5; Kingston Vestry Minutes, 1781–88. 2/6/6; Kingston Parish and Churchwarden's Accounts, 1722–59. 2/6/155; Port Royal Vestry Minutes, 1735–41. 2/19/1; Port Royal Churchwarden Accounts, 1766–93. 2/19/8; St. Andrew's Vestry Minutes, 1781–87. 2/6/40; St. Catherine's Vestry Minutes, 1759–68. 2/2/4.

West India Collection, University of the West Indies Library, Mona

Barham, Henry. *Account of Jamaica c. 1722*. Reproduction of British Library Sloane MS 3918. MR 819.

Knight, James, *History of Jamaica c. 1743*. Reproduction of British Library Add. MS 12418, 12419. MR 822–23.

SOUTH CAROLINA

South Caroliniana Library, University of South Carolina, Columbia

Edward Brailsford, Devotions, 1710–44.
Records of the Welsh Neck Baptist Church, 1737–1935.
William Tennent Letter Album.

South Carolina Division of Archives and History, Columbia

Vestry Minutes and Parish Accounts: St. Philip's Vestry Minutes, 1732–55. L 63002; St. Philip's Vestry Minutes, 1756–74. L 63002; St. Philip's Churchwarden's Account Book, 1725–52. L 63003; Christ Church Parish Vestry Minutes, 1708–59. L 69002; St. John's Parish, Berkeley County, Vestry Minutes, 1731–1911. L 57003; St. John's Parish, Colleton County, Vestry Minutes, 1738–1817. L 71002.

Parish Registers of Baptisms, Marriages, and Burials: St. Andrew's Parish Register, 1719–1856. L 68002; St. Thomas and St. Denis Parish Register, 1693–1778. L 70001.

South Carolina Historical Society, Charleston

Circular Church, Registers of the Corporation, vol. 1, 1695–1796. 28/689/3.
Hutson, William, Diary, 1757–61. 0242.01.01 (D) –02.
Peyre, Samuel, Commonplace Book, 1740–1818. 1082.03.01.
Pringle, Robert, Will, Pringle-Garden Family Papers. 275.01.02(E).

Pugh, Evan, Papers, 1762–1801. 1292.00 28/668/1. Diary: 1762.
St. John the Baptist Lutheran Church, First Consistory Book, translation by Gertha Reinert, 34/524.
St. Michael's Church Records, 1751–1983. 0320.00.
Smith, Robert, Sermon, Smith Family Papers: Writings and Sermons of Bishop Robert Smith. 28–661–3.

Charleston County Public Library
Prince Frederick Parish, Winyah. Vestry Minutes and Registers, 1713–94, 3 vols.
St. Matthew's Parish, Vestry Minutes, 1767–78.

Baptist Historical Collection, James B. Duke Library, Furman University
Ashley River Baptist Church, Charleston District, S.C., Records, 1736–69.
Cashaway Baptist Church Record Book, 1756–78.

Primary Sources: Published

The American Papers of the Society for the Propagation of the Gospel. 17 reels. London: World Microfilms, 1974.
Augustine of Hippo. "On Care to be Had for the Dead." In *A Select Library of the Nicene and Post-Nicene Fathers of the Christian Church.* Edited by Philip Schaff, 3:539–51. Grand Rapids: Eerdmans, 1956.
"The Autobiographical Manuscript of William Senhouse." *Journal of the Barbados Museum and Historical Society* 2 (1935): 61–79, 115–34.
"The Autobiographical Manuscript of William Senhouse." *Journal of the Barbados Museum and Historical Society* 3 (1935): 3–19, 87–99.
Bolzius, Johann Martin. "Reliable Answers to Some Submitted Questions Concerning the Land Carolina." *William and Mary Quarterly* 3rd ser., 14, no. 2 (1957): 223–61.
The Book of Common Prayer and Administration of the Sacraments and Other Rites and Ceremonies of the Church According to the Use of the Church of England. Oxford: Printed by the University Printers, 1703.
Brandow, James V., ed. "The Diary of Joseph Senhouse." *Journal of the Barbados Museum and Historical Society* 37 (1985): 276–95.
———. "The Diary of Joseph Senhouse." *Journal of the Barbados Museum and Historical Society* 37 (1986): 381–414.
———. "Diary of Joseph Senhouse." *Journal of the Barbados Museum and Historical Society* 38 (1988): 179–95.
Bridges, Anne Baker Leland, and Roy Williams III. *St. James Santee Plantation Parish: History and Records. 1685–1925.* Spartanburg, S.C.: Reprint Company, 1997.

Cadbury, Henry J., ed. "A Quaker Account of Barbados in 1718." *Journal of the Barbados Museum and Historical Society* 10 (1943): 118–24.

Cardwell, Edward, ed. *Synodalia: A Collection of Articles of Religion, Canons, and Proceedings of Convocations in the Province of Canterbury*. Oxford: At the University Press, 1842. Reprint, Farnborough, England: Gregg Press, 1966.

Cay, John, ed. *The Statutes at Large, from Magna Charta, to the thirtieth year of King George the second, inclusive*. 6 vols. London, 1758.

Creswell, Nicholas. *The Journal of Nicholas Creswell, 1774–1777*. New York: Lincoln Macveagh, Dial Press, 1924.

Duke, William. *A Course of Plain and Familiar Lectures, on the Christian Covenant, on the Articles of the Christian Faith, and on the Two Sacraments, Baptism and the Lord's Supper, Chiefly Delivered in the Parish Church of St. Thomas, in the Island of Barbados*. Gloucester, England: R. Raikes for J. F. and C. Rivington, 1790.

Eaden, John, ed. *The Memoirs of Père Labat, 1693–1705*. London: Frank Cass & Co., 1970.

"Eighteenth Century Receipts." *South Carolina Historical Magazine* 34 (1933): 170–72.

French, George. *The History of Col. Parke's Administration*. London, 1717.

Further Observations Intended for Improving the Culture and Curing of Indigo. London, 1747.

Garden, Alexander. *The Doctrine of Justification According to the Scriptures, and the Articles, and Homilies of the Church of England, in a Letter to Mr. A. Croswell of Groton, in New England*. Charleston: Peter Timothy, 1742.

Glen, James. *A Description of South Carolina*. London, 1761.

Godwyn, Morgan. *The Negro's and Indians Advocate: Suing for their Admission into the Church*. London, 1680.

Greene, Jack P., ed. *Selling a New World: Two Colonial South Carolina Pamphlets*. University of South Carolina Press, 1989.

Hall, Richard, *An Abridgement of the Acts in Force in the Island of Barbados*. London, 1764.

———. *Acts, Passed in the Island of Barbados from 1643 to 1762*. London, 1764.

Handler, Jerome S., ed. "Father Antoine Biet's Visit to Barbados in 1654." *Journal of the Barbados Museum and Historical Society* 32 (1967): 56–76.

"Historical Notes." *South Carolina Historical and Genealogical Magazine* 26 (1925): 173.

Hooker, Richard J., ed. *The Carolina Backcountry on the Eve of the Revolution*. Chapel Hill: University of North Carolina Press, 1953.

Howe, Mrs. C. G., and Mrs. Charles F. Middleton, eds. *The Minutes of St. Michael's*

Church of Charleston, S.C., *1758–1797*. Historical Activities Committee: South Carolina Society of Colonial Dames of America, 1950.

Hughes, Griffith. *The Natural History of Barbados*. London, 1750.

Interesting Tracts, Relating to the Island of Jamaica: Consisting of Curious State-Papers, Councils of War, Letters, Petitions, Narratives, et c. St. Jago de la Vega, Jamaica: Lewis, Lunan, and Jones, 1800.

Johnson, Elmer D., and Kathleen Lewis Sloan, eds. *South Carolina: A Documentary Profile of the Palmetto State*. Columbia: University of South Carolina Press, 1971.

"Journal of Josiah Quincy, Junior, 1773." *Proceedings of the Massachusetts Historical Society* 49 (1916): 424–81.

Kenyon, J. P., ed. *The Stuart Constitution, 1603–1688: Documents and Commentary*. 2nd ed. New York: Cambridge University Press, 1986.

Klingberg, Frank J., ed. *Carolina Chronicle: The Papers of Commissary Gideon Johnston, 1707–1716*. Berkeley: University of California Press, 1946.

Klingberg, Frank J., ed. *The Carolina Chronicle of Dr. Francis Le Jau, 1706–1717*. Berkeley: University of California Press, 1956.

Knight, James. *History of Jamaica c. 1743*, 29, Reproduction of British Library Add. MS 12418, 12419, West Indies Collection, University of the West Indies, Mona, Jamaica.

Kupperman, Karen Ordahl, John C. Appleby, and Mandy Banton, eds. *Calendar of State Papers, Colonial Series, America and West Indies, 1574–1739*. CD-ROM. London: Routledge, published in association with the Public Record Office, 2000.

Labaree, Leonard Woods, ed. *Royal Instructions to British Colonial Governors, 1670–1776*. New York: D. Appleton-Century Company, 1935.

Lambeth Palace Library. *The Fulham Papers*. Ann Arbor, Mich.: University Microfilms, ca. 1963. 13 reels.

Lawrence-Archer, J. H. *Monumental Inscriptions of the British West Indies*. London: Chatto and Windus, 1875.

The Laws of Jamaica: comprehending all the Acts in force, passed between the thirty-second year of the reign of King Charles the Second, and the thirty-third year of the Reign of King George the Third. St. Jago de la Vega, Jamaica: Alexander Aikman, 1792.

Leslie, Charles. *A New History of Jamaica: from the earliest accounts to the taking of Porto Bello by Vice-Admiral Vernon*. 2nd ed. London: J. Hodges, 1740.

Ligon, Richard. *A true & exact history of the island of Barbados*. 2nd ed. London, 1673. Reprint, London: F. Cass, 1970.

Long, Edward. *The History of Jamaica*. 3 vols. London, 1774. Reprint, New York: Arno Press, 1972.

Manross, William Wilson. *The Fulham Papers in the Lambeth Palace Library: American Colonial Section, Calendar and Indexes.* Oxford: Clarendon Press, 1965.

Marshall, Paul V. *Prayer Book Parallels: The Public Services of the Church Arranged for Comparative Study.* New York: Church Hymnal Corporation, 1989.

Martin, Samuel. *An Essay on Plantership, Humbly Inscrib'd to all the Planters of the British Sugar-Colonies in America.* 2nd ed. Antigua, 1750.

Moreton, J. B. *West India Customs and Manners.* London, 1793.

Morrison, Alfred J., ed. *Travels in the Confederation (1783–1784) from the German of Johann David Schoepf.* Philadelphia, 1911.

Oldmixon, John. *The British Empire in America.* 2nd ed. London, 1741. Reprint, New York: Augustus M. Kelley, 1969.

Oliver, Vere Langford. *The Monumental Inscriptions in the Churches and Churchyards of the Island of Barbados, British West Indies.* London: Mitchell, Hughes, and Clark, 1915. Reprint, San Bernardino, Calif.: Borgo Press, 1989.

Orderson, J. W. *Creoleana: or Social and Domestic Scene and Incidents in Barbados in Days of Yore.* London: Saunders and Otley, 1842. Reprint, Oxford: Macmillan Education, 2002.

Pinckney, Elise, ed. *The Letterbook of Eliza Lucas Pinckney, 1739–1762.* Chapel Hill: University of North Carolina Press, 1972.

Porcher, Anne Alston, ed. "Minutes of the Vestry of St. Stephen's Parish, South Carolina, 1754–1873." *South Carolina Historical Magazine* 45 (1944): 157–71.

Pringle, Elizabeth, ed. *The Register Book for the Parish, Prince Frederick, Winyaw.* Baltimore: Williams & Wilkins, 1916.

"Records of the Vestry of St. Michael." *Journal of the Barbados Museum and Historical Society* 14, no. 4 (1950): 173–80.

"Records of the Vestry of St. Michael." *Journal of the Barbados Museum and Historical Society* 15, no. 2 (1948): 89–102.

"Records of the Vestry of St. Michael." *Journal of the Barbados Museum and Historical Society* 15, no. 3 (1948): 119–31.

"Records of the Vestry of St. Michael." *Journal of the Barbados Museum and Historical Society* 15, no. 4 (1948): 201–15.

"Records of the Vestry of St. Michael." *Journal of the Barbados Museum and Historical Society* 16, nos. 1 and 2 (1948–49): 54–65.

"Records of the Vestry of St. Michael." *Journal of the Barbados Museum and Historical Society* 16, no. 3 (1949): 131–41.

"Records of the Vestry of St. Michael." *Journal of the Barbados Museum and Historical Society* 16, no. 4 (1949): 194–207.

"Records of the Vestry of St. Michael." *Journal of the Barbados Museum and Historical Society* 17, no. 1 (1949): 47–59.

"Records of the Vestry of St. Michael." *Journal of the Barbados Museum and Historical Society* 17, nos. 2 and 3 (1950): 125–38.

"Records of the Vestry of St. Michael." *Journal of the Barbados Museum and Historical Society* 17, no. 4 (1950): 190–204.

"Records of the Vestry of St. Michael." *Journal of the Barbados Museum and Historical Society* 18, nos. 1 and 2 (1950–51): 63–80.

"Records of the Vestry of St. Michael." *Journal of the Barbados Museum and Historical Society* 18, nos. 3 and 4 (1951): 167–76.

"Records of the Vestry of St. Michael." *Journal of the Barbados Museum and Historical Society* 19, no. 1 (1951): 34–45.

"Records of the Vestry of St. Michael." *Journal of the Barbados Museum and Historical Society* 19, no. 2 (1952): 81–91.

"Records of the Vestry of St. Michael." *Journal of the Barbados Museum and Historical Society* 19, no. 3 (1952): 134–44.

"Records of the Vestry of St. Michael." *Journal of the Barbados Museum and Historical Society* 19, no. 4 (1952): 178–89.

"Records of the Vestry of St. Michael." *Journal of the Barbados Museum and Historical Society* 20, no. 1 (1952): 45–50.

"Records of the Vestry of St. Michael." *Journal of the Barbados Museum and Historical Society* 20, no. 3 (1953): 138–46.

"Records of the Vestry of St. Michael." *Journal of the Barbados Museum and Historical Society* 20, no. 4 (1953): 187–99.

"Records of the Vestry of St. Michael." *Journal of the Barbados Museum and Historical Society* 21, no. 1 (1953): 40–48.

"Records of the Vestry of St. Michael." *Journal of the Barbados Museum and Historical Society* 21, no. 2 (1954): 82–96.

"Records of the Vestry of St. Michael." *Journal of the Barbados Museum and Historical Society* 21, no. 3 (1954): 107–17.

"Records of the Vestry of St. Michael." *Journal of the Barbados Museum and Historical Society* 22, no. 1 (1954): 36–49.

"Records of the Vestry of St. Michael." *Journal of the Barbados Museum and Historical Society* 22, no. 4 (1955): 191–204.

"Records of the Vestry of St. Michael." *Journal of the Barbados Museum and Historical Society* 23, no. 2 (1956): 82–94.

"Records of the Vestry of St. Michael." *Journal of the Barbados Museum and Historical Society* 22, no. 3 (1955): 138–49.

"Records of the Vestry of St. Michael." *Journal of the Barbados Museum and Historical Society* 23, no. 3 (1956): 137–46.

"Records of the Vestry of St. Michael." *Journal of the Barbados Museum and Historical Society* 24, no. 2 (1957): 84–90.

"Records of the Vestry of St. Michael." *Journal of the Barbados Museum and Historical Society* 24, no. 4 (1957): 135–48.

"Records of the Vestry of St. Michael." *Journal of the Barbados Museum and Historical Society* 26, no. 1 (1958): 47–52.

"Records of the Vestry of St. Michael." *Journal of the Barbados Museum and Historical Society* 26, no. 2 (1959): 96–97.

Roby, John. *Monuments of the Cathedral-Church and Parish of St. Catharine: Being Part I of Church Notes and Monumental Inscriptions of Jamaica, in the Year 1824*. Montego Bay, Jamaica: Alexander Holmes, 1831.

Salley, Alexander S., Jr., ed. "Letter from Dr. Tucker Harris to His Children." *South Carolina Historical and Genealogical Magazine* 27 (1926): 30–35.

———. *Marriage Notices in the South Carolina Gazette and its Successors (1732–1801)*. Albany, N.Y.: Joel Munsell's Sons, 1902.

———. *Marriage Notices in the South-Carolina Gazette and Country Journal (1765–1775) and in The Charlestown Gazette (1778–1780)*. Charleston, S.C.: Walker, Evans, and Cogswell, 1904.

———. *Minutes of the Vestry of St. Helena's Parish, South Carolina, 1726–1812*. Columbia, S.C.: The State Co, 1919.

———. *Narratives of Early Carolina, 1650–1708*. New York: Charles Scribner's Sons, 1911.

———. "A Quaint Record." *South Carolina Historical and Genealogical Magazine* 32 (1931): 298.

———. *Register of St. Philip's Parish, Charles Town, South Carolina, 1720–1758*. Columbia: University of South Carolina Press, 1971.

Salley, Alexander S., Jr., and Mabel Webber, eds. *Death Notices in The South-Carolina Gazette, 1732–1775*. Columbia: South Carolina Archives Department, 1954.

"Six Letters of Peter Manigault." *South Carolina Historical and Genealogical Magazine* 15 (1914): 113–23.

Sloane, Hans. *A Voyage to the Islands Madera, Barbados, Nieves, S. Christophers and Jamaica, with the Natural History*. London, 1707.

Smith, D. E. Huger, ed. "Broughton Letters." *South Carolina Historical and Genealogical Magazine* 15 (1914): 171–96.

Smith, D. E. Huger, and A. S. Salley, Jr., eds. *Register of St. Philip's Parish, Charles Town, or Charleston, S.C., 1754–1810*. Columbia: University of South Carolina Press, 1971.

South Carolina Gazette, 1732–1775. In *South Carolina Newspapers, 1732–1782*. Charleston: Charleston Library Society, 1956. 12 reels.

South Carolina Historical Society. *The Shaftsbury Papers*. Charleston: Tempus Publishing, 2000.

"St. John's Vestry Minutes." *Journal of the Barbados Museum and Historical Society* 33, no. 1 (1969): 32–49.

"St. John's Vestry Minutes." *Journal of the Barbados Museum and Historical Society* 37, no. 2 (1984): 161–73.

Trott, Nicholas. *The Laws of the British Plantations in America, Relating to the Church and the Clergy, Religion and Learning*. London, 1721.

"T. Walduck's Letters from Barbados, 1910." *Journal of the Barbados Museum and Historical Society* 15 (1947): 27–51.

Ward, Ned. *The London-Spy, Compleat, in Eighteen Parts*. London, 1703.

Webber, Mabel L., ed. "Abstracts of Records of the Proceedings in the Court of Ordinary, 1764–1771." *South Carolina Historical and Genealogical Magazine* 26 (1925): 124–27.

———. "Abstracts of Records of the Proceedings in the Court of Ordinary, 1764–1771." *South Carolina Historical and Genealogical Magazine* 27 (1926): 91–94.

———. "Abstracts of Records of the Proceedings in the Court of Ordinary, 1764–1771." *South Carolina Historical and Genealogical Magazine* 31 (1930): 63–66, 154–57.

———. "Inscriptions from the Independent or Congregational (Circular) Church Yard, Charleston, S.C." *South Carolina Historical and Genealogical Magazine* 29 (1928): 55–66.

———. "Josiah Smith's Diary, 1780–1781." *South Carolina Historical Magazine* 34 (1933): 67–84.

———. "Journal of Robert Pringle, 1746–1747." *South Carolina Historical and Genealogical Magazine* 26 (1925): 21–30, 93–112.

———. "Peter Manigault's Letters." *South Carolina Historical and Genealogical Magazine* 31 (1930): 269–82.

———. "Records of the Quakers in Charles Town." *South Carolina Historical and Genealogical Magazine* 28 (1927): 22–43, 94–107, 176–97.

———. "The Thomas Elfe Account Book, 1768–1775." *South Carolina Historical Magazine* 36 (1935): 7–13, 56–66.

Williams, George, ed. "Letters to the Bishop of London from the Commissaries in South Carolina." *South Carolina Historical Magazine* 78 (1977): 1–31, 121–47, 213–42, 286–317.

Wootton, David, ed., *John Locke: Political Writings*. New York: Penguin Books, 1993.

Wright, Philip, ed. *Lady Nugent's Journal of Her Residence in Jamaica from 1801 to 1805*. Kingston: Institute of Jamaica, 1966.

———. *Monumental Inscriptions of Jamaica*. London: Society of Genealogists, 1966.

Yorke, Philip C., ed. *The Diary of John Baker: Barrister of the Middle Temple, Solicitor-General of the Leeward Islands*. London: Hutchinson & Co., 1931.

Secondary Sources

Addleshaw, G. W. O., and Frederick Etchells. *The Architectural Setting of Anglican Worship: An Inquiry into the Arrangements for Public Worship in the Church of England from the Reformation to the Present Day*. London: Faber and Faber, 1948.

Amussen, Susan Dwyer. *Caribbean Exchanges: Slavery and the Transformation of English Society, 1640–1700*. Chapel Hill: University of North Carolina Press, 2007.

Armstrong, Douglas. *The Old Village and the Great House: An Archaeological and Historical Examination of Drax Hall, St. Ann's Bay, Jamaica*. Urbana: University of Illinois Press, 1990.

Aston, Margaret. *England's Iconoclasts*. Vol. 1, *Laws Against Images*. Oxford: Clarendon Press, 1988.

Bailey, Derrick Sherwin. *Sponsors at Baptism and Confirmation: An Historical Introduction to Anglican Practice*. London: SPCK, 1952.

Beasley, Nicholas M. "Domestic Rituals: Marriage and Baptism in the British Plantation Colonies." *Anglican and Episcopal History* 76 (2007): 327–57.

———. "Ritual Time in British Plantation Colonies, 1650–1780." *Church History: Studies in Christianity and Culture* 76 (2007): 541–68.

———. "Wars of Religion in the Circum-Caribbean: English Iconoclasm in Spanish America, 1570–1702." In *Saints and their Cults in the Atlantic World*, edited by Margaret Cormack, 150–73. Columbia: University of South Carolina Press, 2006.

Beckles, Hilary McD. *Centering Women: Gender Discourses in Caribbean Slave Society*. Kingston, Jamaica: Ian Randle, 1999.

———. *Natural Rebels: A Social History of Enslaved Black Women in Barbados*. New Brunswick: Rutgers University Press, 1989.

———. *White Servitude and Black Slavery in Barbados, 1627–1715*. Knoxville: University of Tennessee Press, 1989.

Bell, Catherine. *Ritual: Perspectives and Dimensions*. New York: Oxford University Press, 1997.

———. *Ritual Theory, Ritual Practice*. New York: Oxford University Press, 1992.

Bell, James B. *The Imperial Origins of the King's Church in Early America, 1607–1783* New York: Palgrave Macmillan, 2004.

Berlin, Ira. "From Creole to African: Atlantic Creoles and the Origins of African-America Society in Mainland North America." *William and Mary Quarterly*, 3rd ser., 53 (1996): 251–88.

———. *Many Thousands Gone: The First Two Centuries of Slavery in North America*. Cambridge, Mass.: Belknap Press of Harvard University Press, 1998.

Bolton, S. Charles. *Southern Anglicanism: The Church of England in Colonial South Carolina*. Westport, Conn.: Greenwood Press, 1982.

Bond, Edward L. *Damned Souls in a Tobacco Colony: Religion in Seventeenth Century Virginia*. Macon, Ga.: Mercer University Press, 2000.

Bonomi, Patricia U. *Under the Cope of Heaven: Religion, Society, and Politics in Colonial America*. Updated ed. New York: Oxford University Press, 2003.

Bonomi, Patricia U., and Peter R. Eisenstadt. "Church Adherence in the Eighteenth-Century British American Colonies." *William and Mary Quarterly*, 3rd ser., 39 (1982): 245–86.

Bossy, John. "The Mass as a Social Institution, 1200–1700." *Past and Present* 100 (1983): 29–61.

Bourdieu, Pierre. *Outline of a Theory of Practice*. New York: Cambridge University Press, 1972.

Bowes, Frederick P. *The Culture of Early Charleston*. Chapel Hill: University of North Carolina Press, 1942.

Brathwaite, Edward. *The Development of Creole Society in Jamaica, 1770–1820*. Oxford: Clarendon Press, 1971.

Breen, T. H. "'Baubles of Britain'": The American and Consumer Revolutions of the Eighteenth Century." *Past and Present* 119 (1988): 73–104.

Bridenbaugh, Carl. *Mitre and Sceptre: Transatlantic Faiths, Ideas, Personalities, and Politics 1689–1775*. New York: Oxford University Press, 1962.

———. *Myths and Realities: Societies of the Colonial South*. Baton Rouge: Louisiana State University Press, 1952.

Bridenbaugh, Carl, and Roberta Bridenbaugh. *No Peace Beyond the Line: The English in the Caribbean, 1624–1690*. New York: Oxford University Press, 1972.

Brinsfield, John Wesley. *Religion and Politics in Colonial South Carolina*. Easley, S.C.: Southern Historical Press, 1983.

Brown, Peter. *The Cult of the Saints: Its Rise and Function in Latin Christianity*. Chicago: University of Chicago Press, 1981.

Brown, Vincent. *The Reaper's Garden: Death and Power in the World of Atlantic Slavery*. Cambridge, Mass.: Harvard University Press, 2008.

———. "Spiritual Terror and Sacred Authority in Jamaican Slave Society." *Slavery and Abolition* 24 (2003): 24–53.

Brydon, G. MacLaren. *Virginia's Mother Church and the Political Conditions Under Which It Grew*. 2 vols. Richmond: Virginia Historical Society, 1947–52.

Bull, Kinloch, Jr. *The Oligarchs in Colonial and Revolutionary Charleston: Lieutenant Governor William Bull II and His Family*. Columbia: University of South Carolina Press, 1991.

Burnhard, Trevor. "'The Countrie Continues Sicklie': White Mortality in Jamaica, 1655–1780." *Social History of Medicine* 12 (1999):45–72.

———. *Creole Gentlemen: The Maryland Elite, 1691–1776*. New York: Routledge, 2002.

———. "A Failed Settler Society: Marriage and Demographic Failure in Early Jamaica." *Journal of Social History* 28 (1994): 63–82.

———. "Inheritance and Independence: Women's Status in Early Colonial Jamaica." *William and Mary Quarterly*, 3rd ser., 48 (1991): 93–114.

———. *Mastery, Tyranny, and Desire: Thomas Thistlewood and His Slaves in the Anglo-Jamaican World*. Chapel Hill: University of North Carolina Press, 2004.

———. "Not a Place for Whites? Demographic Failure and Settlement in Comparative Context: Jamaica, 1655–1780." In *Jamaica in Slavery and Freedom: History, Heritage, and Culture*, edited by Kathleen E. A. Monteith and Glen Richards, 73–88. Mona, Jamaica: University of the West Indies Press, 2002.

———. "'Prodigious Riches': The Wealth of Jamaica before the American Revolution." *Economic History Review* 54 (2001): 506–23.

Bush, Barbara. *Slave Women in Caribbean Society, 1650–1838*. Bloomington: Indiana University Press, 1990.

Bushman, Richard L. *The Refinement of America: Persons, Houses, Cities*. New York: Alfred A. Knopf, 1992.

Butler, Jon. *Awash in a Sea of Faith: Christianizing the American People*. Cambridge, Mass.: Harvard University Press, 1990.

———. *The Huguenots in America: A Refugee People in New World Society*. Cambridge, Mass.: Harvard University Press, 1983.

Caldecott, Alfred. *The Church in the West Indies*. London: SPCK, 1898. Reprint, London: Frank Cass and Co., 1970.

Campbell, P. F. *The Church in Barbados in the Seventeenth Century*. Barbados: Barbados Museum and Historical Society, 1982.

Carney, Judith. *Black Rice: The African Origins of Rice Cultivation in the Americas*. Cambridge, Mass.: Harvard University Press, 2001.

Chaplin, Joyce E. *An Anxious Pursuit: Agricultural Innovation and Modernity in the*

Lower South, 1730–1815. University of North Carolina Press for the Omohundro Institute for Early American History and Culture, 1993.

Chesson, Meredith, ed. *Social Memory, Identity, and Death: Anthropological Perspectives on Mortuary Rituals*. Archeological Papers of the American Anthropological Association, no. 10. Alexandria, Va.: American Anthropological Association, 2001.

Clark, J. C. D. *English Society, 1660–1832*. 2nd ed. New York: Cambridge University Press, 2000.

Clarke, Basil F. L. *The Building of the Eighteenth-Century Church*. London: SPCK, 1963.

Clarke, Colin. *Kingston, Jamaica: Urban Development and Social Change, 1692–1962*. 2nd ed. Kingston, Jamaica: Ian Randle, 2002.

Coclanis, Peter A. *The Shadow of a Dream: Economic Life and Death in the South Carolina Low Country, 1670–1920*. New York: Oxford University Press, 1989.

Cohen, David W., and Jack P. Greene. *Neither Slave Nor Free: The Freedman of African Descent in the Slave Societies of the New World*. Baltimore: Johns Hopkins University Press, 1972.

Colley, Linda. *Britons: Forging the Nation, 1707–1837*. New Haven: Yale University Press, 1992.

Collinson, Patrick. *The Religion of Protestants*. New York: Oxford University Press, 1983.

Connell, Neville. "Church Plate in Barbados." *Connoisseur* 134 (1958): 8–13.

Coster, Will. *Baptism and Spiritual Kinship in Early Modern England*. Burlington, Vt.: Ashgate, 2002.

Craton, Michael. "Reluctant Creoles: The Planter's World in the British West Indies." In *Strangers Within the Realm: Cultural Margins of the First British Empire*, edited by Bernard Bailyn and Philip D. Morgan, 314–62. Chapel Hill: University of North Carolina Press, 1991.

———. *Searching for the Invisible Man: Slaves and Plantation Life in Jamaica*. Cambridge, Mass.: Harvard University Press, 1978.

———. *Testing the Chains: Resistance to Slavery in the British West Indies*. Ithaca: Cornell University Press, 1982.

Craton, Michael, and James Walvin. *A Jamaican Plantation: The History of Worthy Park, 1670–1970*. Toronto: University of Toronto Press, 1970.

Cressy, David. *Birth, Marriage, and Baptism: Ritual, Religion, and the Life-Cycle in Tudor and Stuart England*. New York: Oxford University Press, 1997.

———. *Bonfires and Bells: National Memory and the Protestant Calendar in Elizabethan and Stuart England*. Berkeley: University of California Press, 1989.

Cross, Arthur Lyon. *The Anglican Episcopate and the American Colonies.* Harvard Historical Studies IX, 1902. Reprint, Hamden, Conn.: Archon Books, 1964.

Czarnowski, Stefan. *Le Culte des héros et ses conditions sociales; saint Patrick, héros national de l'Ireland.* Paris: F. Alcan, 1919.

Dalcho, Frederick. *An Historical Account of the Protestant Episcopal Church in South Carolina.* Charleston: E. Thayer, 1820. Reprint, New York: Arno Press, 1972.

Dallett, F. J. "Griffith Hughes Dissected." *Journal of the Barbados Museum and Historical Society* 23 (1955): 3-29.

Davies, Douglas J. *Death, Ritual, and Belief: The Rhetoric of Funeral Rites.* 2nd ed. New York: Continuum, 2002.

Davies, Julian. *The Caroline Captivity of the Church.* New York: Oxford University Press, 1993.

Davis, Kortright. *Cross and Crown in Barbados: Caribbean Political Religion in the Late Nineteenth Century.* New York: Peter Lang, 1983.

Dillow, Kevin. "The Social and Ecclesiastical Significance of Church Seating Arrangements and Pew Disputes, 1500-1740." DPhil diss., University of Oxford, 1990.

Dirks, Robert. *The Black Saturnalia: Conflict and its Ritual Expression on British West Indian Slave Plantations.* Gainesville: University Presses of Florida, 1987.

Doll, Peter M. *Revolution, Religion, and National Identity: Imperial Anglicanism in British North America, 1745-1795.* Madison, N.J.: Fairleigh Dickinson University Press, 2000.

Driver, Tom. *Liberating Rites: Understanding the Transformative Power of Ritual.* Boulder, Colo.: Westview Press, 1998.

Duff, Meaghan N. "Designing Carolina: The Construction of an Early American Social and Geographical Landscape, 1670-1719." PhD diss., College of William and Mary, 1998.

Duffy, Eamon. *The Stripping of the Altars: Traditional Religion in England, c. 1400-c. 1580.* New Haven: Yale University Press, 1992.

Dunn, Richard S. *Sugar and Slaves: The Rise of the Planter Class in the English West Indies, 1624-1713.* New York: W. W. Norton & Co., 1973.

Edelson, S. Max. "The Nature of Slavery: Environmental Disorder and Slave Agency in Colonial South Carolina." In *Cultures and Identities in Colonial British America,* edited by Robert Olwell and Alan Tully, 21-44. Baltimore: Johns Hopkins University Press, 2006.

Edgar, Walter. *South Carolina: A History.* Columbia: University of South Carolina Press, 1998.

Edwards, George Nelson. *A History of the Independent or Congregational Church of Charleston, South Carolina.* Boston: Pilgrim Press, 1947.

Eltis, David. *The Rise of African Slavery in the Americas*. New York: Cambridge University Press, 2000.
Elwood, Christopher. *The Body Broken: The Calvinist Doctrine of the Eucharist and the Symbolization of Power in Sixteenth-Century France*. New York: Oxford University Press, 1999.
Farrar, P. A. "Christ Church." *Journal of the Barbados Museum and Historical Society* 2 (1935): 143–54.
Fincham, Kenneth, ed. *The Early Stuart Church, 1603–1640*. London: Stanford University Press, 1993.
Findling, John E. "The Lowther-Gordon Controversy: Church and State in Barbados, 1711–1720." *Journal of the Barbados Museum and Historical Society* 34 (1973): 131–44.
Frey, Sylvia R., and Betty Wood. *Come Shouting to Zion: African American Protestantism in the American South and British Caribbean to 1830*. Chapel Hill: University of North Carolina Press, 1998.
Fritz, Paul S. "The Trade in Death: The Royal Funerals in England, 1685–1830." *Eighteenth-Century Studies* 15 (1982): 291–316.
———. "The Undertaking Trade in England: Its Origins and Early Development, 1660–1830." *Eighteenth-Century Studies* 28 (1994–95): 241–53.
Gallay, Alan. *The Formation of a Planter Elite: Jonathan Bryan and the Southern Colonial Frontier*. Athens: University of Georgia Press, 1989.
Games, Allison. *Migration and the Origins of the English Atlantic World*. Cambridge, Mass.: Harvard University Press, 1999.
Gaspar, David Barry. *Bondmen and Rebels: A Study of Master-Slave Relations in Antigua, With Implications for Colonial British America*. Baltimore: Johns Hopkins University Press, 1985.
Geertz, Clifford. *The Interpretation of Cultures: Selected Essays*. New York: Basic Books, 1973.
Genovese, Eugene D. *From Rebellion to Revolution: Afro-American Slave Revolts in the Making of the New World*. New York: Vintage Books, 1979.
Gibson, William. *The Achievement of the Anglican Church, 1689–1800: Unity and Accord*. London: Routledge, 2001.
Gilmore, J. T. "Manners, Marriages, and Morals in late Eighteenth Century Barbados: The Case of the Reverend Richard Forster Clarke." *Journal of the Barbados Museum and Historical Society* 36 (1982): 334–41.
Gittings, Clare. *Death, Burial, and the Individual in Early Modern England*. London: Croom Helm, 1984.
Gordon, Shirley C. *Our Cause for His Glory: Christianisation and Emancipation in Jamaica*. Kingston: The Press, University of the West Indies, 1998.

Goveia, Elsa V. *Slave Society in the British Leeward Islands at the End of the Eighteenth Century*. New Haven: Yale University Press, 1965.

Gragg, Larry. *Englishmen Transplanted: The English Colonization of Barbados, 1627–1660*. New York: Oxford University Press, 2003.

Greene, Jack P. *Imperatives, Behaviors, and Identities: Essays in Early American Cultural History*. Charlottesville: University Press of Virginia, 1992.

———. "Liberty, Slavery, and the Transformation of British Identity in the Eighteenth-Century West Indies." *Slavery and Abolition* 21 (2000): 1–31.

———. *Pursuits of Happiness: The Social Development of Early Modern British Colonies and the Formation of American Culture*. Chapel Hill: University of North Carolina Press, 1988.

———. "Society and Economy in the British Caribbean during the Seventeenth and Eighteenth Centuries." *American Historical Review* 79 (1974): 1499–1517.

Greene, Jack P., and J. R. Pole, eds. *Colonial British America: Essays in the New History of the Early Modern Era*. Baltimore: Johns Hopkins University Press, 1984.

Gregory, Jeremy. "The Church of England." In *A Companion to Eighteenth-Century Britain*, edited by H. T. Dickinson, 225–40. Oxford: Blackwell, 2002.

Gundersen, Joan R. *The Anglican Ministry in Virginia, 1723–1775: A Study of a Social Class*. New York: Garland Press, 1989.

Hall, David D. "Religion and Society: Problems and Reconsiderations." In *Colonial British America: Essays in the New History of the Early Modern Era*, edited by Jack P. Greene and J. R. Pole, 317–44. Baltimore: Johns Hopkins University Press, 1984.

Hall, David D., and Ann Brown. "Family Strategies and Religious Practice: Baptism and the Lord's Supper in Early New England." In *Lived Religion in America: Toward a History of Practice*, edited by David D. Hall, 41–68. Princeton: Princeton University Press, 1997.

Hallam, Elizabeth, and Jenny Hockey. *Death, Memory, and Material Culture*. New York: Berg, 2001.

Handler, Jerome. *The Unappropriated People: Freedmen in the Slave Society of Barbados*. Baltimore: Johns Hopkins University Press, 1974.

Handler, Jerome S., and Frederick W. Lange. *Plantation Slavery in Barbados: An Archaeological and Historical Investigation*. Cambridge, Mass.: Harvard University Press, 1978.

Harlow, Vincent T. *A History of Barbados, 1625–1685*. Oxford: Clarendon Press, 1926.

Hatchett, Marion J. *Commentary on the American Prayer Book*. New York: HarperSanFrancisco, 1995.

Hatfield, April Lee. *Atlantic Virginia: Intercolonial Relations in the Seventeenth Century*. Philadelphia: University of Pennsylvania Press, 2004.

Heal, Felicity. *Hospitality in Early Modern England.* Oxford: Clarendon Press, 1990.

Heyrman, Christine. *Southern Cross: The Beginnings of the Bible Belt.* Chapel Hill: University of North Carolina Press, 1997.

Houlbrook, Ralph. *Death, Religion, and the Family in England, 1480–1750.* Oxford: Clarendon Press, 1998.

Hunt, Arnold. "The Lord's Supper in Early Modern England." *Past and Present* 161 (1998): 39–83.

Isaac, Rhys. *The Transformation of Virginia, 1740–1790.* Chapel Hill: University of North Carolina Press, 1982.

James, Fleming H. "Richard Marsden, Wayward Clergyman." *William and Mary Quarterly*, 3rd ser., 11 (1954): 578–91.

James, Mervyn. "Ritual, Drama, and the Social Body in the Late Medieval English Town." *Past and Present* 98 (1983): 3–29.

Johnson, Michael P. "Denmark Vesey and his Co-Conspirators." *William and Mary Quarterly* 58 (2001): 913–76.

———. "The Making of a Slave Conspiracy, Part 2." *William and Mary Quarterly* 59 (2002): 135–202.

Jones, Alice Hanson. *Wealth of a Nation to Be: The American Colonies on the Eve of the Revolution.* New York: Columbia University Press, 1980.

Jones, E. Alfred. *The Old Silver of American Churches.* Letchworth, England: National Society of Colonial Dames of America, at the Arden Press, 1913.

Joyner, Charles. *Down By the Riverside: A South Carolina Slave Community.* Urbana: University of Illinois Press, 1984.

Karant-Nunn, Susan. *The Reformation of Ritual: An Interpretation of Early Modern Germany.* London: Routledge, 1997.

Klein, Rachel N. *Unification of a Slave State: The Rise of the Planter Class in the South Carolina Backcountry, 1760–1808.* Chapel Hill: University of North Carolina Press, 1990.

Klingberg, Frank. *An Appraisal of the Negro in Colonial South Carolina: A Study in Americanization.* Washington, D.C.: Associated Publishers, 1941.

Koslofsky, C. M. *The Reformation of the Dead: Death and Ritual in Early Modern Germany, 1450–1700.* New York: St. Martin's Press, 2000.

Kulikoff, Allan. *Tobacco and Slaves: The Development of Southern Cultures in the Chesapeake, 1680–1800.* Chapel Hill: University of North Carolina Press for the Omohundro Institute of Early American History and Culture, 1986.

Kupperman, Karen Ordahl. "Errand to the Indies: Puritan Colonization from Providence Island to the Western Design." *William and Mary Quarterly* 45 (1988): 531–55.

Laing, Annette. "'All Things to All Men': Popular Religious Culture and the Anglican Mission in Colonial America, 1701–1750." PhD diss., University of California Riverside, 1995.

———. "'Heathens and Infidels'? African Christianization and Anglicanism in the South Carolina Low Country, 1700–1750." *Religion and American Culture: A Journal of Interpretation* 12 (2002): 197–228.

———. "'A Very Immoral and Offensive Man': Religious Culture, Gentility, and the Strange Case of Brian Hunt, 1727." *South Carolina Historical Magazine* 103 (2002): 6–29.

Lewis, Lesley. "English Commemorative Sculpture in Jamaica." *Jamaican Historical Review* 9 (1972): 9–124.

Linder, Suzanne Cameron. *Anglican Churches in Colonial South Carolina: Their History and Architecture*. Charleston: Wyrick and Company, 2000.

Little, Thomas J. "The Origins of Southern Evangelicalism: Revivalism in South Carolina, 1700–1740." *Church History: Studies in Christianity and Culture* 75 (2006): 768–808.

Livingstone, E. A. *The Oxford Dictionary of the Christian Church*. 3rd ed. New York: Oxford University Press, 1997.

Luria, Kenneth P. "Cemeteries, Religious Difference, and the Creation of Cultural Boundaries in Seventeenth-Century French Communities." In *Memory and Identity: The Huguenots in France and the Atlantic Diaspora*, edited by Bertrand Van Ruymbeke and Randy J. Sparks, 58–72. Columbia: University of South Carolina Press, 2003.

Marsh, Christopher. "'Common Prayer' in England 1560–1640: The View From the Pew." *Past and Present* 171 (2001): 66–94.

———. "Order and Place in England, 1580–1640: The View From the Pew." *Journal of British Studies* 44 (2005): 3–26.

———. "Sacred Space in England, 1560–1640: The View From the Pew." *Journal of Ecclesiastical History* 53 (2002): 286–311.

Matthews, Donald G. *Religion in the Old South*. Chicago: University of Chicago Press, 1977.

Menard, Russell R. *Sweet Negotiations: Sugar, Slavery, and Plantation Agriculture in Early Barbados*. Charlottesville: University of Virginia Press, 2006.

Merrens, H. Roy, and George D. Terry. "Dying in Paradise: Malaria, Mortality, and the Perceptual Environment in Colonial South Carolina." *Journal of Southern History* 50 (1984): 533–50.

Metcalf, Peter, and Richard Huntington. *Celebrations of Death: The Anthropology of Mortuary Ritual*. Cambridge: Cambridge University Press, 1991.

Minter, R. A. *Episcopacy Without Episcopate: The Church of England in Jamaica before 1824*. Upton-upon-Severn, England: Self Publishing Association, 1990.

Mintz, Sidney, and Douglas Hall. "The Origins of the Jamaican Internal Marketing System." *Yale University Publications in Anthropology* 57 (1960): 3–36.

Monteith, Kathleen E. A., and Glen Richards, eds. *Jamaica in Slavery and Freedom: History, Heritage, and Culture*. Mona, Jamaica: University of the West Indies Press, 2002.

Moore, Cornelia Niekus. "The Magdeburg Cathedral Pastor Siegfried Saccus and Development of the Lutheran Funeral Biography." *Sixteenth Century Journal* 35 (2004): 79–95.

Morgan, Edmund S. *American Slavery, American Freedom: The Ordeal of Colonial Virginia*. New York: Norton, 1975.

Morgan, Philip D. *Slave Counterpoint: Black Culture in the Eighteenth-Century Chesapeake and Lowcountry*. Chapel Hill: University of North Carolina Press, 1998.

Morrill, John S. *The Revolt of the Provinces*. London: Allen & Unwin, 1976.

Muir, Edward. *Ritual in Early Modern Europe*. New York: Cambridge University Press, 1997.

Mulcahy, Matthew. *Hurricanes and Society in the British Greater Caribbean, 1624–1783*. Baltimore: Johns Hopkins University Press, 2006.

Mullin, Michael. *Africa in America: Slave Acculturation and Resistance in the American South and the British Caribbean, 1736–1831*. Urbana: University of Illinois Press, 1992.

Nelson, John K. *A Blessed Company: Parishes, Parsons, and Parishioners in Anglican Virginia, 1690–1776*. Chapel Hill: University of North Carolina Press, 2001.

Nelson, Louis P. *The Beauty of Holiness: Anglicanism and Architecture in Colonial South Carolina*. Chapel Hill: University of North Carolina Press, 2009.

———. "Building Cross-Wise: Reconstructing Jamaica's Eighteenth-Century Anglican Churches." *Jamaican Historical Review* 22 (2003): 11–39, 70–76.

———. "The Material Word: Anglican Visual Culture in Colonial South Carolina." PhD diss., University of Delaware, 2001.

Olwell, Robert. "Becoming Free: Manumission and the Genesis of a Free Black Community in South Carolina, 1740–1790." In *Against the Odds: Free Blacks in the Slave Societies of the Americas,* edited by Jane G. Landers, 1–19. London: Frank Cass, 1996.

———. *Masters, Slaves, and Subjects: The Culture of Power in the South Carolina Lowcountry*. Ithaca: Cornell University Press, 1998.

Oman, Charles. *English Church Plate, 597–1830*. London, 1957.

O'Shaughnessy, Andrew Jackson. *An Empire Divided: The American Revolution and the British Caribbean.* Philadelphia: University of Pennsylvania Press, 2000.

Palmetto Silver: Riches of the South. Columbia: University of South Carolina Press, 2003.

Parent, Anthony S., Jr. *Foul Means: The Formation of a Slave Society in Virginia, 1660–1740.* Chapel Hill: University of North Carolina Press for the Omohundro Institute of Early American History and Culture, 2003.

Pares, Richard. *War and Trade in the West Indies, 1739–1763.* New York: Routledge, 1963.

———. *A West-India Fortune.* New York: Longmans, Green, 1950.

Parker, Kenneth. *The English Sabbath: A Study of Doctrine and Discipline from the Reformation to the Civil War.* New York: Cambridge University Press, 1988.

Parry, Graham. *The Arts of the Anglican Counter-Reformation: Glory, Laud and Honour.* Rochester, N.Y.: Boydell Press, 2006.

Patterson, Orlando. *The Sociology of Slavery: An Analysis of the Origins, Development and Structure of Negro Slave Society in Jamaica.* Cranbury, N.J.: Associated Universities Press, 1969.

Pearson, Edward. "'Planters Full of Money': The Self-Fashioning of the Eighteenth-Century South Carolina Elite." In *Money, Trade, and Power: The Evolution of Colonial South Carolina's Plantation Society,* edited by Jack P. Greene, Rosemary Brana-Shute, and Randy J. Sparks, 299–321. Columbia: University of South Carolina Press, 2001.

Pestana, Carla Gardina. *The English Atlantic in an Age of Revolution, 1640–1661.* Cambridge, Mass.: Harvard University Press, 2004.

Peterson, Mark. "Puritans and Refinement in Early New England: Reflections on Communion Silver." *William and Mary Quarterly* 58 (2001), 307–41.

Porcher, Jennie Rose, and Anna Wells Rutledge. *The Silver of St. Philip's Church, Charles Town/Charleston, 1670–1970.* Charleston: St. Philip's Church, 1970.

Raboteau, Albert J. *Slave Religion: The "Invisible Institution" in the Antebellum South.* New York: Oxford University Press, 1978.

Rath, Richard Cullen. *How Early America Sounded.* Ithaca: Cornell University Press, 2003.

Raven, James. *London Booksellers and American Customers: Transatlantic Literary Community and the Charleston Library Society, 1748–1811.* Columbia: University of South Carolina Press, 2002.

Reece, J. E., and C. G. Clark-Hunt. *Barbados Diocesan History.* London: West India Committee, 1925.

Robertson, James. *Gone is the Ancient Glory: Spanish Town, Jamaica, 1534–2000.* Kingston, Jamaica: Ian Randle Publishers, 2005.

Robinson, W. Stitt. *James Glen: From Scottish Provost to Royal Governor of South Carolina.* Westport, Conn.: Greenwood Press, 1996.

Roeber, A. G. *Palatines, Liberty, and Property: German Lutherans in British Colonial America.* Baltimore: Johns Hopkins University Press, 1998.

Rogers, George C., Jr. *Charleston in the Age of the Pinckneys.* Norman: University of Oklahoma Press, 1969.

———. *The History of Georgetown County, South Carolina.* Columbia: University of South Carolina Press, 1970.

Roper, L. H. *Conceiving Carolina: Proprietors, Planters, and Plots, 1662–1729.* New York: Palgrave Macmillan, 2004.

Roussel, Bernard. "'Ensevelir les corps': Funeral Corteges and Huguenot Culture." In *Society and Culture in the Huguenot World, 1559–1685,* edited by Raymond A. Mentzer and Andrew Spicer, 193–208. Cambridge: Cambridge University Press, 2002.

Rowland, Lawrence S., Alexander Moore, and George C. Rogers, Jr. *The History of Beaufort County, South Carolina. Vol. I, 1514–1861.* Columbia: University of South Carolina Press, 1996.

Rubin, Miri. *Corpus Christi: The Eucharist in Late Medieval Culture.* Cambridge: Cambridge University Press, 1991.

Russell, Conrad. *The Causes of the English Civil War.* New York: Oxford University Press, 1990.

Ryden, David B. "'One of the fertilest pleasantest Spotts': An Analysis of the Slave Economy in Jamaica's St. Andrew Parish, 1753." *Slavery and Abolition* 21 (2000): 32–55.

Schomburgk, Robert H. *The History of Barbados.* London: Longman, Brown, Green, and Longmans, 1847. Reprint, London: Frank Cass, 1971.

Sensbach, Jon F. *Rebecca's Revival: Creating Black Christianity in the Atlantic World.* Cambridge, Mass.: Harvard University Press, 2005.

———. "Religion and the Early South in an Age of Atlantic Empire." *Journal of Southern History* 63 (2007): 631–42.

Sheridan, Richard. *The Development of the Plantations to 1750* [and] *An Era of West Indian Prosperity, 1750–1775.* Barbados: Universities Press, 1970.

Sirmans, M. Eugene. *Colonial South Carolina: A Political History.* Chapel Hill: University of North Carolina Press, 1966.

Smith, Jonathan Z. *To Take Place: Toward Theory in Ritual.* Chicago: University of Chicago Press, 1987.

Smith, Mark M. "Remembering Mary, Shaping Revolt: Reconsidering the Stono Rebellion." *Journal of Southern History* 67 (2001): 513–34.

———, ed. *Stono: Documenting and Interpreting a Southern Slave Revolt*. Columbia: University of South Carolina Press, 2005.

Spicer, Andrew. "'Defyle not Christ's kirk with your carrion': Burial and the Development of Burial Aisles in Post-Reformation Scotland." In *The Place of the Dead: Death and Remembrance in Late Medieval and Early Modern Europe*, edited by Bruce Gordon and Peter Marshall, 149–69. Cambridge: Cambridge University Press, 2000.

Spurr, John. *The Restoration Church of England, 1646–1689*. New Haven: Yale University Press, 1991.

Stannard, David E. *The Puritan Way of Death: A Study in Religion, Culture, and Social Change*. New York: Oxford University Press, 1977.

Steele, Ian K. *The English Atlantic: An Exploration of Communication and Community*. New York: Oxford University Press, 1986.

Stevenson, Kenneth W. *Covenant of Grace Renewed: A Vision of the Eucharist in the Seventeenth Century*. London: Darton, Longman, and Todd, 1994.

———. *Nuptial Blessing: A Study of Christian Marriage Rites*. London: SPCK, 1982.

Stewart, Dianne M. *Three Eyes for the Journey: African Dimensions of the Jamaican Religious Experience*. New York: Oxford University Press, 2005.

Stewart, Robert J. *Religion and Society in Post-Emancipation Jamaica*. Knoxville: University of Tennessee Press, 1992.

Stone, Lawrence. *The Family, Sex, and Marriage in England, 1500–1800*. New York: Harper and Row, 1977.

———. *Uncertain Unions: Marriage in England, 1660–1753*. New York: Oxford University Press, 1992

Sypher, Wylie. "The West Indian as a Character in the Eighteenth Century." *Studies in Philology* 36 (1939): 503–20.

Tait, Clodagh. *Death, Burial, and Commemoration in Ireland, 1550–1650*. New York: Palgrave Macmillan, 2002.

Taylor, Alan. *American Colonies*. New York: Penguin Books, 2002.

Taylor, S. A. G. *The Western Design: An Account of Cromwell's Expedition to the Caribbean*. Kingston, Jamaica: Institute of Jamaica, 1965.

Thornton, John K. "The Development of an African Catholic Church in the Kingdom of Kongo, 1491–1750." *Journal of African History* 25 (1984): 147–67.

———. "African Dimensions of the Stono Rebellion." *The American Historical Review* 96 (1991): 1101–13.

Tittler, Robert. "Seats of Honor, Seats of Power: The Symbolism of Public Seating in the English Urban Community, c. 1560–1620." *Albion* 24 (1992): 205–23.

Todd, Margo. *The Culture of Protestantism in Early Modern Scotland*. New Haven: Yale University Press, 2002.

Turner, Mary. *Slaves and Missionaries: The Disintegration of Jamaican Slave Society, 1787–1834*. Urbana: University of Illinois Press, 1982.

Turner, Victor. *The Anthropology of Performance*. New York: PAJ, 1986.

———. *The Ritual Process: Structure and Anti-Structure*. Chicago: Aldine, 1969.

Underdown, David. *Revel, Riot, and Rebellion: Popular Politics and Culture in England, 1603–1660*. New York: Oxford University Press, 1985.

Upton, Dell. *Holy Things and Profane: Anglican Parish Churches in Colonial Virginia*. Cambridge, Mass.: MIT Press, 1986.

Watson, Karl. *The Civilised Island: Barbados A Social History, 1750–1816*. Barbados: Caribbean Graphic, 1979.

Weir, Robert M. *Colonial South Carolina: A History*. Millwood, N.Y.: KTO Press, 1983.

Welch, Pedro L. V. *Slave Society in the City: Bridgetown, Barbados, 1680–1834*. Kingston, Jamaica: Ian Randle Publishers, 2003.

Westerkamp, Marilyn. "Religion." In *A Companion to Colonial America*, edited by Daniel Vickers, 382–83. Malden, Mass.: Blackwell Publishing, 2003.

Williams, George W. "Charleston Church Music, 1562–1833." *Journal of the American Musicological Society* 7 (1954): 35–40.

———. *St. Michael's, Charleston, 1751–1951*. Columbia: University of South Carolina Press, 1951.

Willis, Eola. *The Charleston Stage in the Eighteenth Century, with Social Settings of the Time*. Columbia, S.C.: The State Co, 1924.

Wood, Bradford J. "'A Constant Attendance on God's Alter': Death, Disease, and the Anglican Church in Colonial South Carolina, 1706–1750." *South Carolina Historical Magazine* 100 (1999): 204–20.

Wood, Peter H. *Black Majority: Negroes in Colonial South Carolina from 1670 through the Stono Rebellion*. New York: W. W. Norton & Co., 1975.

———. "The Changing Population of the Colonial South." In *Powhatan's Mantle: Indians in the Colonial Southeast*, edited by Gregory A. Waselkov, Peter H. Wood, and Tom Hatley, 57–132. Revised and expanded ed. Lincoln: University of Nebraska Press, 2006.

Woolverton, John Frederick. *Colonial Anglicanism in North America*. Detroit: Wayne State University Press, 1984.

Yates, Nigel. *Buildings, Faith, and Worship: The Liturgical Arrangement of Anglican Churches, 1600–1900*. Revised ed. New York: Oxford University Press, 2000.

Zaceck, Natalie. "A Death in the Morning: The Murder of Daniel Parke." In *Culture and Identities in Colonial British America*, edited by Robert Olwell and Alan Tully, 223–43. Baltimore: Johns Hopkins University Press, 2006.

INDEX

Page numbers in italics refer to maps and photos.

Act for the governing of Negroes of 1688 (Barbados), 42, 157n96
Act of Toleration of 1689 (England), 86
Act of Uniformity of 1662 (England), 21, 169n110
African American churches, 36, 108, 139–41. *See also* Baptist Church; evangelicalism
African Methodist Church (Charleston, S.C.), 139
Africans (British plantation colonies): degree of autonomy of, 18; differences from, in Virginia, 17–18, 148n33; issues in constructing identity of, 73–74; as majority, 8; as proportion of enslaved, 188n23; religious/cultural practices of, 43, 44, 45, 53, 111–14, 133–34, 142, 181n18. *See also* Creole slaves; free people of color; people of color; slaves
agricultural cycles, 37–38, 154n61
All Saints' Day, 39, 48
altarpieces, 104–5
American religious historiography. *See* historiography of American religion
Anglicanism. *See* Church of England
Antigua: mortuary rituals in, 114, 121, 129; slave rebellions, 44, 45, 47, 106
Antiguan conspiracy (1736), 44, 47, 106

Ashley River Baptist Church (Charleston, S.C.), 93, 95, 101, 176n36
"Atlantic frame" of analysis, 15, 17–19

Bahamas, 65, 71
baptism: Anglican clergy monopoly on, 71, 169n98; and baptismal fonts, 68, 167–68nn76–77; demand for, 65, 166nn51–52; of English royalty, 164n33; fees for, 66–67, 71, 76, 171n124; of free people of color, 63–64, 69–70, 74, 78–82, 170n115, 171n138, 172n144, 173n157; and godparents, 70–71, 72, 168n92, 169n101, 169n103; legal privileges gained through, 78; legitimating power of, 11, 54, 77, 78–79, 80–83; location of, 66–67, 68–70, 167n60, 167n62, 168n79; and Quakers, 65, 66, 68, 166n57; recording of, 72–73, 169n109, 169–70n110, 170n115; as requirement for marriage, 63, 78; ritual variations on, 66, 74, 166n55, 166n58; role of, in creating American systems of race, 65; of slaves, 70, 74–77, 80–82, 170nn119–21, 170–71n123, 171n130, 171n132, 171n135, 172nn150–51; as social event, 67–68, 167n69
Baptist Church: baptism in, 66, 166n55; the Eucharist in, 93, 94, 95, 101, 176n36, 176n43. *See also* black churches; evangelicalism

213

Barbados: ban of, on church courts, 56, 162n10; baptism in, 65, 66, 71, 75, 78–79; church attendance/seating in, 23–24, 33, 143, 154n56; Church of England in, 143; the Eucharist in, 91–92; marriage in, 56–57, 58, 59, 60, 163n22; minor holy days in, 47; mortuary rituals in, 120, 125–27; office holding and transubstantiation oaths in, 87, 173n8; parishes of, *4*, 5; political notices during Sunday worship in, 42; religiosity/irreligiosity of, 14; Sabbatarian laws in, 40, 42–43, 44; slave owner absenteeism in, 148n31; slave population of, 109–10, 188n23; slave rebellions in, 8, 10; state holidays in, 49; transition to slave society of, 17. *See also* British plantation colonies

Beaver Creek, S.C., 77

Bermuda, 62, 65, 73, 170n119

bishops (Church of England), 2–3, 56, 106, 141, 162n10. *See also* Church of England; laity vs. clergy balance of power

black churches, 36, 108, 139–41. *See also* Baptist Church; evangelicalism

Black Majority (Wood), 15

Book of Common Prayer: on burial of unbaptized, 117; on the Eucharist, 91, 93; on liturgical year, 21, 48; on marriage, 55–56, 161n8; plantation colonies' use of, 2, 14; on Thanksgiving of Women after Child-birth, 73

Brick Church. *See* St. James's Santee Parish

Bridenbaugh, Carl and Roberta, 15

British Caribbean, 141. *See also* British plantation colonies

British cultural identity: Anglicanism as key to, 2, 10–12, 48, 52, 147n16; challenges in plantation colonies to, 1, 6, 8; and Creole whites, 1, 6; and English royalty, 115, 129–30, 164n33; and ethnic-patronal holidays, 51, 160n135; and naturalization, 89, 175n23; and state holidays, 48, 52; supercession of place and maintenance of, 21, 51. *See also* white anxiety

British plantation colonies: American Revolution disruption of, 141; common religious culture among, 2, 20; comparison of, with New England, 3, 14–16; comparison of, with Virginia, 16–18, 110, 148nn32–33, 148n37; defined, 145n1; historiography on religiosity/irreligiosity of, 13–14, 18, 26, 46, 83, 84, 90, 148n37; as pathological societies, 15; reliance on slave labor in, 8; scholarship on religion in, 18; as unit for historical analysis, 2, 19–20, 143. *See also* Barbados; Jamaica; South Carolina

burial. *See* mortuary rituals

calendar cycles: agricultural cycles, 37–38, 154n61; disease cycles, 38; liturgical year, 21, 37, 39, 48–49, 52, 154n62; meteorological cycles, 36–37

Carolina. *See* South Carolina

catechetical instruction, 32, 45, 63, 64, 76, 82, 94

Chesapeake, the, 6, 16–19, 110, 147nn32–33, 148n37, 153n50, 154n53

childbirth, 64, 73

Christ Church Parish (Barbados): baptism in, 68; marriage in, 58, 64; mortality rates in, 110; mortuary ritu-

als in, 125, 182n30; transubstantiation oaths in, 88
Christ Church Parish (S.C.), 22, 93, 102
christening parties, 67–68, 167n69. *See also* baptism
Christian rites. *See* baptism; Eucharist, the; marriage; mortuary rituals
Christmas, 39, 44–45, 85, 91–93, 157n97, 158n108
Church Act of 1706 (S.C.), 32, 173n8
church attendance, 12, 22–24, 32–33, 34, 143, 149–50n6; and weekday prayers, 46–47, 159n111. *See also* holidays; Sunday worship
church calendar. *See* liturgical year
church courts, 56, 166nn9–11
church design: baptismal fonts in, 68, 167–68nn76–77; communion tables in, 103–5; pelican iconography in, 97, 177n53; of St. Andrew's Church (S.C.), *23, 24*; of St. James Goose Creek Parish (S.C.), 96–98, *97, 98*. *See also* ritual space and time
Church of England: adaptations of, to colonial life, 40, 56, 107–8, 155nn73–74, 158n100, 159n111; baptism of slaves urged by, 75; baptismal records of, 73, 169–70n110; in Barbados, 143; and British cultural identity, 2, 10–12, 48, 52, 147n16; and church courts, 56, 162nn9–11; conversion to, 42, 64, 88–89, 99, 165n44, 177–78n59; high church vs. low church distinction, 3, 146n5; in Jamaica, 5; legal disestablishment of, 136–37, 142, 169–70n110; legal establishment of, 2, 5, 14, 21; as link to Britain, 10, 19, 51, 52, 116; metropolitan practices of, 39, 55–56, 72, 141, 162n9; metropolitan vs. lay control over, 2–3, 5; non-Anglican objections to holy days of, 47–48; post–American Revolution reform of, 141; reform of Christian liturgical year by, 39; social hierarchy / spiritual egalitarianism tension in, 11, 21, 31, 52, 53, 85, 139; in South Carolina, 5, 136, 137–39, 142. *See also* bishops; clergy (Anglican); liturgical year; Sunday worship; *and specific rites*
church seating: design of, 22; and intramural burial sites, 28, 123, 126–27; for people without pews, 25, 30–31, 152n35, 152n39, 153n50; and pews, 22, 25–29, 150n16, 151nn24–27, 151n29, 152nn31–32, 152nn34–35, 154n56; and racial hierarchy, 31, 33–36, 52, 153nn49–50, 154n53; and social hierarchy, 11, 26–27, 29–31, 51; and women returning from childbirth, 73. *See also* ritual space and time
churching of women, 73
Clarendon Parish (Jamaica), 78
clergy (Anglican): and balance of power with laity, 2–3, 5, 56, 81–83, 96, 141–42; communication of, with bishop of London, 149n5; monopoly of, over marriage rites, 59–60; performance by, of rites across parish lines, 62. *See also* Church of England
clergy (non-Anglican), 50, 59, 65, 164n31
coffins, 117, 118, 130–31. *See also* mortuary rituals
cohabitation outside of marriage, 62–63. *See also* interracial sexual relationships; marriage; sexual relationships
communion. *See* Eucharist, the
communion tables, 102–5

Creole slaves, 13, 74, 77, 82, 121, 174n18. *See also* mulattoes; people of color; slaves
Creole whites, 1, 6. *See also* British cultural identity
creolization, 18, 76, 106, 143
Curtin, Philip, 109–10

daily prayers, 46–47, 159n111
death rites. *See* mortuary rituals
demographics: and gender, 5; mortality rates, 109–11, 180n2; overall population decrease, 54, 161n1; and race, 6–8, 17, 146n12; of slaves/Africans, 18, 109–11, 148n33, 188n23; of whites, 110
Denmark Vesey rebellion, 139
disease cycles, 38, 180n2; and mortality rates, 109–11
Dunn, Richard, 15
Durham Cathedral (S.C.), 27–28

Easter, 39, 44–45, 85–86, 158n102
election writs, 42
elite slaves, 52, 74, 77, 82, 116. *See also* slaves
English naturalization, 89, 175n23
Englishness. *See* British cultural identity
Eucharist, the: Baptist practices of, 93, 95; barriers to receiving, 91; church design focus on, 96–98, 103–5; English history of, 84–86; frequency of celebration of, 90–93, 96, 176n36, 176n47; and pastoral care, 93–94, 96; and people of color, 12, 98–100, 105–8, 141; personal experience of, 94–95, 104–5; political meaning and transubstantiation oaths, 86–90, 173–74nn8–9, 174n17, 174n22; religious instruction regarding, 94, 176n43; silver and linen for, 100–103, 178n74, 179n83, 179n89; and sin, 91, 95, 97; social control and power in, 98–100
evangelicalism: American historiographical overemphasis on, 14, 18, 147n20, 148–49n30; attitudes of, toward slavery, 188n7; biracial worship in, 139; and Methodist Church, 137, 139, 140; and preaching of George Whitefield, 137; revolutionary potential of, 139. *See also* Baptist Church; black churches

fast days, 49–51, 160n131. *See also* holidays
First African Church (Savannah, Ga.), 140
free people of color: baptism of, 63–64, 69–70, 74, 78–82, 170n115, 171n138, 172n144, 173n157; church attendance of, 33, 52, 153n46; legitimation of, through Christian rites, 13, 54, 78, 80–83; and Maroons, 5, 8; marriage of, 54, 58–59, 63–64, 82–83, 165–66n47; mortuary rituals of, 115, 123–25, 182n31, 187n122. *See also* mulattoes; people of color
funerals. *See* mortuary rituals

godparents, 65, 70–72, 80–81, 168n92
Godwyn, Morgan, 33
Good Friday, 48, 158n104
Goose Creek, S.C. *See* St. James's Goose Creek Parish
governors, 29–30, 49, 56, 152nn31–32. *See also* political elites
great festivals. *See* Christmas; Easter; holidays; Whitsunday (Pentecost)
Greene, Jack P., 15–16, 147–48n25
Gunpowder Treason Day, 47, 48

Hall, David D., 19
hatchments, 130, 186n105. *See also* mortuary rituals
historiography of American religion: and "Atlantic frame" of analysis, 15, 17–19; failure to acknowledge nonevangelical Christianity in, 14–15, 107, 144; neglect of Christian ritual in everyday life in, 48–49; overemphasis of New England in, 14–16; and people of color, 13; on religiosity/irreligiosity of British plantation colonies, 13–14, 18, 26, 46, 83, 84, 90, 147–48n25, 148n37
holidays: danger to whites on, 53, 158n107; fast days, 49–51, 160n131; minor, 47–48, 51; as opportunity for slave rebellion, 44, 45, 47, 157n98, 158n107; slave/indentured servant activities on, 45, 47. *See also* liturgical year; state holidays; *and specific holidays*
Huguenots, 69, 93, 128
hurricanes, 36–37

indentured labor, 17, 45, 142
Independent Church (Charleston, S.C.): church seating in, 22, 25, 30; the Eucharist in, 101; mortuary rituals in, 119
interracial sexual relationships: and baptism of slaves, 64, 77, 166n48, 171n135; frequency of, 55, 161n5; and mortuary rituals, 115, 133. *See also* mulattoes; people of color; sexual relationships
intramural burial, 121–23, 184n75

Jamaica: African religious/cultural traditions in, 142; attitudes toward interracial relationships in, 77; ban of, on church courts, 56, 162nn10–11; baptism in, 66–67, 76–77; black churches in, 140–41; church attendance in, 24–25, 33, 153n46; Church of England in, 5; the Eucharist in, 87, 88, 92, 94; Maroons in, 5, 8; marriage in, 57, 60; minor/state holidays in, 47, 49–50; mortuary rituals in, 115, 120, 125; negro markets in, 43, 44; office holding and transubstantiation oaths in, 87, 173–74n9; parishes of, 7; Sabbatarian laws in, 41; slave population of, 110, 188n23; slave rebellions in, 8, 140–41. *See also* British plantation colonies
Jews, 77, 89, 171n132

Kingston Parish (Kingston, Jamaica): altarpieces in, 104–5; baptism in, 75, 78; church attendance/seating in, 24, 29, 33, 35; and Eucharistic silver and linens, 102; and frequency of worship, 46; and holiday decorations, 44; and minor/state holidays, 48, 49–50, 51; mortuary rituals in, 115, 118, 121, 122, 125, 131; religious instruction in, 45

laity vs. clergy balance of power, 2–3, 5, 56, 81–83, 141–42. *See also* bishops
Le Jau, Francis: burial of, 122; on the Eucharist, 88, 93, 96–100; on marriage, 59; on mortuary rituals, 115; and promotion of literacy among enslaved, 178n62; on slave work on Sundays, 43, 47. *See also* St. James's Goose Creek Parish
Lent, 39, 45, 158n103
Leslie, Charles, 113, 117
Liele, George, 139, 140

linens and silver (the Eucharist), 100–103, 178n74, 179n83, 179n89
Little, Thomas J., 18
liturgical year: Book of Common Prayer prescriptions for, 21; Church of England reform of, 39; compliance/dissension with, 48–49, 158n100; as dovetailing with economic cycles, 37, 154n62; as link to Britain, 52. *See also* Church of England; holidays; ritual space and time; Sunday worship; *and specific holidays*
Long, Edward: on African religious/cultural practices, 63, 90, 112, 133; on Christian rites for people of color, 76, 116; on Englishness of Jamaica, 8
Lord's Supper. *See* Eucharist, the
low country. *See* South Carolina
Lutherans, 48, 103, 120, 128, 159n118

Maroons, 5, 8. *See also* free people of color
marriage: Anglican clergy monopoly on rites of, 59, 164n31; banns and licenses, 42, 58–59, 61–62, 163n23, 163nn26–27, 164n28; baptism as prerequisite for, 63, 82, 165n44; clandestine, 61–62, 162n17; cohabitation outside of, 62–63; fees for, 58, 59, 163n23, 163n26; of free people of color, 54, 58–59, 63–64, 82–83, 165–66n47; as legitimating sexuality, 11, 54, 55, 81–83; location and time of, 55–58, 141–42, 161n8, 162nn15–16, 162n19, 163n22; of slaves, 58, 59, 63, 82, 165n45; as social event, 60
Maryland, 16–17
meteorological cycles, 36–37
Methodist Church, 137, 139, 140. *See also* evangelicalism

ministers. *See* clergy (Anglican); clergy (non-Anglican)
missionaries, 20, 140, 142
mortality rates, 109–11, 180n2; and disease cycles, 38. *See also* demographics
mortuary rituals: and African funeral traditions, 43, 111, 112–14, 121, 133–34, 181n18; and burial locations, 121–28, 151n24, 184n75, 185n78; coffins in, 117, 118, 130–31; for English royalty, 129–30; exclusion of unbaptized from, 117; fees for, 116, 119, 120, 121, 122, 131, 183n42, 184n75, 185n78; and funeral attire, 128–29; and hatchments, 130, 186n105; as link to culture of origin, 111, 130; as means for coping with high mortality rates, 116, 134–35; for people of color, 115, 116, 117, 182nn30–32, 187n122; and sanitary reasons for prompt burial, 117; similarities/differences of, between whites and people of color, 12, 112–16, 120–21, 134; for slaves, 114, 117, 123–25, 132–33; as social events, 113–15, 132, 181n18, 181–82n23; social hierarchy in, 119–21, 121–25, 127–28, 185n87, 186n105, 186n108; and tombstones, 185n87; and use of palls, 119–21, 183n49; of whites, 116–21
mulattoes: baptism of, 33, 52, 63–64, 70, 76–78, 171n132; burial of, 115, 116, 123, 125; and Christian worship, 13, 74, 108; church attendance/seating of, 33, 52; interracial sexual relationships involving, 161n5. *See also* free people of color; interracial sexual relationships; people of color; slaves

Native Americans, 76, 145n2
natural disasters, 49–50

naturalization, and the Eucharist, 89, 175n23
negro markets, 43, 44
New England, in American religious historiography, 14–16
No Peace Beyond the Line (Bridenbaugh and Bridenbaugh), 15

obeah, 77
Olwell, Robert, 32, 106

pallbearers, 118, 183n42
palls, 119–21, 183n49. *See also* mortuary rituals
parishes: of Barbados, *4*, 5; burial responsibilities of, 117, 183n42; of Jamaica, 7; lacking ministers, 55; of South Carolina, *9*. *See also* vestries; *and specific parishes*
pelican iconography, 97, 177n53
Pentecost. *See* Whitsunday
people of color: attitudes of, toward Christian rituals, 32, 52, 64, 78, 108, 134; baptism of, 73–81; and black churches, 36, 108, 139–41; burial of, 115, 116, 117, 182n32; and church attendance/seating, 33–35, 52, 153n46, 153n49, 153n50; and evangelical Christianity, 130; exclusion of, from Christian rites, 10–11, 12, 52, 54, 82, 84; and Maroons, 5, 8; marriage of, 54, 58–59, 63–64, 82–83, 165–66n47; rejection of European mortuary rituals by, 111. *See also* Africans; Creole slaves; free people of color; interracial sexual relationships; mulattoes; slaves
pews. *See under* church seating
Pinckney, Eliza Lucas, 22, 36, 46, 77

plantation colonies. *See* British plantation colonies
plantocracy. *See* British plantation colonies
political elites: church seating for, 29–30, 151n29; donations of Eucharistic silver by, 101–2; and holidays, 47, 50–51; office holding of, and the Eucharist, 86–87; and Sunday worship attendance, 41–42, 156n83. *See also* governors
poor whites: baptism of, 69, 82, 168n80; burial of, 117–18, 125; church seating for, 35, 153n50; cohabitation of, outside of marriage, 62–63; marriage of, 82. *See also* whites
population. *See* demographics
Port Royal Parish (Jamaica): altarpieces in, 104; church attendance in, 24; the Eucharist in, 92; festival decorations in, 44; marriage in, 62; mortuary rituals in, 118, 120; negro markets in, 43, 44; state holidays in, 49–50; weekday prayers in, 46
Presbyterians, 48, 73, 89, 137
Prince Frederick Parish (S.C.): church seating in, 27; the Eucharist in, 93, 100; marriage in, 59; mortuary rituals in, 118, 131
Prince William's Parish (S.C.), 107, 122
probate matters, 56
Protestants (non-Anglican): experience of the Eucharist by, 95; flourishing of, in South Carolina, 137; objections of, to Anglican holy days, 47–48. *See also* Church of England; *and specific denominations*
Puritanism, 14, 73, 147n19

Quakers: attitude of, toward minor/state holidays, 48; and baptism, 65, 66, 68, 166n57; and the Eucharist, 89, 99; marriage of, 59–60

racial hierarchy: and burial locations, 121, 125; and church seating, 31, 33–36, 52; in the Eucharist, 107; role of baptism in creating, 65. *See also* social hierarchy
religious instruction, 32, 45, 63, 64, 76, 82, 94
rice plantation, 37
ritual space and time: of baptism, 66–67; of the Eucharist, 96–98, 103–5; of marriage, 55–58, 141, 161n8, 162n15, 163n22. *See also* church design; church seating; liturgical year
ritual year. *See* liturgical year
Roman Catholicism: and conversion to Anglicanism, 42, 88–89, 99, 165n44; and exclusion from holding public office, 86–87, 88, 107, 173–74n9; intolerance in British colonies of, 2

Sabbatarian laws, 40–41
saints' days: St. Andrew's, 51; St. George's, 51, 52–53, 160n133; St. Patrick's, 39, 51, 160n135
sexual relationships: and cohabitation outside of marriage, 62–63; marriage as legitimating, 11, 54, 55, 81–83; and punishment of vice, 56, 162n9; white views on African, 82–83, 133. *See also* interracial sexual relationships
silver and linens (the Eucharist), 100–103, 178n74, 179n83, 179n89
slave owners: absenteeism of, 148n31; attitudes of, about slave participation in Christian ritual, 63, 64, 70, 75, 80–82, 137; and Sunday/holiday slave work requirements, 43, 45. *See also* white anxiety
slave rebellions, 8, 10, 146–47n13: and black churches, 139–41; dangers to whites of, on holidays, 53, 158n107; Sundays/holidays as opportunities for, 44, 45, 47, 157n98, 158n107. *See also* slaves; white anxiety; *and specific rebellions*
slavery: as central to British plantation colonies, 1–2, 6; metropolitan criticism of, 6, 141; as threatened by black churches, 141; Virginia vs. British plantation colonies differences in, 17–18, 148nn32–33. *See also* white anxiety
slaves: attitudes of, toward Anglican worship, 137–39; baptism of, 70, 74–77, 80–82, 170nn119–21, 170–71n123, 171n130, 171n132, 171n135, 172nn150–51; burial of, 114, 117, 123–25, 132–33; and church attendance/seating, 32–34, 52; demographics of, 18, 109–10, 148n33, 188n23; elite, 52, 74, 77, 82, 116; and the Eucharist, 99–100, 105–6; legal exemption of, from public records, 76; literacy of, 99, 178n62; marriage of, 58, 59, 63, 82, 165n45; mortality rates of, 109–10; and negro markets, 43, 44; numerical superiority of, 8; religious conversion of, 64, 99, 175n26, 177–78n59; rice agriculture knowledge of, 37; Sunday and holiday activities of, 40, 43, 44, 45, 53, 157n96; work week of, 38. *See also* Africans; Creole slaves; mulattoes; people of color; slave rebellions

Sloane, Hans, 45, 112, 114–15, 127
Smith, Jonathan Z., 52
social events: baptisms as, 67–68; funerals as, 115; and legislative sessions, 38–39, 155n67
social hierarchy: in church seating, 11, 26–27, 29–31, 51; and degree of privacy in marriage and baptism, 11, 56–59, 61, 66, 68–70, 78, 82; and donation of Eucharistic silver and linens, 101–3; in Eucharist participation, 84, 85; in marriage, 61–62, 83; in mortuary rituals, 119–21, 121–25, 127–28, 185n87, 186n105; tension of, with community ideals / spiritual egalitarianism, 11, 21, 31, 52, 53, 85, 139. *See also* racial hierarchy
social history methodology, 15
Society for the Propagation of the Gospel. *See* SPG
South Carolina: backcountry religious/cultural differences, 69, 137, 139, 159n111; baptism in, 65–66, 70, 76–77, 79–80; Church of England in, 5, 136, 137–39, 142; and disease cycles, 38; and the Eucharist, 87–89, 92–93, 95; historiographical marginalization of, 149n41; law on arming of churchgoers in, 44, 157n97; local government role of vestries in, 87–88; marriage in, 55, 57, 63; minor/state holidays in, 47, 48, 51; Native Americans in, 145n2; non-Anglican Protestants in, 137; parishes of, *9*; religiosity/irreligiosity of, 18, 148n37; Sabbatarian laws in, 40–41; slave population of, 110; slave rebellions in, 8, 10. *See also* British plantation colonies

Spanish Town, Jamaica (St. Jago de la Vega), *124*
SPG (Society for the Propagation of the Gospel), 5, 96, 106, 110
spiritual egalitarianism: in evangelical churches, 139, 188n7; and exclusion of people of color from Christian rites, 10–11, 12, 52, 54, 82, 84; tension of, with racial/social hierarchy, 11, 21, 31, 52, 53, 85, 139. *See also* racial hierarchy; social hierarchy
St. Andrew's Day, 51
St. Andrew's Parish (Barbados), 23
St. Andrew's Parish (Jamaica): baptism in, 77, 78; church seating in, 30; the Eucharist in, 89, 102; marriage in, 59, 64; mortuary rituals in, 118, 121, 122, 123, 182n32
St. Andrew's Parish (S.C.): baptism in, 66, 74, 76–77, 79; church design in, *23*, *24*; church seating in, 22; the Eucharist in, 92; marriage in, 64; political notices in, during Sunday worship, 91; religious instruction in, 45
St. Ann's Parish (Jamaica), 92
St. Catherine's Parish (Spanish Town, Jamaica): baptism in, 75, 78; church design in, 103–4, 177n53; the Eucharist in, 92; frequency of worship in, 47; mortuary rituals in, 13, 117, 118, 120, 125, 131; state holidays in, 50
St. Denis's Parish (S.C.), 69, 93
St. Dorothy's Parish (Jamaica), 92
St. Elizabeth's Parish (Jamaica), 24, 33, 59, 65, 92
St. George's Day, 51, 52–53, 160n133

St. George's Parish (S.C.): baptism in, 170n121; church seating in, 32, 34; the Eucharist in, 93, 106; religious instruction in, 45

St. Helena's Parish (Beaufort, S.C.): church seating in, 30, 31; the Eucharist in, 93, 94, 102; mortuary rituals in, 122, 132

St. Jago de la Vega, Jamaica (Spanish Town), *124*

St. James's Goose Creek Parish (S.C.): church design in, 96–98, *97*, *98*, 177n53, 177nn55–57; church seating in, 12, 22, 32; the Eucharist in, 88–89, 93, 96–100, 103, 106; marriage in, 59; minor holy days in, 47; mortuary rituals in, 115, 122. *See also* Le Jau, Francis

St. James's Parish (Barbados): baptism in, 66, 67, 69, 70, 74, 77, 78, 167n60, 167–68n77, 168n79; marriage in, 58, 59

St. James's Santee Parish (S.C.): church attendance in, 22, 149–50n6; the Eucharist in, 93; marriage in, 57, 58, 163n19; minor holy days in, 47

St. John's Colleton Parish (S.C.), 27, 88, 121

St. John's Parish (Barbados), 58, 118, 126

St. John's Parish (Jamaica), 24, 92

St. Joseph's Parish (Barbados), 23, 74, 75, 91–92, 104

St. Mary's Parish (Jamaica), 75, 94

St. Matthew's Parish (South Carolina), 88

St. Michael's Parish (Bridgetown, Barbados): baptism in, 69, 75, 78–79; black attendance in, 143; church seating in, 22, 23, 26–28, 29, 30, 34, 35, 126–27; the Eucharist in, 91–92, 93, 100, 102, 103; frequency of worship in, 46; minor/state holidays in, 47, 48, 49, 51; mortality rates in, 110; mortuary rituals in, 115, 118, 119, 125, 126, 127–28, 129–30, 131, 182n31, 183n42

St. Michael's Parish (Charleston, S.C.): altarpieces in, 105; church design in, 28, *138*; church seating in, 25, 26, 27; the Eucharist in, 103; frequency of worship in, 46; as hub of social activity, 41; mortuary rituals in, 119, 120

St. Patrick's Day, 39, 51, 160n135

St. Peter's Parish (Speightstown, Barbados), 23, 46

St. Philip's Parish (Bridgetown, Barbados): altarpiece in, 104; baptism in, 70, 75, 77; church seating in, 23; the Eucharist in, 91–92; marriage in, 59, 64

St. Philip's Parish (Charleston, S.C.): baptism in, 69, 80, 110; church seating in, 22, 25, 29, 30, 31; the Eucharist in, 88–89, 92, 93, 94, 103, 107; marriage in, 58; minor/state holidays in, 48; mortality rates in, 110; mortuary rituals in, 115, 118, 119, 121, 128, 132; worship services in, 14, 46

St. Stephen's Parish (S.C.), 29, 100–101

St. Thomas's in the East (Jamaica), 24, 50, 92

St. Thomas's in the Vale Parish (Jamaica), 24, 92

St. Thomas's Parish (Barbados), 23

St. Thomas's Parish (S.C.), 22, 32, 92

state holidays: and British cultural identity, 48, 52; evangelical rejection of, 139; as observances of political events / natural disasters, 49. *See also* holidays

Stono Rebellion, 8, 44, 47

Sugar and Slaves (Dunn), 15
sugar plantation, 37–38, 110
Sunday markets, 43, 44
Sunday secular activities, 40–45
Sunday worship: danger of attending, 44, 157nn97–98; number of services for, 155n74; reading of political notices in, 42, 156n85, 156nn87–88, 157nn90–91; Sabbatarian laws concerning, 40–41; as social event, 41, 156n81; as spectacle of political elites, 41–42, 156n83; vs. weekday prayers, 46–47, 159n111. *See also* church attendance; Church of England; holidays; liturgical year

Tacky's Revolt (Jamaica), 8, 45
Tennent, William, 136–37
Test Act of 1673 (England), 86–88, 173n8
Thanksgiving of Women after Child-birth (rite), 73
Tidewater colony. *See* Virginia
transubstantiation: oaths against, 86–88, 173–74n9, 174n17; perceived similarities of, with African religious beliefs, 90, 175n26
Turner, Victor, 19

Vere Parish (Jamaica), 75, 87, 127
vestments, 103
vestries: local government role of, 87–88; regulation of mortuary rituals by, 116–17; role in plantation colonies of, 21. *See also* parishes
Virginia: church seating in, 153n50, 154n53; differences of, from British plantation colonies, 16–19, 110, 148nn32–33, 148n37; wealth in, 6

weddings. *See* marriage
weekday prayers, 46–47, 159n111. *See also* Sunday worship
Welsh Neck Baptist Church (S.C.), 66, 166n55
Wesleyan Chapel (Kingston, Jamaica), 140
Wesleyan Church (Bridgetown, Barbados), 140
Westmoreland Parish (Jamaica), 76, 92
white anxiety: over baptism of people of color, 78, 80–81; and creation of black evangelical churches, 140–41; and the Eucharist, 106; religious/cultural means for coping with, 6–8, 10, 21, 35, 52, 106, 111, 161n138; and segregated church seating, 35. *See also* British cultural identity; demographics; slave rebellions; slavery; whites
whites: attitudes of, about African mortuary rituals, 111–14, 133–34; gender imbalance of, 3; as indentured servants, 17, 45; as minority population, 6, 8, 17, 146n12; mortality rates of, 110–11; repatriation of, 17; wealth of, 6. *See also* poor whites; white anxiety
Whitsunday (Pentecost), 39, 44–45, 85, 91, 93
Wood, Peter H., 15
Woodmason, Charles: baptisms by, 65, 69, 77; on marriage, 55, 63; ministry of, to South Carolina backwoods, 137; on minor/state holidays, 48
Woolverton, John, 90
worship. *See* holidays; Sunday worship
Worthy Park Plantation, 110

www.ingramcontent.com/pod-product-compliance
Lightning Source LLC
Chambersburg PA
CBHW021756230426
43669CB00006B/99